Cheating the Government

Cheating the Government

The Economics of Evasion

Frank A. Cowell

The MIT Press
Cambridge, Massachusetts
London, England

This book was set in Palatino by Asco Trade Typesetting Ltd. in Hong Kong and was printed and bound in the United States of America.

Library of Congress Cataloging-in-Publication Data

Cowell, Frank A. (Frank Alan)
  Cheating the government : the economics of evasion / Frank A. Cowell.

    p.   cm.
  Includes bibliographical references.
  ISBN 0-262-03153-1
  1. Tax evasion—United States. 2. Informal sector (Economics)—
United States. I. Title.
HJ2348.6.C68   1990
336.2—dc20   89-12921
                                                                  CIP

This book is dedicated to Nicholas Edmond Thomas Cowell.

Contents

Contents

Preface

Public finance is not always perceived as the most fascinating branch of economics. Tax evasion is seldom regarded as its most prominent sub-branch. What, then, of an entire book on the subject?

There is a case to be made that tax evasion raises some important issues for economic analysis. I hope that *Cheating the Government* will make that case. Of course, it may just confirm the reader's belief that the subject is rather boring. If so, this is accidental—"for *deliberate* and *intentional* boring," according to Hilaire Belloc, "you must have a man of some ability to practise it well, as you must practise any art well." I am not sure of my own ability in this respect. However, I am sure that this book would have been a lot less interesting had it not been for the valuable assistance of many people.

I am grateful to several colleagues in the Suntory Toyota Centre for Economics and Related Disciplines who discussed with me some of the basic ideas I explore in the book. I would especially like to acknowledge the help of Tony Atkinson, Dieter Bös, Luis Corchon, Jim Gordon, Jonathan Kesselman, and Agnar Sandmo, who read through and commented constructively upon much of the text. Many thanks also to Jane Henderson, who provided expert advice, and to Sue Kirkbride, who reprocessed my word-processed diskettes. As will be evident from the bibliography, I have drawn freely on the extensive literature that has been developing, and have benefited from access to the unpublished work of several authors. Finally, Robert Bolick, then at The MIT Press, took the initiative in suggesting that I do a book on this topic. I am very glad that he did.

Cheating the Government

1   Introduction

The man who says to one, go, and he goeth and to another come, and he cometh, has, in most cases, more sense of restraint and difficulty than the man who obeys him.
John Ruskin, *The Stones of Venice*

What Is the Problem?

According to the experts, nearly 40 percent of all garden sheds in the Soviet Union were built in the black economy. This official revelation might raise no more than a bemused eyebrow, until one realizes who revealed it and why.

The information comes from a statement[1] by no less a personage than the Procurator General—the most senior official responsible for law enforcement in the Union of Soviet Socialist Republics. Thrusting aside more fanciful thoughts (Who were these "experts"? Did they carry out an economic census of Soviet back gardens?), it is not hard to see why such an eminent figure should comment upon apparently homespun trivia: The black economy is a fact of life in the USSR, and the authorities there, as in other countries, are concerned lest it undermine the effectiveness of the mechanisms of government control. Elsewhere it would be the Treasury Minister expressing anxiety at the erosion of the tax base through evasion. The form of the problem may be different from one type of economic system to another; the economic issues to which it gives rise are, in substance, intriguingly similar.

Indeed, Soviet garden sheds, shares in Newmarket stallions,[2] and the Universal Life Hidden Valley Church[3] have a serious side to them. In an area of study where many conventional methods of observation and measurement are plainly out of the question, casual evidence should not be casually dismissed. Odd anecdotes and bizarre examples of officialdom's ignorance or lack of control may actually be symptoms of a significant economic problem. The "shadow economy"—tax evasion, illegal employment, welfare fraud—is widely claimed to be a growing phenomenon. Whatever the substance of this claim, it is certainly true that scholarly and journalistic writing about the shadow economy is a growing phenomenon.[4] It is evidently a topic that grips the popular imagination.

An economics monograph on the subject ought perhaps to start by identifying the economic issues. To a harrassed Finance Ministry these might be summarized in a single question of brutal practicality: How does the government get its cash? This concern for simple fiscal housekeeping leads into a set of more complex and analytically challenging questions relevant to any government that attempts to influence the running of the economy: To what extent will it be constrained by the private recalcitrance of the members of the public in whose interests it purports to act? This book is principally concerned with the economic aspects of this sort of question: what the underlying economic problem is, why it arises, and how the government or its agents can usefully react to it.

Before I launch into this, though, two questions about the general line of approach need to be dealt with: Is economic analysis an appropriate tool to apply to the study of what is simply unlawful behavior? On what basis should this particular form of unlawful behavior be singled out for special treatment?

Breaking the Rules

Playing by the rules becomes a habit of thought among econo-mists; the orderly market, the respect for property rights, the calm acceptance of legal regulation are all part of run-of-the-mill model building. Of course the phenomenon of crime upsets a lot of these rules, and to the tidy-minded this might appear quite disturbing: If we throw aside so many of the standard tenets of microeconomics, are we to be left in a wilderness of analytical chaos?

Evidently not; the substantial and thought-provoking litera-ture on the topic testifies to that.[5] Actually, many elements of the phenomenon of crime are recognizably economic in nature and can usefully be analyzed with standard economic apparatus. Hijackers, whores, and hit men all weigh the prospective costs and benefits of their labors. The public perception that "crime pays" prompts populist demands for stiffer sentences. The en-trepreneurial spirit displays itself in bootlegging and drug traf-ficking. "Crime is a logical extension of the sort of behavior that is often considered to be perfectly respectable in legitimate business."[6]

Yet there remains a nagging feeling that the economic ap-proach to lawbreaking and law enforcement neglects some im-portant issues that are bound to have a bearing upon criminal activity and therefore upon the way in which it might be prevented or counteracted.

Take, for example, the issue of motivation. Standard economic models take the position that people are criminals simply be-cause it pays them to be criminals, but at best this can be only a part of the story. Some people just will not engage in certain types of crime; for them there is no well-defined tradeoff be-tween the proceeds of crime and the rewards of a blameless, upright life. To say this is not to subscribe to the notion that criminals are genetically predisposed to their criminality. But some motivation other than pure rate of return must surely influence the potential lawbreaker. I am fairly sure that I would never engage in a bank robbery, no matter how big the prospective haul and how small the chance of being caught; still less would I ever be tempted to murder my granny *for her money*. Are these additional influences just a matter of taste? Or is there a deeper analytical point to be developed—and, if so, what implications does this have for the enforcement of social rules?

Or take the issue of social control. The economist's approach to law enforcement is akin to the regulation of a public nuisance, such as pollution: Offer the right scheme of incentives and you can reshape the behavior of uncooperative citizens to an appropriate—law-abiding—pattern. However, this presupposes that the state's carrots and sticks are more effective than changing the environment that induces the noncooperation, and that individual cooperation is bound to fail. It also presupposes some accepted standard of what constitutes acceptable behavior; from where does this standard come? These issues deserve consideration but are normally outside the scope of economic models.

Such reservations about the simplistic versions of the economics of crime apply similarly (although perhaps with less force) to the study of tax evasion and the black economy. One of the tasks of this book is to deal with them in a systematic fashion—to examine how certain types of economic analysis can be brought to bear on private behavior that is intended to frustrate the instruments of government economic policy, and what counteracting measures might be appropriate.

What Is Special about Tax Evasion?

It is tempting to lump tax evasion with business fraud, shoplifting, and burglary as just another form of theft. By treating it as one special case in the economics of crime, we might hope to infer all the necessary analytical results concerning tax evaders from general propositions about the rational economic behavior of criminals. However, to do so would be to miss some of the most important economic aspects of tax evasion. The theoretical and practical problems to which these special economic aspects of tax evasion give rise will form the subject matter of later chapters. I will mention three of them briefly here.

First, tax evasion is a fraud that is committed against a very special economic agent: the government. The government is special in that it has, presumably, the power to set and to enforce some of the "rules of the game" by which economic relationships are supposed to abide. It sets the structure and the level of taxes. It also has ultimate control over the mechanism used to enforce the payment of taxes and over the structure of penalties for offenders. It combines the roles of rulemaker, victim, and umpire. Contrast this centralized, unitary authority with the victims of burglary and business fraud: Companies and individuals do not normally have anything like the resources, the power, or the organization available to the government with which to combat those crimes.[7] In fact, rather than stress the apparent analogy between tax evasion and common theft, it is more useful to consider evasion as one of a special class of "economic crimes."

The second reason for singling out this subject for special treatment is the delicate interplay of information among those involved in the black economy (evaders, investigators, the government). This gives rise to some particularly interesting economic problems. In some cases the decision between tax compliance and tax evasion explicitly involves the contents of a report to the authorities, a feature that is absent from crimes such as theft[8]; in others the behavior of an individual evader (his consumption or his occupation, for example) can be interpreted by investigators as a useful signal of what may be going on unseen. This feature of the problem can afford some insight into the design of public policy, since information—in the form of known characteristics of people and organizations, or of observable behavior—is essential to an operational tax system. The government's awareness of the scope for evasion, and its (imperfect) knowledge of how the tax-evading sector operates, can play a crucial role in determining the structure of taxation.

Third, there is a special relationship between tax evasion and certain other topics central to the study of public economics. Evasion is a particular "economic crime"—one that involves a breach of the laws designed to ensure that people act in the economic interests of the community and not just in their own economic interests. The need for such laws arises from an ambivalent relationship between the individual citizens and the state that is supposed to act on their behalf. There may be genuine public support underlying government programs for providing collective goods, for redistributing income, for managing the economy; yet, even if that support were universal, individuals might still try to act contrary to the program they publicly support. The precise form that such economic crimes take—tax evasion, fiddling government controls, smuggling, trading on "black" markets—will differ according to the type of society, the economic structure, and the legal system.[9] Because of this ambivalent relationship and the associated incentives to economic crime, a goverment usually recognizes the restraints on its choices of economic policy. It is not as simple as saying to one, go, and he goeth and to another come, and he cometh.

In short, the issue of evasion is, unlike other illegal activities, inseparably bound up with the instruments of fiscal control that the government attempts to use in carrying out its economic policy. The quest for effective policies of taxation and public expenditure makes the topic of evasion interesting in its own right.

An Outline of the Approach

The idiosyncratic and sometimes faintly comic snippets that emerge about the black economy are often symptoms of an important problem: dissent and defection from government control. To understand this problem, and to evaluate its significance, we need to set up a coherent theoretical framework within which we can incorporate the "economics of dissent" as a natural phenomenon. We can then use this to examine the design and the implementation of policies that take this phenomenon into account.

I shall try to adhere to two guidelines: facts before theory and analysis before prescription. Unfortunately, it is not always possible to maintain this order of precedence. The problem is a subtle one, and it is sometimes necessary to spend some time sorting out what might be supposed to be going on *in principle* before one knows where one might try looking for the facts. Nevertheless, it is with the facts—such as they are—that we shall begin.

2   The Scope of the Problem

The income tax has made more liars out of the American people than golf has.
Will Rogers

Like many of the people who work in it, the "black economy" goes under several different names. One hears of the "shadow economy," the "second economy," the "unofficial economy," the "informal sector," the "underground," "clandestine," and "parallel" economies, and more.

This chapter is, to a large extent, about names. There is a lot to be sorted out before we can start on numbers, let alone analysis. However, the reader who is afraid of being confronted with a tedious taxonomy should be assured that the discussion of names leads directly to substantive issues concerning the scope of the subject. "Scope" here refers to both the meanings of the underlying concepts and the magnitudes involved.

The first basic question concerns what constitutes tax evasion. (There is considerable ambiguity about the boundaries of the subject, as we have already seen.) The second question flows from this: How can the black economy be identified, in principle and in practice? The third is a question of measurement: How big is the black economy, and is it getting bigger?

What Is Tax Evasion?

We are dealing with a corner of taxation analysis in which there is much loose talk. Stop the layman in the street and you are likely to find that he has only a very hazy idea of the difference between tax evasion and tax avoidance. Stop the *tax-evading* layman in the street and you may well find the same vagueness about this distinction. Even some professional economists use one of these terms in circumstances where their more pernickety colleagues would insist that the other is more appropriate.

In fact, there appears to be fairly general confusion in the usage of English in this area, where context and nuance play a significant role in the formation of policy and the application of statute. A similar sort of difficulty with nuances seems to apply in other languages too,[1] which does not make life easy for those who like to make international comparisons. Furthermore, the confusion over terminology can lead to a rather more unfortunate confusion of analytical concepts; and although names themselves may not matter very much, it is important to be precise about the fundamental issues we seek to discuss. Different activities that might be categorized under the heading of "evasion" could actually differ markedly in terms of their associated economic behavior, or in terms of their implications for social welfare.

Hence, a prime concern of this chapter is whether it is possible to draw a clear and practical line around the economic activities that are to be understood as "tax evasion." Can, indeed, the concept of "evasion" be usefully distinguished from "tax avoidance" or "tax planning"? And if so, how? The usual answers fall roughly into three categories:

Legalistic   The distinction between evasion and avoidance can be taken as purely a question of legal boundaries: Evasion is outside the law; avoidance is not.

Moralistic   It is sometimes argued that certain types of avoidance are just as morally wrong as evasion and therefore should be treated the same as evasion for the purposes of analysis.[2]

Agnostic   "Evasion" and "avoidance" are merely two arbitrary segments of a continuum that stretches from innocent tax planning to outrageous fraud.[3]

Each of the above views has some force, but each appears to be remarkably difficult to apply on a consistent basis. The legal distinction between "tax evasion" and "tax avoidance" and the distinction between "tax avoidance" and "tax planning" (or other similar terms) differ in specification and interpretation from country to country.[4] Moral views are difficult to translate from worthy generalities into specific concepts of economic analysis, and may turn out to be surprisingly flexible. The "continuum" thesis may be pressed almost to the point of vacuity. Moreover, in some respects each of the above views misses the main point of this book, which is the *economic analysis* of tax evasion.

At first blush the economic approach to questions of this sort seems to be quite different from the approach based on the niceties of legal definition. The economist usually takes as his basic ingredients resources, incentives, and opportunities, whereas the lawyer focuses on the interpretation of statute and on the supposed intentions of the parties involved. As far as the courts are concerned, the problem of distinguishing among (illegal) evasion, (legal) tax planning, and (possibly legal but questionable) avoidance relies to a large extent on the judge's perception of the intentions underlying the taxpayer's action. But intention seems to be scarcely a reliable basis on which to draw up watertight classifications of different economic transactions, which may in practice be closely related to one another.[5]

Yet the contrast in approach may not be as great as superficial appearances might suggest. In some cases the law attempts to make what are essentially economic distinctions among "evasion," "avoidance," and the milder forms of "tax planning."[6] Motive—which clearly has an important role in legal distinctions—also plays a part in the construction of models of economic behavior. In fact, this observation leads to a method of characterizing the specific economic problem labeled "tax evasion," and to a way of differentiating it from other apparently closely related activities, such as "avoidance" and "tax planning."

Indeed, for the purposes of the rest of this book, economic behavior is the basis for determining the scope of evasion. The economic approach to the whole issue of tax evasion is founded on the analysis of the behavior of individual tax evaders. The way in which the individual perceives his economic opportunities to be affected by the tax code and by the instruments of tax enforcement is particularly relevant. The system of taxation and its enforcement may induce the taxpayer to conceal or misrepresent some of his activites. By themselves such concealment and misrepresentation do not constitute evasion; in fact, the state may actually acquiesce in such apparent deviousness. However, the taxpayer may perceive certain choices with regard to tax declaration, financial transactions, or economic activity to be potentially costly in that they are subject to the threat of exposure and penalty.[7] If so, then this perception will influence such choices, hence influencing the response of the economy as a whole to the fact of evasion and the apparatus of control.

In the light of this, we see that "evasion" activities typically involve the individual taxpayer either in making decisions under uncertainty (concerning his eventual liability to taxes and penalties) or in trying to eliminate that uncertainty by more thorough concealment.[8] By contrast, "tax planning" implies certainty on the part of the taxpayer at the time when he makes his decisions about the deployment of his assets and his report to the tax authority. "Avoidance" is essentially similar to this but may also involve an attempt to frustrate the intention of the tax law by such deployment. In some cases the success of such attempts may depend on the rulings of tax administrators; in others the legislature or the judiciary may respond to such frustrated intentions by changing or clarifying the law.[9]

Thus, if the administration effectively turns a blind eye to a particular transaction which the law classifies as "tax evasion," then engaging in that transaction is equivalent to engaging in legitimate tax avoidance, in terms of both the consequences to the individual taxpayer and the implications for the economy as a whole. It becomes impossible to evade a provision of the tax law that is never actually enforced; you know you are never going to be chased, so there is no point taking evasive action. Conversely, if a particular "avoidance" scheme is actually the subject of legal doubt, or is liable to substantial arbitrary penalty, then the perceived consequences to the taxpayer of engaging in that scheme may be equivalent to those of participating in manifestly illicit tax evasion.

The contrast in approach can be explained as follows: Whereas the law attempts to make distinctions on the basis of *entitlement*, the appropriate distinction from the viewpoint of economic analysis is one of *function*.[10] The law attempts to specify the portion of your resources to which the state is entitled; evasion is a violation of that entitlement. How the law places such entitlement in principle may correspond to economic function. But in an economy of complex structure the two may not exactly coincide—for example, what the law describes as your income for tax purposes may not exactly coincide with what the economist means by income.[11] In practice, the scope of the economic problem of tax evasion is likely to be broader than the boundaries set by the legal definition.[12]

The above distinction between tax evasion and tax avoidance nevertheless leaves some questions open. Popular discussion of the subject suggests that somehow one can clearly divide up all activity in the economy, setting all "aboveboard" production and exchange on one's right hand and all "evasion" activities on one's left.[13] However, it could be argued that our classification of evasion in terms of economic function, though well suited for the purposes of economic modeling, gives little practical guidance as to how this separation might take place. For this reason we need to examine more closely the meaning of the term "black economy."

What Is the Black Economy?

"Black economy" or "underground economy" is a convenient catch phrase,[14] but what constitutes a sensible definition of the economic reality underlying the phrase is far from self-evident. Nor is it self-evident on what criteria such a definition should be based. The common perception is that of a chunk of largely useful activity which an overrestrictive or inept public administration has forced into a hole-and-corner existence. On this perception, the black economy is the continuation of production by other means. How is such production to be identified in principle?

The usual approach is to try to set up some sort of accounting framework within which to place different types of economic activity.[15] The focus of our inquiry has thus shifted from the relationship between legal definition and economic behavior to a more pragmatic question: How does the "black economy" fit into conventional systems of classifying the economy into sectors?

This is not solely a definitional matter; it raises several questions of economic analysis. The national-income accountant may reasonably wish to incorporate certain types of concealed or illicit activities within an idealized "production boundary" for the economy. The finance minister may reasonably wish to distinguish between activities that may properly be considered tantamount to tax evasion and other activities in the "informal" sector (which also includes household production and some barter transactions). However, making such clear distinctions is a task that is full of analytical imponderables and empirical pitfalls, and the task is complicated further by the activities of officialdom. For example, the informal sector—or "shadow economy"—is to some extent an artifice of accounting convention, which usually differs among countries and which may change over time.[16] To deal with the subject thoroughly would seem to require an exhaustively detailed discussion of a wide variety of activities and transactions. In fact, however, I am not going to attempt to draw up something so complex (and perhaps fruitless) as a standardized system of national accounts for the black economy. It is probably best just to accept the hotchpotch of concepts and definitions found in the substantial literature on the subject, and to try to see how they relate to one another.

To this end, examine figure 2.1, a rough schematic depiction of the relationship among different types of economic transaction. Let us start with the boundaries sketched there. Boundary

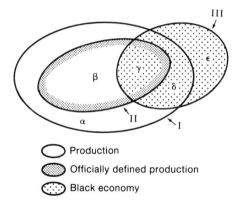

⬭ Production
⬭ Officially defined production
⬭ Black economy

Figure 2.1
The scope of the black economy. α: housework, do-it-yourself work, voluntary organizations. β: legal official production, private and public sectors. γ: black economy allowed for in official accounts. δ: black economy not allowed for in official accounts. ε: benefit fraud and tax evasion outside production sector. I, II, III: boundaries (discussed in text).

I represents the borderline—on which we suppose economists to agree—that lies between transactions that constitute production and those that do not. As is well known, this is a tricky line to draw. One attempts to make a distinction between the use of time in ways that contribute to the national income (even if it is not actually paid for) and the use of time purely as leisure; between (notional or actual) remuneration for services rendered and pure transfers. Do-it-yourself housebuilding almost certainly ought to be inside the boundary; bodybuilding probably ought to be outside. Paying one's wife for secretarial work constitutes an appropriate return to a productive factor; paying her alimony does not.

Boundary II is the *official* production boundary, the one that determines what actually appears in a country's national accounts. It has been drawn wholly inside boundary I because, for a number of reasons, official statistical bureaus define what constitutes production more restrictively than most economists. Hence, even if everyone got religion and became perfectly honest there would still be an "informal sector"; boundary II would still lie inside boundary I.

Boundary III delimits the black economy. Because it intersects the other boundaries, there are at least three separate types of economic activity that may be subsumed within the broad category "black economy."[17] The regions labeled γ and δ may contain moonlighting, off-the-books sales, production of illegal goods and services, black-market transactions, and the like; the reason that such activities may fall into both categories is that statistics on national accounts are usually compiled, and cross-checked, from several sources, so that some activities that may successfully be concealed from the tax authorities, and hence escape the conventional income measure, may nevertheless show up in, say, estimates of expenditure. Finally, note that one portion of the black economy (ε) contains forms of evasion that are very close to activities within δ in terms of the definition of the preceding section but which lie outside the production boundary—for example, benefit fraud and the evasion of taxes on the transfer of capital.

Finer distinctions than the above are possible, and may be of great interest to the national-income accountant, but they are of secondary importance in the analysis of economic behavior in comparison with those discussed above concerning the distinction between avoidance and evasion. In fact, we can probably leave to one side the niceties of specification, providing we take careful note of two warnings: First, what one identifies as the black economy is to some extent influenced by what one perceives to be the underlying economic problem, if any, that is in need of remedy. Second, the definition of the perceived problem differs among different societies, between developed and underdeveloped countries, and between market and planned economies. This difference naturally affects estimates of the size of this sector and the meaning to be attached to them.

There remains the important preliminary question of whether tax evasion and the black economy are quantitatively important.

How Large Is The Black Economy?

We have come back to Will Rogers' original assertion: Can we in fact determine *how many* Americans the U.S. income tax has made liars? Are their ranks increasing?

Establishing the nature and the extent of activities that by their very nature are intended to be covert is not easy. The degree of success that one can hope to achieve differs according to the country one examines and the range of evasion activities one wishes to cover. Although there is no instance of any government's statistical office publishing regular figures on the size and composition of the "shadow economy" as part of its standard national-income figures, there are instances where direct estimates of evasion are available. Nevertheless, it is rather unlikely that government statistical offices in all countries are going to begin providing official tables giving the details of the quantitative structure of the "shadow" sector. Thus, it usually is necessary—and will continue to be necessary—to resort to ingenious indirect methods to arrive at some figure that will yield a plausible approximation.

Let us start with the principal direct methods of estimating the size and growth of the black economy. There are two. (1) In circumstances where the taxing authority has the power, the resources, the will, and the competence to carry out its own investigation, an estimate of the extent of underreporting of incomes can be obtained by "grossing up" the results of an intensive audit of a sample of taxpayers.[18] (2) One can ask people in a survey of economic activities and attitudes. Obviously, method 2 is likely to run into a particularly acute form of the difficulties of nonresponse, evasiveness, or misrepresentation that are well known in the theory of survey design (although this can be mitigated if the questionnaire used in the survey focuses on other legitimate activities, so that the evidence of evasion can be inferred).[19] Method 1, if carefully pursued, can avoid this problem of unreliable response, but imposes upon itself certain limitations (a taxation authority can be expected to report on only those violations of tax law over which it has direct jurisdiction; one also has to be careful to take into account differences in auditing policy that may apply over time or that may apply to different groups of the taxpaying population). Nevertheless, direct methods based on such compliance studies can promise a relatively reliable, if conservative,[20] estimate of the size of the black economy.

As has been noted, the occasions when one can use direct methods are likely to be exceptions. The alternative is to try to infer the extent of activity in the shadow economy by one or more of four indirect routes. This approach is a bit like counting molehills in your lawn. It relies on the underground economy's leaving some special signs on the surface, from which you might be able to deduce the extent of what is going on beyond the view of the statistician. In three of the four indirect routes the focus is on just one particular phenomenon among those that seem to be inescapably bound up with successful evasion activity (product is created, labor hours are used up, cash changes hands). Accordingly, in addition to the two direct methods above we may categorize four indirect methods as follows: (3) the "expenditure-income discrepancy" method, (4) the "employment census" method, (5) the "monetary aggregates" method, and (6) "soft modeling" (a kind of amalgam method, explained below). Unfortunately, each of these approaches has some serious shortcomings.

The "expenditure-income discrepancy" approach can be applied to the entire economy or on a disaggregated basis. It relies on the assumption that, although incomes may be concealed or understated, expenditures will eventually show up somewhere. Given that these two concepts should, in principle, be of equal magnitude under suitably well-defined conditions, one can estimate the size of the black economy by looking at the observed discrepancy. The limitations of this on an aggregative basis are obvious—for example, both components in the simple difference that one computes are in fact measured subject to error, so there is a considerable risk of confounding these unremarkable measurement errors with the real and remarkable phenomenon of "black" economic activity. At a disaggregated level the situation may be more promising, since evidence of extraordinarily high expenditures (relative to income) can be used to identify those groups of individuals or households that may be active in the black economy; the behavior of these groups can then be analyzed and used to derive an estimate of concealed income.[21]

The "employment census" method employs both crude projections of participation rates (from which one estimates the size of the black economy by deducting reported employment from projected employment) and questionnaire surveys of firms and workers (which indirectly reveal the extent of secondary, concealed employment). The former variant faces the same criticism as method 3; the latter is really another version of method 2.

The crudest version of the "monetary aggregate" approach is the observation that there are more large-denomination banknotes around than there used to be.[22] Although this is undoubtedly true (along with the observation that operators in the black economy tend to handle large wads of folding money), it does not get one very far in determining whether the black economy has increased in size, and it is useless in determining its absolute magnitude at any particular date. A rapid increase in the number of £20 notes or $50 bills in circulation could be simply the result of inflation, and need have nothing to do with an increase in illicit transactions. Unfortunately, the same type of criticism can also be leveled at the more sophisticated versions of the "monetary aggregate" approach. Gutmann's (1977) approach relies on a stable relationship between cash held by the private sector and the total monetary base (somehow defined).[23] Fixing a particular baseline date at which the black economy is assumed not to exist then enables one to determine the size of the undergound economy by observing the growth of currency in excess of the monetary base. Feige's (1979) approach relies on the quantity equation to predict the "true" size of the gross national product (total transactions) from observations of the money stock: Estimate the velocity of circulation, deduct from this estimate the measured value of the GNP, hope that the answer does not come out negative, and you have an estimate of the size of the black economy. Clearly, either approach depends on an accurate estimate of, and on the stability of, the "mole-to-molehill" ratio. In the one case this is the ratio of currency to money; in the other it is the monetary velocity. Moreover, the estimate of the absolute size (not the growth) of the unobserved sector is likely to be sensitive to the baseline date.[24] If you were dealing with a period so short that you could be confident of the stability of the parameters, the Guttmann and Feige approaches might be valid for measuring changes in the size of the black economy; however, such a period might well be too short to be useful. Trying this method over longer periods must be approached with great caution. The results from such aggregate behavioral methods, which rely heavily on some supposed relationship that is assumed to remain stable over time, are at best extraordinarily limited; at worst, in James Thurber's famous phrase, they are "not unmeaningless."

"Soft modeling"—an approach pioneered by Frey, Pommerehne, and Weck in a number of papers[25]—attempts to reverse the usual procedure of constructing an econometric model. Rather than employing observations of the dependent variable (the size of the shadow economy) on the left-hand side and observations of independent variables (tax rates, income, indices of tax attitudes, etc.) on the right-hand side of a standard regression design, and then estimating the coefficients, one "plugs in" various assumptions about the coefficients on the explanatory variables on the right-hand side and then reads the size of the (unobserved) shadow economy off the left-hand side. The procedure is likely to be highly sensitive to the model specification[26] and to the assumptions of similarity between the economy under consideration and the economy on which the guesses or estimates of the parameters are based.

The reservations just noted are particularly important when one tries to make comparisons. Does it make sense to contrast a figure for the black economy of, say, 5 percent of the GNP in the United Kingdom with, say, 30 percent in India? As we have seen, the definition of the perceived problem differs with different types of community, and the methodologies differ widely as to their plausibility, never mind their numerical results. So I have not attempted to present a neat table of percentages, country by country. For similar reasons, I have avoided sketching a graph of spurious time trends over a few decades.

As a second-best solution I offer two tables. Table 2.1 is a summary listing of some of the more readily available studies

Table 2.1
Empirical studies of the extent of tax evasion and the black economy.

Australia	Tucker 1980 [5]	United Kingdom	Board of Inland Revenue 1981 [1]
Austria	Franz 1985 [4]		Brown et al. 1984 [2]
	Skolka 1984, 1985 [2, 5]		Dilnot and Morris 1981 [3, 5]
Belgium	Frank 1972, 1976, 1977, 1987 [3]		Feige 1981 [3, 5]
	Geeroms and Mont 1987 [5]		Macafee 1980 [3, 5]
	Ginsburgh et al. 1987 [2]		Matthews 1982, 1983 [5, 3]
	Pestieau 1985 [2]		O'Higgins 1980, 1981a [3, 5], 1981b [3, 1989 [1, 2, 3, 5]
Canada	Mirus and Smith 1981 [5]		Smith 1986 [3]
Denmark	Frey and Pommerehne 1982 [3]	United States	Crane and Nourzad 1986 [3]
France	Barthelemy 1989 [5]		Feige 1979 [5]
India	Acharya 1985 [3]		Groves 1958 [2]
	Chopra 1982 [3]		Gutmann 1977 [5]
Israel	Tanzi 1982b [3]		US, IRS 1979 [1]
Italy	Contini 1981 [4]		Kenadjian 1982 [1]
	De Grazia 1980 [4]		Long 1980 [1]
	Patrizi 1986 [4]		Molefsky 1982 [3, 5]
	Rey 1965 [3]		Park 1981, 1983 [3]
Jamaica	Alm and Bahl 1985 [1]		Ross 1978 [5]
	Bahl and Murray 1986 [1]		Tanzi 1982a, 1982b [1, 5]
			Weck, Pommerehne, and Frey 1984 [6]

Table 2.1 (cont.)

Netherlands	Aaron 1981
	Broesterhuizen 1985 [3]
Norway	Isachsen and Strøm 1985 [2]
	Isachsen, Klovland, and Strøm 1982 [2, 5]
	Klovland 1980, 1983 [5]
Spain	Lafuente 1980 [5]
	Moltó 1980 [5]
	Ruesgo Benito 1987 [4]
Sweden	Hansson 1980 [5]
	Hansson 1982a, b [2, 3, 4, 5]
	Klovland 1983 [5]
	Wärneryd and Walerud 1982 [2]
Switzerland	Weck-Hanneman and Frey 1985 [2, 3, 4, 5, 6]
USSR	Ofer and Vinakur 1980 [2]
West Germany	Frey et al. 1982 [6]
	Kirchgässner 1983 [5]
	Petersen 1982 [5]

Key: [1] audit sample; [2] voluntary interview; [3] expenditure-income discrepancy; [4] employment "census"; [5] monetary aggregate; [6] "soft modeling."

using each of these six methods. (This is only a partial listing of the literature, because it is often the case that detailed estimates are provided only as internal memoranda within finance departments and tax administrations. Furthermore, it overrepresents developed countries and market economies.[27]) Table 2.2 gives an official picture of underreporting in the United States.[28]

On the whole, there appears to be a consensus that the black economy probably constitutes from 2 to 10 percent of the GNP in Western-style industrialized economies,[29] but this conclusion should be heavily qualified. The quantitative answer to the general question "How large is the black economy" depends on the way in which the question is understood in detail and on the method of direct or indirect estimation used. The availability of data depends crucially on the social institutions of the country in question; this factor, above all, affects the estimates of the size of the black economy.

There is also a comparative dearth of hard evidence on the *growth* of this sector. There are few countries for which consistent series of evidence (other than the highly questionable aggregative methods 3 and 5) are available, and such evidence as exists does not suggest rapid growth of the black economy in recent years.[30]

Summary

Names are always important insofar as they help us to latch onto ideas clearly and precisely. However, this apparent truism is well worth repeating in connection with tax evasion and the black economy, where preconceptions and misconceptions abound and where so much of the raw material is concealed or confused.

It would be a mistake to blur the boundary between "evasion" and "avoidance" (or other euphemisms) by means of some analytical or terminological fudge. The distinction is subtle and

Table 2.2
Internal Revenue Service estimates of the unreported legal-sector income in United States, 1976 (billions of dollars). Source: Kenadjian 1982.

| Type of income | Lower estimates | | | | Higher estimates |
| | Underreporting based on | | | | |
	TCMP[a]	Other sources	Nonfiling	Total	
Self-employment[b]	19.8	3.5	9.7	33.0	39.5
Wages and salaries	3.5	5.0	12.8	21.3	26.8
Interest	1.4	1.8	2.2	5.4	9.4
Dividends	1.4	—	0.7	2.1	4.7
Rents and royalties	2.6	—	0.6	3.2	5.9
Pensions, annuities, estates, trusts	2.1	—	1.5	3.6	5.4
Capital gains[c]	2.9	1.0	—	3.9	5.1
Other[d]	1.7	0.6	—	2.3	2.9
Total[e]	35.4	12.0	27.5	74.9	99.7

a. Taxpayer Compliance Measurement Program.
b. Covers net earnings of farm and nonfarm proprietorships and partnerships (at times referred to as unincorporated business income) as well as net earnings of self-employed individuals working outside the context of regularly established businesses in the legal sector.
c. Excluded from the National Income and Product Accounts (NIPA) income concept, which defines income as earnings arising from the current production of goods and services.
d. Includes alimony, lottery winnings, prizes and awards, and other types of income. Most of the incomes included here are excluded from NIPA, since they represent transfer payments.
e. Rounded off.

does not usually accord exactly with the legal definitions. However, there is an important connection between what the law says and how the economy behaves. The issue of what is and what is not wrong might be taken to be essentially a matter for legal decision, but the *perception* of wrongdoing by individual citizens is of direct concern to economic analysis. Such a perception affects people's choices, and hence affects the way in which the economy as a whole responds to the system of taxation and to its enforcement. It is for this reason that economic function rather than arbitrary definition has been emphasized here.

The problem of what to call things also affects comparisons that we might want to make in terms of the sector known as the "black economy." Casual observation suggests that the nature of the black economy differs significantly among countries with different structures. It also suggests that there are in fact stark contrasts in the size of the black economy among countries, although problems with the comparability of data make it particularly hard to recast such casual observation as a precise empirical proposition. However, there is just too little specific evidence to confirm or refute the most extreme claims for the size of the black economy in certain countries. There is also little evidence to suggest that the problem of the black economy is accelerating out of hand in the United Kingdom or the United States. Nevertheless, it is clear that, whatever reservations one might reasonably have about some of the methodologies discussed in the preceding section, the problem of tax evasion cannot be dismissed as quantitatively trivial in either developed or underdeveloped economies.

No matter what method is used to estimate the size of the black economy, by the very nature of the phenomenon the data are inadequate. Moreover, any conceivably improved data set is also likely to be inadequate, because of a "catch-22": If official or unofficial institutions existed that could provide really accurate and reliable data in this area, then presumably there would be enough information available to the authorities to ensure that evasion would not exist in the first place. In view of this endemic problem concerning data, economic *theory* plays a particularly important role in helping us to understand the workings of the black economy.

Accordingly, our next step is to follow up the tentative leads concerning economic theory that emerged in this chapter. In view of the special economic importance of the interaction between the tax laws and their enforcement and the behavior of taxpayers, tax evasion must be discussed in the general context of public economics.

3   Taxation, the Taxpayer, and the State

There can be no taxation without misrepresentation.
J. B. Handelsman

The subject of tax evasion sometimes appears to be a poor relation in the family of public economics. In view of its comparatively recent appearance in the analytical literature and its neglect in most textbooks on public finance,[1] a newcomer to the topic might well suppose that it is peripheral to the main body of economic analysis.[2] This view is, perhaps, unfortunate.

A superficial reading of the mainstream literature on public economics can leave a deceptively neat impression of the economic relationships among the government, the public agencies, and the general public. There is considerable advantage in portraying these relationships as a system of smoothly operating linkages—a mechanism of fiscal connecting rods by which the government's policy can be transmitted. It would be convenient indeed if the public sector worked like this, but it does not.

There are, of course, some well-known sources of slippage in the mechanism. By altering the incentives to work, to save, and to take entrepreneurial risks, the structure of taxation can affect the supply of productive factors and hence the size of the tax base. Increasing the tax rates on income or expenditures reduces the aggregate demand in the economy and hence the size of the tax base. Such effects are not only well known but well recognized. Despite difficulties in estimating them in practice, they are, by and large, built in as standard features of analytical models of the public sector; the machinery of control is adjusted to take account of them. Tax evasion also is an important source of slippage in the fiscal mechanism, but the way it operates is less well understood, even though it is endemic to tax-financed systems.

This takes us back to a question posed in chapter 1: Why is tax evasion special? As I suggested there, the answer lies in the special role that it plays within public economics. Tax evasion is one manifestation of the general "black economy" phenomenon, which is bound to emerge under various systems of public control of the economy (ranging from the mildest forms of intervention up to full-blown state direction of all economic activity). Let us look at this more closely.

Some Basic Questions

To demonstrate the special role of tax evasion does not require any special apparatus. We do not have to set out a specific formal model of the economy or of its constituent parts. That task can be left until later, when we will examine the detail of the rewards and incentives open to the dishonest taxpayer and the possible mechanisms of control. For the moment, we can imagine an economic system in quite general terms. Let us begin by assuming that this system has a "public sector" and posing two very elementary questions.

Why Do Governments Levy Taxes?

The obvious answer is that they need the money in order to finance the programs of public expenditure and transfer that they wish to carry out. However, the question does have a deeper significance if we rephrase it slightly: Why do governments finance these programs by taxation rather than by some alternative route? Consider the alternatives.

The government might try *borrowing* the funds it needs. It is clear that governments do use this method of finance—successfully—in situations where there is a sufficiently well-developed capital market. It is also clear that there are limits to the extent to which they can pursue this course.[3] At the very least, some other method of finance has to be found to pay for the interest charges on such publicly issued debt. Borrowing alone will not do.

The government might try *selling* the goods and services that it provides. The argument is that if, for whatever reason, the government chooses to provide bread for the masses, why should the masses not be charged the market price for the bread? The two principal objections to such an approach are that a pricing scheme may be impracticable and that it may be inefficient.[4] Either or both of these objections may be valid, depending on the type of things on which the government wants to spend money. If the publicly supplied goods and services take the form of broadcast television rather than bread, then financing the expenditure through sales may be impracticable; there may be no relatively low-cost mechanism that would force those who want a particular good or service to pay for it. Again, if the government wants to spend money on bridges and bus lines, then, although it may be feasible to extract from people their willingness to pay in hard cash, it may be undesirable to do so. The reason for this is that the price that the government would have to charge the second, the third, and the millionth customer in order to cover the cost of the public good might greatly exceed the marginal cost of supplying it, and such a pricing scheme would force customers into consuming too little of the publicly supplied good. And trying to charge the public for battleships would be both infeasible and inefficient.

Clearly neither borrowing nor selling things is going to be suitable as a general form of public finance, even though each method will have a role to play in the broad spectrum of the government's economic activities. There are, of course, yet other forms of finance that could be considered as alternatives to taxation. Perhaps the most notable of these involves voluntary contributions or subscriptions by the populace for the programs that their government wishes to undertake. Before we see why this voluntary approach raises difficulties, let us examine the second of our two elementary questions.

Why Do People Try to Escape Their Obligation to Pay Taxes?

This question too seems to have a blindingly obvious answer: that people try to duck out of paying their taxes because they will be financially better off. However, once again there are deeper points to be made. First, people may deliberately evade taxes for reasons other than personal gain—perhaps for reasons of political dissent. Second, even if we set aside these additional reasons, the blindingly obvious answer neglects any consideration of the true personal interest of the citizen, in the broadest sense. It is a mistake to assume automatically that public expenditures are of no value to him; if the level of these expenditures were unilaterally reduced, he might well be worse off.

To see what is involved here, let us examine the public-expenditure options facing a very simple community. Imagine that there are just two persons (they may be representatives of larger interest groups), whom we shall call the *Greek* and the *Roman*. There are also two types of good, *private* goods and *collective* goods, which both the Greek and the Roman find desirable to some extent. The Greek has by right a stock of resources, which could all be devoted to his own consumption of private goods or which could be sacrificed (to some extent) in order to provide collective goods; the Roman is in a similar situation. There are three important points to note:

Collective goods really are collective in that, once provided, they are available to all.

Collective goods have to be paid for by contributions from the resources of one or both of the two people.

Each person strictly prefers more collective goods to less, if he does not have to pay for them.

For the moment let us leave the method of "contribution" unspecified; we will assume only that, one way or another, a person's contributing means that he has less to spend on his own private consumption.

To simplify the situation, let each person's contribution be like an on/off switch: Either he contributes a given sum (denoted by [+]) or he does not (denoted by [−]). There are no fractional or multiple contributions. Then there are only four possible social states:

Both contribute [+ +], so that there is plenty of the collective good.

Only one person contributes [+ −].

Only the other contributes [− +].

No one contributes [− −], so there is no collective good provided at all.

These four social states will be ranked in different ways according to the Greek's or the Roman's preferences, because, although they have a common interest in there being some collective goods rather than none, their interests are opposed when it comes to the matter of who shall pay for the goods.

Two interesting possibilities are set out in tables 3.1 and 3.2; which of these two cases is relevant depends on the type of collective good that is being provided and on the tastes of the

Table 3.1
An inferior equilibrium.

		Roman	
		[+]	[−]
Greek	[+]	β,B	δ,A
	[−]	α,D	γ,C

Table 3.2
Two lopsided equilibria.

		Roman	
		[+]	[−]
Greek	[+]	β,B	γ,A
	[−]	α,C	δ,D

two persons for the good. These two tables are to be read in the same fashion. The Greek's preferences over the states (from best to worst) are represented as α, β, γ, and δ; the Roman's as A, B, C, and D. The upper left entry in each grid refers to the evaluation by the Greek and by the Roman when they both contribute [+ +]; the upper right corner gives their evaluations when the Greek contributes but the Roman does not [+ −]; and so on. (The fact that the Greek comes before the Roman the way the diagrams have been arranged is just a matter of convention and is not meant to imply that his decisions have precedence.)

Observe that in both diagrams [+ +] is ranked as (β, B): [− +] gets an α from the Greek and [+ −] gets an A from the Roman. In other words, *from the standpoint of purely personal interest* the state where both parties contribute is considered inferior to the state where the other fellow pays for the collective good and you do not. Thus, if the provision of the collective good is left to voluntary action, it seems quite clear that [+ +] will not emerge as a solution. What does happen in each case is as follows: In table 3.1 each person, left to his own devices, will automatically choose the [−] option over the [+] option, *irrespective of what he knows or believes the other person to be doing.*[5] The solution that emerges is evidently that at the lower right corner, [− −]. This has the paradoxical property that, although it is freely chosen, both the Greek and the Roman consider it to be *strictly worse* than the [+ +] state —it is evaluated as (γ, C). Such a paradox does not arise in table 3.2, because the lower right corner is evaluated as (δ, D). In this case either the Greek or the Roman will willingly contribute of his plenty to make sure that *some* collective good will be provided rather than none at all.[6] Either [+ −] or [− +] is a candidate for an equilibrium at any given moment, although common sense suggests that if the problem were to be repeated year after year one might find oscillation between the two states.

Neither the inferior equilibrium of table 3.1 nor the pair of lopsided equilibria in table 3.2 seems very attractive. However, the hint at the role of time at the end of the last paragraph suggests a way in which a sensible solution can be reached. Let us make an additional assumption: When the Greek and the Roman talk the situation over, they agree that the [+ +] state is the best *from the standpoint of the community.* Fine; but how is this to be made consistent with the standpoint of personal interest as it was just explained? Will not individual selfishness inevitably win out over "community spirit"? Not necessarily. Suppose that the economy is that of table 3.1, and that in year 1 the state [+ +] is tried. Suppose now that in year 2 the Roman defects, yielding the state [+ −]. In year 3 the Greek, rightly exasperated, defects too, and thereafter the economy may be stuck at [− −] forever and ever. The awful prospect of remaining interminably stuck in this position may deter the Roman from defecting in the first place—taking the long view, he sees a connection between his present action and the future action of the other party, with its attendant implications for himself. A similar story could be told for table 3.2.

This appears to convey a message of greater generality: If a person's failure to contribute to the public purse has as its immediate consequence a reduction in the supply of publicly provided goods and services, or in the other presumably desirable activites of the state, may we not reasonably conclude that his perception of this straightforward cause and effect is sufficient to deter him from undercontributing?[7]

Unfortunately, the simple tale of enlightened self-interest falls down once one looks a bit more skeptically at the nature of the enlightenment. In fact, not only self-interest is involved but also some form of *reciprocity*. Reciprocity may take the form of an established custom or a social code, which may spring from a number of different motivations (such as not wanting to let one's side down, or wanting the esteem of one's fellows, or the fear that others will copy one's own publicly reprehensible behavior). In a small community, where each citizen can costlessly monitor the contributions made to the public purse by every other citizen, such reciprocity may be self-actuating; however, such communities may well be intriguing exceptions to the main concerns of public economics.

In a very large community a person may perceive his self-interest quite differently. He may suppose that, being just an individual citizen, his choices and actions are of so little significance relative to the rest of the universe that he may as well ignore any reciprocal actions by other citizens.[8] Whether or not he puts in his tuppenyworth toward the common good will thus appear to be of not the slightest consequence, since it is unlikely that anyone else will know or care what he is doing.

This assumption of insignificance is obviously invalid if the agent is sufficiently large relative to the community—for example, a large private firm or a public institution. It is also invalid if there are sufficient interconnecting social or economic links between the apparently "small" individual and many of his fellows so that the individual's action will induce a chain reaction that is large relative to the community. Leaving aside trend-setters, multimillionaires, and multinational corporations, the conjecture by an economic agent that he is (globally) insignificant, and that he may therefore disregard any appreciable social impact from his socially irresponsible behavior, is understandable, though unfortunate.

The story of the Greek and the Roman makes it plain that defection has little to do with either the perceived worth of the uses to which public funds are put or the impossibility of tying one's contributions to specific uses. Despite any moral commitment a person might feel to part of the government's expenditure (for example, the government's domestic policy of income support for the disadvantaged, or its program of aid to the Third World), he could still be tempted to renege on his payment to the government. Even if each person considered that the government acts as a trustee for those concerns in which he had a direct interest, he still might not be prepared to make voluntary contributions to the full extent required of him. There is always the hope that someone else will pay up.

The financing of a government cannot be organized like the financing of Oxfam or like that of a parish church. Though this remark seems trite, it touches on one of the major reasons for economists' concern with tax evasion. To see the application of the argument to the problem of evasion, return to tables 3.1 and 3.2 and suppose that the collective good is financed not by voluntary contributions but through taxation. If the government[9] concurs in the assessment that $[++]$ is the preferred state, then it will need some means of checking up on its Greek and Roman taxpayers; otherwise they might start trying to dodge their payments. The system of investigation and enforcement is a social institution that obviates the threat of eternal deprivation of collective goods as a means of ensuring socially responsible behavior.

Evasion is thus seen to be endemic to the economy because of a kind of myopic self-centered rationality. It appears to be in each person's interest to sneak out of making his contribution to the public purse, even though, if such antisocial behavior were to be followed by one's fellow citizens, one would lose out thereby. Unless the community develops powerful social codes or institutions to correct it, this myopia will lead to antisocial behavior even in a community of like-minded individuals; it is likely to be exacerbated in a community formed of uneasy coalitions of individuals with very different tastes, resources, and aspirations. There is a fundamental clash between a person's interests when he is "wearing his private hat" and his interests when he is "wearing his public hat." This clash of interests lies at the heart of the economic analysis of the behavior of taxpayers in an economy where the government is not omniscient.

Tax Evasion and Information

The lack of omniscience is clearly a difficulty that besets the economic policies of most governments, outside the world of Orwellian fantasy. As far as the specific matter of tax evasion and the black economy is concerned, this information problem enters the analysis by two important routes: It has a fundamental influence on the design of the underlying tax system—the fiscal expression of the "art of the possible"—and it also affects the scope for official enforcement and control.

Take the issue of tax design first. Income taxes, sales taxes, value-added taxes, and the rest are so much part of the furniture of our personal and business lives that it may never occur to us why governments use these forms of taxation rather than other forms. Familiarity with the fiscal institutions around us creates an impression of well-defined boundaries to taxation in general and to the domain of particular tax instruments. Yet even the most elementary categorization of taxes—the distinction between direct and indirect taxation—can be seen as largely an issue of information: What do the authorities know about you? Or, what do they *choose* to know about you?

The general nature of the problem can be described roughly as follows. Imagine that for each citizen there is a list of personal attributes—call it the *a* list—which itemizes all that could ever be imagined to be relevant about him: age, IQ, marital status, number of dependent children, height, collar size.... From this list we might extract certain key items upon which it seems appropriate—according to our principles of taxation—to condition taxes, allowances, public transfers, and subsidies (retirement pensions, married man's tax allowance, child benefit,...). It is obvious that this procedure has severe limitations; some of the attributes in the *a* list could conceivably be manipulated by the individual to his own advantage,[10] and others, although highly relevant in determining a person's economic status, may not be quantifiable. This second category includes such attributes as industriousness and willingness to take risks, which are crucial in terms of their income-generating potential but which are extremely hard to observe, let alone to measure objectively.

In response to this lack of direct information about items in the *a* list, tax laws usually specify certain types of observable behavior *b*, or the results of that behavior, as the basis for tax liability. Thus we find taxes on income, on purchases of particular commodities, on certain types of transactions, and so on. This is a manifestation of the standard "second-best" problem of public policy. However, drawing up this "*b* list" is not an easy task; someone has to determine what the government assumes to be knowable and therefore taxable. Some types of behavior (like some component attributes in the *a* list) will never be within the bounds of public knowledge; others are, up to a point, and these assorted bits of information and potential information can give rise to an apparently haphazard pattern of taxes.[11] Furthermore, because malleable behavior rather than a set of fixed attributes is used as a tax base, the tax system itself is bound to modify behavior. There will be a diversion of resources into other legitimate but officially unobservable activities[12]; and because of the difficulty in specifying the exact boundaries of observable, taxable behavior, the drafting of tax law may inadvertently set the stage for profitable "avoidance" schemes.[13] Intelligent governments and tax administrations know that this happens and accept it as the price of getting things done in a foggy world.

Thus, in this foggy world people quite legitimately take actions to present information about themselves that puts them in a favorable light; very few go out of their way to advertise their taxable capacity to the tax authority. However, these actions do not constitute misrepresentation. Misrepresentation is essentially a problem of the second route by which the information problem emerges—the effect on the scope for enforcement and control.

This brings us back to the generic "black economy problem" which was mentioned in chapter 1: Because of the structures of many economic relationships, there is an inherent advantage to individuals in behaving dishonestly and in providing false information. Distortion of information lies at the heart of the state's problem of exercising control and authority in the economy. In a centrally planned economy this can take the form of "report padding" (making additions and other distortions to accounts concerning the fulfillment of the plan[14]); in Western-style economies it is expressed in the form of tax evasion and related activities. We have seen the basic reason why this happens in the tale of the Greek and Roman: Each would love to renege on the commitment to the full-contribution [+ +] solution if the direct personal consequences of doing so appeared to be slight. If it would reduce his tax liability, each would willingly lie, cheat, and bear false witness. In this sense there is indeed no taxation without misrepresentation.

There are two principal versions of the misinformation problem. We have already had a glimpse of the first of these—the version in which individuals manipulate their personal attributes, or the outcomes of apparently exogenous events, to their own advantage. Insofar as entitlements to tax reliefs or to benefits are made conditional upon personal attributes related to certain specific events (unemployment, sickness, parenthood, ...), there is clearly the potential for abuse of the system: People may create the appearance of need by malingering. The other version of the misrepresentation problem highlights the phenomenon of *private knowledge*. Some of the observable attributes in the *a* list used to determine tax liability (or benefit eligibility) may be susceptible to dissimulation. One can pretend to have a low innate taxable capacity[15] by falsifying accounts, by lying, or by just not filing tax returns.[16] Because these pretenses violate the state's criteria of what is knowable and reportable, they are considered illegal and punishable.

The intelligent government or tax administration will recognize these problems of misinformation too, and will attempt to allow for the anticipated lies of the citizens in its own plans for tax enforcement. How this is done depends on the quality of the available information and the perceptiveness of the players in the tax-evasion game—the taxpayers and the tax collectors. The game may be a simple one of hide and seek, or it may have the sophistication of a hand of poker, with each player trying to make sense of signals that—deliberately or inadvertently—are being broadcast by the actions of other participants. In the first case the economic problem of control and enforcement is an exercise in "quality control"; in the second it often becomes a variant of the well-known "principal and agent" or "master and servant" relationship.[17] (The public servants charged with tax administration are the masters, of course; you and I are the servants.)

Because the misinformation problem is by nature complex, general rules for tax enforcers are not easy to come by. One point worth making at this stage, is that it is usually a good idea to make it difficult for people to avoid telling the truth in the first place, in order to prevent evasion and fraud in advance. To do this requires careful planning not only of the system of enforcement but also of the way in which information is transmitted from taxpayer to tax collector. It is for this reason that many countries tax income from employment on a "pay as you earn" basis rather than relying on the earners to report their income. It is for this reason, too, that the tax authorities, mindful of the problem of tax evasion, pay particular attention to the *structure* of taxation.

Tax Evasion and the Tax Structure

As we have just seen, the structure of taxation is important because of the patchy information with which the tax gatherers must work. But the tax structure also has a direct bearing on the emergence and development of tax evasion within an economy. The way in which the authorities have designed the structure of taxes in the community will significantly affect not only the amount of evasion that is likely to take place but also the means by which it takes place. The structure can also be a root cause of individuals' refusal to comply with the tax authority.

The main difficulty in investigating the relationship between tax design and tax dodging is that there are so many dimensions to the problem. If we speak of reforming the tax structure, several distinct issues spring to mind: the theoretical base of the tax, the intended progressivity, the method of collection, the institutions, the forms of reporting. This difficulty is evident when we consider the way in which the tax structure affects the opportunities for evasion. Two taxes with the same formal tax base may have quite different implications. Take as examples a tax on personal expenditures and a supposedly equivalent sales tax. A tax on personal expenditures is likely to offer opportunities for evasion similar to those offered by conventional income or wealth taxes—after all, the *person's* economic circumstances are being used as the basis on which detailed messages are transmitted to the tax authority.[18] In the case of the sales tax—where individual *transactions* are the basis for the mes-

sage—effective evasion will probably require collusion between the buyer and the seller, which may have as a consequence the concentration of such activity in a separate "black"
sector of the economy. If so, then we have to take into account
the impact of the structure of taxation on the structure of
markets, and the distinction between direct and indirect taxation in the evasion activity.

The difficulty is compounded by the possibility that the tax
structure is itself a cause of evasion. Here we encounter yet
another aspect of the information problem: It is often people's
perception of their taxes that matters in determining their responses to the fiscal system, rather than the actual tax rates or
the actual tax base. If there were perfect certainty, then the way
in which people perceive the tax system would be relatively
unimportant. In the absence of such certainty, perceptions can
be crucial in influencing people's choices as to their work, the
things they buy, and the risks they are prepared to take—including the risks involved in breaking the law. Are people
aware of the rate of the sales tax or the value-added tax on
the items they buy in the supermarket, or of the income-tax
schedules that affect them personally?[19] Moreover, it is not just
their perceptions of their tax rates and their personal liabilities
which are important in the analysis of tax evasion; we should
also be concerned with the more nebulous concept of people's
perception of the *justice* of those taxes.[20]

The sense of justice in taxation can be outraged by issues of
collective concern, such as the constitution of the government
demanding the tax, the size of the public revenue required, or
the purpose to which the revenue is apparently put. This outrage
occasionally takes the form of open, isolated acts of political
dissent by principled individuals.[21] In the extreme it finds expression as an outright tax revolt—the Boston Tea Party or
California's famous Proposition 13.[22] However, constituents'
collective rejection of the state as a "benevolent dictator" is comparatively rare and presupposes a degree of common interest.[23]

The sense of outrage against the system is also expressed in a more commonplace form: tax evasion. In fact, evasion is often a series of small revolts against minor irritants in different parts of the fiscal system. The various instruments of government tax programs each impinge in their own way upon the problem of evasion. This is not to suggest that the stealthy tax evader is in fact a Caped Crusader dedicated to the fight for social justice. But, along with the issues just cited, people's sense of justice may also be offended by what they perceive about the structure of taxation and its unfairness in relation to income, wealth, or special needs. In such cases the taxpayer's *own* standpoint in the system, rather than a sense of common concern, may be the driving force. "Inequity" is in the eye of the beholder. The sense of distributional injustice gives additional leverage to other, more selfish motives for evading taxes: "Why should I worry about my little bit of evasion when the rich all have their tax avoidance schemes sewn up by their accountants?"

Why indeed?

Why Worry About It?

As was noted on page 1, the government needs the money. Therefore it has to be concerned about tax evasion. This consideration alone makes it worth worrying about the problem of how to enforce the payment of taxes. But common sense suggests that there must be more to the answer than that. If revenue raising were all that mattered to government fiscal planners, then they might not be too worried about inefficiencies and injustices along the way: who cares if a sniper's rifle or a howitzer is used, as long as the revenue target is somehow hit?

Of course there are other substantive economic issues involved, and we should consider the basis for concern about evasion at a rather deeper level than simply saving the finance minister some embarrassment. However, just as the apparently easy questions raised above (Why do governments levy taxes? Why do people try to evade taxes?) turned out to have instructive answers, so too does the question addressed by this section. There are in fact two principal reasons for concern about tax evasion: It harms the interests of the general public, and it harms the means by which the state can look after the interests of the general public. Each of these reasons encompasses several issues.

The interests of the general public are broadly represented by goals that are commonly pursued elsewhere in the domain of economic policy. These might be summarized as the cardinal fiscal virtues of social justice and efficiency. In this respect there is nothing particularly special about tax evasion. The presumption is that the activity of tax evaders will frustrate the pursuit of each of these two objectives.

Nevertheless, it is not self-evident that tax evasion is all bad from the government's point of view when judged on the grounds of these two cardinal virtues.

Take social justice. Evasion induces transfers between citizens. To the extent that the rich get away with it and the poor take the blame, this may offend one's sense of distributional justice. To the extent that *anybody* gets away with evasion while others do not, one might conclude that some principles of equity are being violated. Yet, as we have seen, under some circumstances evasion may be seen as a vehicle whereby prior injustices are redressed to some extent—as a chance for the modern-day Robin Hood or Ned Kelly to even the score against an oppressive or unfair tax regime.

Or consider efficiency. The idea that tax evasion is a bad thing prompts economists to try to work out its cost. Yet in conventional economic terms these costs seem a bit elusive—exchequer losses are pure transfers; the balance between private goods and public goods can be adjusted by adjusting the tax rates; the administrative costs of enforcing taxes are positive but are not likely to be extraordinarily large. There is an argument that the uncertainty caused by the game of hide and seek imposes a burden, but even this is not overwhelmingly persuasive; in some cirumstances it can be shown that social welfare would be *enhanced* by permissiveness toward (or even encouragement of) such uncertainty.[24]

The presumed interests of the general public evidently raise several ambiguities, which we shall pursue further in later chapters. By contrast, the second reason for concern about evasion— the loss of the means of control—is relatively free of ambiguity. It is clear from our previous discussion that evasion erodes the tax base and can, in some circumstances, make the effect of alterations in tax rates indeterminate and unpredictable. Evasion can also have a major impact on the structure of prices and incomes, and can distort the effectiveness of macroeconomic policy.[25] It can also mislead the government as to what is actually going on in the economy (and therefore what ought to be done, if anything) or as to the effectiveness of policy (and therefore the extent to which adjustments need to be made, if any). Observed-unemployment figures may be unreliable indicators of the economy's performance if a substantial proportion of workers are in the black economy. The apparent elasticity of labor supply and public revenue with respect to tax rates may have less to do with conventional factors, such as work disincentives, than with the inducement to conceal income and productive activity.[26] And a fiscal system that forces many moderately substantial incomes into internal exile within the black economy could be mistaken for a genuinely progressive tax structure.[27]

Toward an Analytical Framework

In the absence of intolerable authoritarianism, taxation operates through a kind of social consent. This consent is often grudging or, where willingly granted, accompanied by a weakness of resolve or a failure of perception. Even if I lived in a country of like-minded clones, I should still expect to find that each of my alter egos would, if left unsupervised, cheat on his portion of the public duty to which we had all pledged ourselves. I would probably be doing the same. Whether this is the result of shortsightedness or malice does not matter much, since the lesson is the same: There is a kind of unanimous schizophrenia by which people will pursue their own private interests to the neglect of the public purse, even though they know that they would actually benefit from the public purse. Consent must therefore be buttressed by routine policing of the citizenry on behalf of their own interests. In this respect the topic of evasion, far from being a Cinderella subject, is arguably *central* to many issues of tax design and implementation.

Instead of dealing with a somewhat peripheral problem, we would find that an adequate treatment of tax evasion would require a comprehensive account of the political economy of the state. To do justice to such a demanding agenda would make this book far too long, so I shall try to attain a more modest objective. The general aim of the next five chapters is to build up a coherent account of how the black economy works from the viewpoint of standard microeconomic analysis: how the individual makes his decisions, how this fits into an elementary economic system with a public sector, and what the implications are for those who try to control the individual's activities through the system.

We start, in chapter 4, with the most elementary of models and the basest of motives: the greedy, calculating individual who lives in a legal and moral vacuum.[28] He produces nothing, has no sense of public duty, and habitually evades the income tax in the same way that others bet on horses or play the stock market. He is a rational rat. Understandably, not everyone sees the "black economy" in quite this way; so we move on to two important issues that are absent from simple models of solitary tax dodging. Chapter 5 examines the black economy as a productive sector. Chapter 6 reintroduces the relationship between the individual and the community which we glimpsed in the fable of the Greek and Roman; it also has a tiny bit to say about morals. In chapters 7 and 8 we turn to some important questions that arise from the normative economics of tax evasion: On what principles should a policy of enforcement be based? How far should "routine policing" go?

As was noted at the end of chapter 2, the economic analysis of evasion entails a special difficulty: By the very nature of the subject, factual evidence is neither plentiful nor of good quality. However, lest the impatient practical-minded reader give up in horror at the prospect of an unbroken diet of flimsy theoretical models based on even flimsier concepts (such as taxpayers' "perceptions"), let me offer some reassurance. There is in fact an interesting patchwork of empirical studies which have been carried out on the behavior of tax evaders and black-economy operators, using a variety of methodologies and drawing upon disciplines other than economics. So we shall examine the limited evidence that is available as we go along.

4   Rational Taxpayers

Stand firm in your refusal to remain conscious during algebra. In real life,
I assure you, there is no such thing as algebra.
Fran Lebowitz, *Tips for Teens*

It is time for more rigor. The purpose of this—Miss Lebowitz's advice notwithstanding—is to develop a framework of analysis that will help us understand the workings of the black economy. It seems advisable that such a framework be consistent with the economic modeling that is routinely used in related fields.

What counts as a "related field" in the context of tax evasion? Clearly, the term ought to cover the standard microeconomic theory of the effects of taxation. Many powerful results reported in the literature on public economics are founded on the assumption of utility-maximizing behavior by individuals and households, and this suggests that a similar approach might be fruitfully employed in an analysis of tax dodging. In addition, the element of risk taking involved in tax dodging suggests that the demand for financial assets is also a relevant related field: taking risks in legitimate activity may not be far removed from taking risks by being dishonest—in terms of the economic principles involved, not the morality.

In this chapter we will examine the elements of a simple formal model of the phenomenon of tax evasion, based on standard assumptions about rational decision-making in the face of risk. There are two sorts of economic agents whose behavior needs to be analysed: the individual taxpayers, and the government on whose behalf the tax authority acts. After considering how each of these may be modeled, we will use this structure to examine how changes in tax instruments and in the method of enforcement affect the amount of evasion. Then we will look at the results of this model in the light of the available evidence on the behavior of tax evaders.

The Basic Model: Private Sector

We begin by analyzing the choice problem of a rational taxpayer who is predisposed to dishonesty. The word "rational" is used here because we assume that the individual chooses whether to evade taxes, and by how much, according to the same sort of criteria that one would apply to other areas of rational consumer choice. And the expression "predisposed to dishonesty" is used because here we do not impute to the taxpayer any views about duty, honor, or civic pride that would compel him to put some responsibility to the state before his own money-grubbing interests. He is prepared to evade his due taxes if he thinks it might be worth his while financially.

The basic idea is that the taxpayer is confronted by a classic economic problem of choice under risk. He knows his own financial resources, he knows the tax legislation and the taxes that he should pay, and he knows the penalty for getting caught and convicted of failing to pay. He also knows that the taxation authority is not psychic and cannot know his true tax liability unless he reports it or unless the authority spends time and trouble finding out for itself. It is possible, then, that the taxpayer could get away with concealing part of his resources, falsifying his report to the authority, or even making no report at all. Being without moral scruples, he is tempted to take the opportunity of evasion.

So at the heart of the analysis lies an elementary lottery: Is it worth taking the chance of being caught and suffering a financial penalty? To focus on this problem, let us assume that the taxpayer's initial resources and all gains and losses can be measured in terms of a single consumption good, which can be interpreted as "income." We can simplify the discussion further by making two important assumptions about time and uncertainty:

• Time is compressed into a single period, within which the taxpayer has to decide whether to attempt to evade paying tax and, if so, how much to evade.

• Once the decision to evade has been taken, one of two possible states of the world must obtain: Either the taxpayer escapes detection and enjoys a consumption level c', or he is caught, convicted, and punished, in which case his consumption is c''. If he chooses to be perfectly honest, then $c'' = c'$; otherwise, $c'' < c'$.[1]

The exact nature of the lottery will be determined by the taxpayer's financial resources, by the tax system, and by the penalty system in force. To keep the discussion simple, let us take it that the tax is specifically based on income,[2] and for the moment let us make these crude assumptions about all three factors:

A1   The taxpayer has a fixed gross income, y, which is liable to tax.

A2   There is a proportional income tax at rate t.

A3(a)   There is a fixed probability, p, that tax evasion will be discovered and punished.

A3(b)   The tax on any income found to have been concealed from the authorities is subject to surcharge at a rate s.

It will be convenient to refer to the collection $\tau := (p, s, t)$ as the *tax-enforcement parameters*.

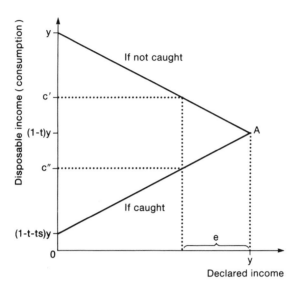

Figure 4.1
Payoffs to evasion.

Consider the situation that then confronts each taxpayer: For every dollar of gross income, he would receive \$[1 − t] if he honestly declared it to the tax authority, \$1 if he dishonestly failed to declare it but managed to escape detection, and \$[1 − t − ts] if he were dishonest and got caught. This situation is illustrated in figure 4.1, where declared income is measured along the horizontal axis and where disposable income (consumption) in the two states "if not caught" and "if caught" is related to declared income by the two sloping straight lines that meet at A. If the taxpayer is absolutely honest, he declares y and has disposable income [1 − t]y; this is represented by point A. If he is dishonest, his disposable income depends on how much he evades. If he chooses to conceal an amount of income e (so that he reports and amount y − e), his consumption is c′ if he is not caught and c″ if caught. If he is blatantly

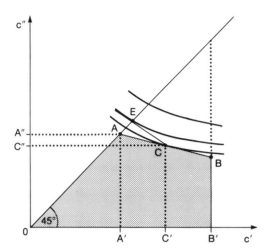

Figure 4.2
The evader's equilibrium.

dishonest and reports nothing, his consumption is y if he is not caught and $[1 - t - ts]y$ if he is caught.

We may use figure 4.1 to construct the taxpayer's *budget set*, illustrated in figure 4.2. This set consists of all the feasible pairs (c', c''), given the person's income y and the tax-enforcement parameters τ. Any point in the wedge-shaped area bounded by the 45° line and the horizontal axis represents a stochastic consumption prospect **c** with realizations c' and c'' respectively in the two states of the world such that $c'' \leq c'$; the area above the 45° line is irrelevant. Within this wedge we may draw the budget set as follows: This situation yields a budget set like the shaded area in figure 4.2 with a linear boundary AB. Point A on the 45° ray represents the case of absolute honesty, and point B the case of blatant dishonesty. The coordinates of A are $([1 - t]y, [1 - t]y)$; those of B are $(y, [1 - t - ts]y)$; accordingly, the slope of the boundary AB is $-s$. The coordinates (c', c'') of each of the points along the straight line AB represent the payoffs in the two states corresponding to different amounts of evasion e in figure 4.1. The budget set is then the whole of the shaded area $OABB'$, although only the boundary AB is of particular interest.

An alternative fruitful way to look at the opportunities facing the tax evader is as follows: Once again let evasion be measured by e, the amount of income concealed from the authorities, and let the system of tax evasion and enforcement be represented by the collection of parameters τ. Then consumption can be represented as the stochastic variable

$$\mathbf{c} = [1 - t]y + \mathbf{r}te \tag{4.1}$$

where $\mathbf{r}$ is the rate of return to a dollar of evaded tax and is given by

$$\mathbf{r} = \begin{cases} 1 & \text{with probability } 1 - p \\ -s & \text{with probability } p \end{cases} \tag{4.2}$$

so that the *expected* rate of return is $\bar{r} := \mathbf{E}\mathbf{r} = 1 - p - ps$, where $\mathbf{E}$ denotes the expectations operator. Putting it this way, we can see that the economic problem of the tax evader is almost identical to the analysis of portfolio selection, where gross income, y, is the initial endowment and where "declared income" and "concealed income" play the role of a safe asset (with a zero return) and a risky asset (with return $\mathbf{r}$) respectively. In effect, the evader asks himself "How much of the 'risky asset' should I 'purchase,' given the known distribution of the rate of return $\mathbf{r}$?" We shall find that the similarity between the two problems enables us to draw a number of conclusions about tax evasion from results that are standard in portfolio theory.

Let us now analyze the taxpayer's optimal evasion decision, given that he is constrained to be in the above budget set. Refer back to figure 4.2. Clearly, if the taxpayer is not satiated with the consumption good, then the optimal choice must lead to a point in the closed line segment AB. To be more precise than this we have to be more specific about the taxpayer's preferences regarding the state-contingent consumption levels c' and c''. As far as these preferences are concerned we shall again make a very simple assumption:

A4 The taxpayer has a von Neumann-Morgenstern utility function that is concave in consumption. It may be written $U(c', c'') = [1 - p]u(c') + p\,u(c'')$, where u is a concave *cardinal utility* function.

The use of the von Neumann-Morgenstern assumptions to characterize preferences appears, in some respects, to be quite restrictive. It rules out state-dependent utility, and hence it rules out any feeling of shame or intrinsic delight at successful evasion. It also rules out regrets and rules out misperceptions by the taxpayer of the probabilities of the two possible states of the world.[3] Under this restriction on preferences, the absolute value of the slope of any indifference curve at the point where it intersects the $45°$ ray through the origin must be exactly $[1 - p]/p$ (the betting odds on the person's succeeding in his evasion).[4] Finally, concavity rules out the phenomenon of the risk-lover—someone who would be prepared to accept unfair gambles. Everyone is supposed to be either risk-averse (in which case the indifference curves are strictly convex to the origin, as in figure 4.1) or risk-neutral (in which case the indifference curves are straight lines).

Using the expectations operator **E** again, we may write the expected utility in assumption A4 above as $\mathbf{E}u(\mathbf{c})$. With $\mathbf{c}$ given by equations 4.1 and 4.2, we find that the first-order condition for maximizing $\mathbf{E}u(\mathbf{c})$ with respect to e is given by

$$\mathbf{E}(u_c(\mathbf{c})\mathbf{r}) \begin{cases} \leq 0 \text{ if } e = 0 & (4.3a) \\ \geq 0 \text{ if } e = y & (4.3b) \\ = 0 \text{ if } 0 < e < y & (4.3c) \end{cases}$$

where $u_c(\mathbf{c})$ denotes the first derivative of u. Inequalities 4.3a and 4.3b represent, respectively, the cases where the person

chooses to be absolutely honest and blatantly dishonest. However, if we adhere to assumption A4, if the taxpayer is not
satiated in consumption goods, and if $\bar{r} > 0$, case 4.3a is irrelevant. The reason is that, given this structure of preferences, the
marginal impact of evasion on expected utility, evaluated at the
point of zero evasion, must be $u_c([1 - t]y)\bar{r}$. Since marginal
utility and the expected rate of return are both positive, it is
clear from this expression that an increase (away from zero) in
evasion would increase expected utility. The person is, by assumption, an amoral gambler, risk-averse but greedy; he is
being offered a "better than fair" gamble, so he takes it.[5]

Equation 4.3c characterizes the interesting case where the
taxpayer attempts to conceal just a part of his income from the
authorities. This case is represented in figure 4.2 as the point C,
where the indifference curve is tangent to the budget line AB.
So, out of a gross income equal to the distance OB', the taxpayer pays an amount $C'B'$ in tax and evades an amount $A'C'$.
If his dishonesty goes undetected, this results in a consumption
level equal to OC'. However, if the authorities detect the evasion he pays the full tax ($A'B'$) *plus* a penalty equal to the
surcharge rate times the evaded tax, represented on the diagram by the distance $A''C''$. This results in a consumption level
equal to OC''. The expected consumption, given this strategy,
is represented by point E on the $45°$ ray, where EC forms the
tangent to an indifference curve at E.

Now imagine that we have a whole community of these
taxpayers, with differing personal characteristics. The two principal ways in which individual taxpayers differ from one another are in their incomes (y) and in their preferences (given by
the shape of the cardinal utility function). Let each person have
a list of attributes a which, among other things, determine the
shape of this function, which we may now write as u^a. How
might we expect evasion behavior to differ across individuals?

Let us assume that, apart from their taxable income, all individuals—honest or dishonest—face the same economic opportunities. Their behavior is thus completely characterized by

their personal characteristics (y, a) and by the tax-enforcement parameters $\tau = (p, s, t)$. We may write the evasion activity of a (y, a)-type person confronted by tax-enforcement parameters τ as $e(\tau, y, a)$, where $0 \leq e(\tau, y, a) \leq y$. We need to consider how e is affected by differences in y or in a for a given τ. Let us begin with preferences, a.

Of course, some a-type individuals may be pathologically disposed toward honesty, whatever the rewards of evasion. Among the remainder, one particularly important way in which they may differ in their preferences is in their attitude toward risk. This is captured by the concavity—or, loosely, the curvature—of the cardinal utility function. We shall say that a person with attributes a^* exhibits greater risk aversion than a person with attributes a if it is possible to write their cardinal utility funtions as

$$u^{a^*} = f(u^a) \tag{4.4}$$

where f is a strictly concave transformation (see figure 4.3).

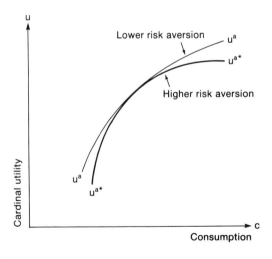

Figure 4.3
An increase in concavity.

Let us examine the effect of an increase in risk aversion on the taxpayer's optimum evasion in the case of an interior solution such as equation 4.3c. Use the left-hand side of equation 4.3c to define a function g of e:

$$g(e; y, a) := \mathbf{E}(u_c^a(\mathbf{c})\mathbf{r}),$$

where $\mathbf{c}$ is given by equation 4.1 and $\mathbf{r}$ is given by equation 4.2. Differentiating this with respect to e, we find

$$g_e(e; y, a) = \mathbf{E}(u_{cc}^a(\mathbf{c})\mathbf{r}^2)$$

where u_{cc}^a denotes the second derivative of u^a. In view of the strict concavity of u^a, it is clear that the derivative g_e must be strictly negative; therefore, the function g has the shape indicated in figure 4.4. Now suppose that u^a is replaced by u^{a*}, as in equation 4.4. Clearly we may use equation 4.4 to write

$$g(e; y, a^*) = \mathbf{E}(f_u(u^a(\mathbf{c}))u_c^a(\mathbf{c})\mathbf{r}).$$

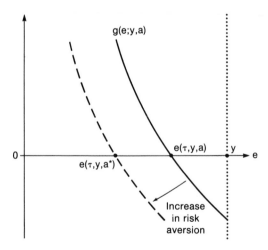

Figure 4.4
Risk aversion and evasion.

Because f is strictly concave, f_u is a strictly decreasing function of u, and so it can be seen that the shift of the attributes from a to a^* must reduce g at any given value of e: The curve shifts downward in figure 4.4. Hence it is clear from figure 4.4 that, if a^* exhibits greater risk aversion than a and if $e(\tau, y, a) > 0$, then

$$e(\tau, y, a^*) < e(\tau, y, a).$$

Now consider the relationship between personal incomes and evasion in the community. To obtain a clear-cut result, we introduce an apparently reasonable restriction on preferences: that of decreasing absolute risk aversion. Thus we require the following:

A5 Absolute risk aversion—defined as $-u_{cc}^a(c)/u_c^a(c)$—is a decreasing function of c.

It is well known that one important implication of such a restriction is that a risk-averse individual who holds a mixed portfolio of a safe asset and a risky asset would increase his holding of the risky asset if his endowment were to increase.[6] This can be illustrated with the aid of the elementary apparatus of figure 4.2. An increase in income y shifts the budget line AB outward with unchanged slope and proportionately increased length, so that both A and B move upward and to the right. It follows from the above-noted implication of assumption A5 that, for any particular a,

$$e(\tau, y, a) < e(\tau, y^*, a)$$

if and only if $y < y^*$. Thus, such a shift in the budget constraint will increase the absolute amount of tax evasion so that the new equilibrium point C^* must lie to the right of C. (See figure 4.5, where the new budget line is A^*B^*.) Notice that A5 does not permit anything definite to be said about the *proportion* of taxable income that is being concealed. To do so we would have to restrict the possible structure of the indifference map yet further. It can easily be established that an increase in y will

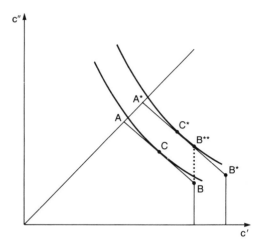

Figure 4.5
A cut in the tax rate.

increase, or leave unchanged, or decrease the proportion of income concealed from the authorities according as the *relative risk aversion*, $- c\, u_{cc}^a(c)/u_c^a(c)$, is respectively a decreasing, or constant, or increasing function of c.[7]

Thus, an elementary analysis of behavior in the face of risk results in two simple propositions about the incidence of tax evasion in the community: that people with higher risk aversion tend to evade less, and that people with higher income tend to evade more. This appears to yield a powerful insight into the anatomical structure of the black economy, although it is important to remember that many factors that may play important parts in determining individuals' participation in tax evasion— or even their *opportunities* for tax evasion—have not yet been modeled.

The Basic Model: Public Sector

We now "close" the model by looking at the situation from the government's point of view. Let us suppose that the government's only source of revenue is the income tax that we considered above (plus, of course, the proceeds of any surcharges imposed upon convicted malefactors).

If the economy is large, the government may take as *determinate* the total amount of revenue that it receives through the penalties imposed on proven tax evaders, even though the amount that each individual taxpayer has to pay (tax plus sucharges, if any) is still a stochastic variable. For the present we shall assume that the numbers of taxpayers is effectively infinite and that the distribution of individuals in the community by a (y, a) type may be described by means of a continuous distribution function $F(y, a)$.

There are several ways in which the appropriate budgetary constraint on the government might be modeled. If the government has a specific net revenue target[8] R, then the constraint that it faces is given by

$$R \leq tY - \overline{r}tE - \Phi(p), \tag{4.5}$$

where aggregate income is

$$Y := \int y \, dF(y, a),$$

aggregate evasion (one measure of the size of the black economy) is

$$E := \int e(\tau, y, a) dF(y, a),$$

and $\Phi(p)$ is the dollar cost to the government of enforcing the probability of detection p everywhere.[9]

However, the assumption of a required level of net government revenue R, fixed somewhere outside the model, is not entirely satisfactory. As was discussed in chapter 3, it is useful to see the phenomenon of evasion as part of a general problem in public economics—namely, that people in a large economy have, individually, an innate temptation to renege on payments for goods and services which they collectively desire. Let us incorporate this by supposing that the amounts raised through the tax system are used to finance publicly supplied goods and services which, ultimately, the taxpayers enjoy. Suppose that there is a single, homogeneous public good, of which the government provides a quantity z measured in the same units as the private-consumption good.[10] An individual with attributes a now has a cardinal utility function $u^a(\mathbf{c}, z)$, where z is the quantity of the public good. Because it is a public good, the same amount z appears as an argument in each person's utility function, regardless of his or her (y, a) type; the quantity of the private good $\mathbf{c}$ will, of course, usually differ with the (y, a) type of the taxpayer. In the background of this model we make a simple assumption regarding technology:

A6 The private consumption good can be transformed by the government into the public good at a constant marginal rate of transformation $\overline{\psi}$.

Thus, in this case, rather than the revenue constraint 4.5, we have

$$z \leq [tY - \overline{r}tE - \Phi]/\overline{\psi}. \tag{4.6}$$

Assuming that people are not satiated with public goods, we may take this as holding with equality.

Consider the evasion decision by any one particular taxpayer. In view of the assumption of an infinite population of infinitesimally small taxpayers, each individual may reasonably conjecture that any change in his own evasion behavior will have a significant impact on his own consumption prospect $\mathbf{c}$, but that it will have a negligible effect on the government's finances and hence on the supply of the public good z; however, this does rest crucially on the taxpayer's assumption that he is "too small to matter," and it is clear that changes in everybody else's attitude to evasion or in the distribution of income may affect E and hence affect the amount of public goods available under constraint 4.6. Because of this negligible impact of one isolated person's evasion upon z, the first-order conditions for an optimum are essentially the same as in 4.3a–4.3c, with $u(\mathbf{c})$ replaced by $u^a(\mathbf{c}, z)$:

$$E(u_c^a(\mathbf{c}, z)\mathbf{r}) = 0 \tag{4.7}$$

if $0 < e(\tau, y, a) < y$, with appropriate inequalities for the two corner solutions. Nevertheless, despite the very close similarity of the first-order conditions between the two versions of the model, the model that includes public goods (constraint 4.6) can perform quite differently from that without public goods (constraint 4.5).

We have now assembled a simple three-sector model of the economy, consisting of the legitimate private sector, the public sector, and the black economy. Let us look more closely at how it operates.

The Effects of Changes in Policy

The elementary models of the two preceding sections can be used to answer some straightforward questions about the effects of changes in taxes and in the system of enforcement: Will increased zeal or efficiency of enforcement have the desired effect upon evasion? Does the overall level of evasion rise if the tax system is made more progressive? Does the black economy increase or decrease as the public sector grows relative to the private sector?

Because of the very close relationship between our model of the private sector and standard portfolio analysis, many of the comparative-static results can be deduced directly from the literature on taxation and risk-taking in wealth-allocation models.[11] In fact, some results *for a particular individual* are immediately evident from an inspection of figures 4.2 and 4.5.

First, let us reexamine figure 4.2 and assume that the original solution to the optimization problem was at C, in the interior of the line segment AB. Let us look at what happens if enforcement is tightened. Recall that the slope of the budget line AB is $-s$ and that the slope of an indifference curve is

$$-\frac{1-p}{p}\frac{u_c(c')}{u_c(c'')}.$$

Now rotate the line AB clockwise through A; the distance $A'C'$ must fall. Hence an increase in the surcharge s must reduce tax evasion. Alternatively, if p is increased, then the slope of each contour everywhere on the indifference map is reduced; again it is clear that the distance $A'C'$ must fall. In other words, increasing the probability of detection must reduce tax evasion.[12]

Second, let us analyze the impact on an individual's behavior of changes in the tax system. Examine figure 4.5 and consider a simple cut in the marginal tax rate t without any alterations to the penalty structure, to the individual's pre-tax income, or to the quantity of public goods enjoyed by the individual. The effect of this is similar to that of an increase in y, which was discussed above: The tax cut moves the budget line AB outward, with the slope unchanged (equal to $-s$) but this time with the abscissa of point B unaltered (equal to y); accordingly, AB moves to A^*B^{**}. It is then immediately clear that the assumption of diminishing absolute risk aversion implies that the new solution must be at a point to the right of C, such as C^*, and that tax evasion must increase.[13] We can also deduce what happens if there is an increase in tax progression.[14] Reexamine figure 4.2; suppose that the values of p and s are held constant and that the marginal tax rate t is increased at the same time that a lump-sum grant is made to the taxpayer in such a way that his expected utility is held constant. Constant s and constant utility imply that equilibrium must stay at C (point A and the slope of AB stay put). Thus, evaded tax stays unchanged as the marginal tax rate rises; hence, concealed income must have fallen. Tax evasion is reduced.

Other results of changes in policy instruments follow directly from elementary reasoning about the theory of portfolio selection by risk-averse individuals. Notable among these is a mixture of such changes that generates a "mean-preserving spread" of the returns to evasion activity. There are several possible ways of constructing such mean-preserving spreads that may be interesting from the viewpoint of tax policy—for example an increase in the surcharge may be accompanied by a decrease in the probability of detection such that $\bar{r}$, the expected return per dollar of evasion activity (equal to $1 - p - ps$), remains unaltered; or a simultaneous increase in the marginal tax rate and an increase in the surcharge with an unchanged detection probability so as to keep $\bar{r}t$ constant. In all of these cases we can apply a standard result that such a change will induce a reduction in risk-taking—in other words, less evasion.[15]

However, all of these results have to do with the evasion behavior of an *isolated individual*, $e(\tau, y, a)$. Let us see what happens to aggregate evasion E where, to keep the analysis interesting, we assume that the tax-enforcement parameters τ have been set such that $E > 0$. The impact of p or s at the aggregate level is fairly clear; one has only to integrate over the individual effects of evasion to see that, unless there is an extraordinarily large feedback effect on the supply of public goods, an increase in either parameter will reduce the aggregate level of evasion. The effects of changes in tax rates are less straightforward, though. The principal reason for this is that changes in taxation will have a major impact on the size of the public sector relative to the private sector, as can be seen from an examination of constraint 4.6.[16]

To see the implications of this, let us work out the *total* impact of a change in the marginal tax rate t, including its implications for the supply of public goods. Let us begin with the first-order condition 4.7 for those taxpayers who are already involved in some tax evasion. Let there be an infinitesimal increase in the marginal tax rate t, and let the induced change in the supply of the public goods be z_t, where z_t can be evaluated from equation 4.6 and the set of solutions to equation 4.7. Differentiating equation 4.7 with respect to t and simplifying, we have, for anyone of the (y, a) type,

$$te_t(\tau, y, a) + e(\tau, y, a) = [-\mathbf{E}(u_{cc}^a \mathbf{r})y + \mathbf{E}(u_{cz}^a \mathbf{r})z_t]/D \qquad (4.8)$$

where $D := -\mathbf{E}(u_{cc}^a \mathbf{r}^2)$, which is strictly positive in view of the strict concavity of cardinal utility.[17] Let us examine equation 4.8 term by term. The two terms on the left-hand side give the total effect on *evaded tax* $(te(\tau, y, a))$ of a small increase in the tax rate. The first term on the right-hand side is unambiguously negative if $e(\tau, y, a) > 0$ and assumption A5 holds[18]; the sign of the second term on the right-hand side is ambiguous,[19] and in order to obtain some insight into this and into the sign of the whole expression 4.8 we shall look more closely at the structure of preferences for public goods.

Refer back to the discussion in chapter 3 concerning the optimal level of public goods. The standard result is that, for an optimum, the sum of the individuals' marginal rate of substitution of the private good for the public good shall equal the marginal rate of transformation of the private good for the public good. In the present model, this would imply

$$m = \bar{\psi} \qquad (4.9)$$

where $m := \int m^a dF(y, a)$ and where m^a denotes u_z^a/u_c^a, the marginal rate of substitution of a person with attributes a. However, this first-best solution is not in fact practicable because, as we know, a government tax-enforcement policy that has values of the parameters $\tau = (p, s, t)$ as considered above will induce a certain amount of evasion. As we can see from equation 4.6, transferring a dollar from private pocket to public purse (via a tax hike) does *not* call forth $1/\bar{\psi}$ of public goods;

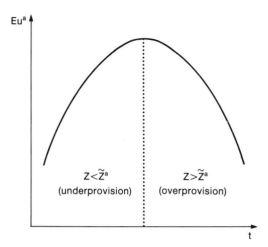

Figure 4.6
The tax rate and the taxpayer's welfare.

rather we have

$$dz = [d(tY) - d(\overline{r}tE)]/\overline{\psi}. \tag{4.10}$$

In fact, if we differentiate the expected utility with respect to t, allowing for the induced effect on evasion and the resulting z, we can see that for a (y, a)-type person the expected utility behaves as in figure 4.6 and achieves a maximum where $m^a = y/z_t$. Call the value of z that achieves this maximum $\tilde{z}^a$. If $z < \tilde{z}^a$, we shall say that a (y, a)-type person considers public goods are *underprovided*, and that if $z > \tilde{z}^a$ he considers them *overprovided*.

To see the implications for the aggregate amount of evaded tax tE, let us take a particularly illuminating special case in which all individuals are identical (so that $E = e$ and there is unanimity on the optimal level of provision of public goods: $\tilde{z}^a = \tilde{z}$) and in which individual preferences are such that there are zero income effects (the *Ziff assumption*). The Ziff assumption implies that m is independent of c (see figure 4.7) and hence is independent of r; it also implies that the second

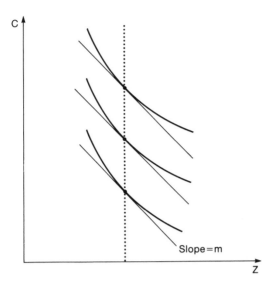

C

Slope = m

Z

Figure 4.7
Preferences for public and private goods.

term on the right-hand side of equation 4.8 can be written $m\mathbf{E}(u_{cc}^a \mathbf{r})z_t$.[20] Moreover, we see that the expression 4.8 must then have the sign of $m - y/z_t$, which in turn is positive if $z < \bar{z}$ and vice versa. So it is clear from equation 4.8 that the effect of a tax increase on the quantity of the evaded tax is positive or negative according as public goods are underprovided or overprovided.

The intuition is as follows: An increase in the tax rate for a single individual in the model without public goods simply reduces his resources and so (in virtue of A5) reduces evasion via a wealth effect. But if tax increases imply a concomitant increase in public goods z, then a typical citizen perceives total resources (private disposable income plus public goods) to rise if public goods are underprovided, and to fall if they are overprovided.

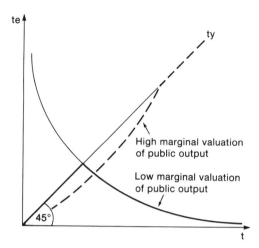

Figure 4.8
Evasion response to the tax rate.

Does the result generalize? Certainly it does if one allows for heterogeneous individuals and retains the assumption of Ziff public goods[21]; in such a case a (y, a)-type taxpayer will evade more or less tax ($te(\tau, y, a)$ will rise or fall) according as m^a is greater or less than y/z_t. Evidently, low-income persons and those with a relatively high marginal valuation for public goods will evade more; rich people and those who place little value on public goods will evade less. This is illustrated in figure 4.8 for two individuals, one with a high marginal valuation of public goods and one with a low marginal valuation of such goods but both with the same income. Notice the kink as each schedule hits the line $te = ty$—one could have points above that line only if it were possible to have $e > y$, as in the case of benefit fraud. For the case of heterogeneous taxpayers, then, what happens in the group as a whole must depend on the joint distribution of income y and the marginal rate of substitution m^a; but it also depends on the way in which risk aversion is distributed amongst the members of the community. To see the reason for this, suppose that all individuals are at an equilibrium of type 4.3c. Then

$$tE_t + E = \int [e_y(m^a z_t - y)] \, dF(y, a)/(1 - t). \tag{4.11}$$

To extend the idea of public goods being under- or overprovided, we must weight the individual terms m^a by the expression e_y, the income effect on evasion (equal to $-\mathbf{E}(u^a_{cc}\mathbf{r})/\mathbf{E}(u^a_{cc}\mathbf{r}^2)$), which will depend on the risk aversion of a (y, a)-type person as well as upon his income.

Clearly there are other simple, qualitative questions that could be answered with the aid of this basic model,[22] but the particular comparative-static exercises that we have examined above should be sufficient to deal with these fairly briskly. It is time to look at some real numbers again.

Empirical Evidence

Manipulation of the simple models outlined in the preceding section suggests some simple, testable propositions about tax rates, tax enforcement, and tax evasion. However, the fundamental problem of unreliable or unavailable data (discussed in chapter 2) might suggest that empirical models of evasion are impossibly difficult to construct. Even the standard way of dealing with the lack of an adequate set of microdata—going out and conducting one's own purpose-built sample survey—does not appear to be promising in this particular field.[23]

Nevertheless, in some countries there is a convenient way around the problem of inadequate microdata: to make use of the information that becomes available to the tax authority in the course of its investigation of potential tax evaders. One of the primary sources of data for this type of approach is the Tax Compliance Measurement Program, in which the U.S. Internal Revenue Service conducts thorough audits of a stratified sample of taxpayers. This program provides detailed data on audit and prosecution rates, severity of sentences, income sources, regions, and the demographic and social classification of taxpayers.[24]

The availability of such compliance data suggests the construction of an econometric model of evasion. If we neglect the influence of public goods, our theoretical model gives aggregate evasion (or concealed income) as

$$E = \int e(\tau, y, a) \, dF(y, a).$$

This suggests that an appropriate empirical version of the model ought to have tax and enforcement parameters, personal income, and indicators of the type of income recipient as explanatory variables; the dependent variable would be some measure of underreported income. The model could be estimated for different categories of taxpayers (broadly defined a-types) or for taxpayers in general.[25] One might then use such an empirical model to test some of the elementary hypotheses in the relationships between evasion and the tax-enforcement parameters.

There are a number of difficulties with so simple a model specification. Foremost among these is the "rationing" of evasion: Individuals' opportunities for participating in evasion can differ greatly among occupations and social groups, even though it may be the case that they have deliberately selected those groups for themselves. In addition, there may be underlying problems of bias in the sample selection, since the system of intensive audits excludes those individuals who do not file a tax return at all (so that the Program will underestimate the total amount of evasion). Despite these reservations, the Tax Compliance Measurement Program is probably one of the most reliable official sources, and the empirical work carried out on it provides valuable evidence on the determinants of taxpayer dishonesty in practice. The principal results of this work can be summarized as follows:

Evasion behavior varies considerably by income type and population group. In fact it is for this reason that the IRS separates taxpayers into audit classes. Clotfelter (1983) found that personal taxpayers have a rather low value of the income elasticity of underreporting (about 0.3) compared with that for farm business income (about 0.65). Married people evade more than single persons, and younger people more than the old.[26]

Disposable income and enforcement parameters have the expected effects on evasion behavior. However, Witte and Woodbury (1985) found only a weak relationship between taxpayer compliance and the probability and severity of criminal penalties, and Alexander and Feinstein (1987) found that the *source* of income, rather than its level, is a significant determinant of evasion.

Evasion increases with the tax rate. Again this is suggested by Clotfelter's work; there is less taxpayer compliance in audit classes with higher marginal tax rates.

The last two of these findings also appear to be supported by time-series evidence. Poterba (1987) used a series of observations obtained from six rounds of the TCMP to investigate the effect of marginal tax rates on the reporting of capital gains; his estimates of the elasticity of evasion with respect to the marginal tax rate are very similar to Clotfelter's cross-section results. Crane and Nourzad (1986) used a synthetic series of an "adjusted gross income gap," the difference between aggregate income estimated by the Bureau of Economic Analysis and the (smaller) estimate of the IRS; this is clearly a version of the aggregate-discrepancies method discussed in chapter 2.[27] Tax evasion (this gap) was modeled as a function of tax rates, enforcement parameters, income, and the inflation rate. However, as far as tax rates are concerned, the time-series results may be picking up a quite different black-economy phenomenon. We would expect to see a positive relationship between marginal tax rates and the overall size of the black economy if, on average, public goods were perceived to be underprovided; accordingly, we might expect a period in which a popularly supported expansion of the public sector took place to be accompanied by a growth in the relative size of the black economy.

A final cautionary remark about the interpretation of the cross-section evidence: In any sample of taxpayers taken at any particular time, those persons facing different marginal tax rates may belong to groups that have different economic opportunities, or that have significantly different preferences for risk and attitudes toward evasion. We shall investigate these issues further in the next two chapters.

Provisional Conclusion

The predictions of the most elementary of the economic models of evasion, in which tax evasion is treated just as a simple form of gambling, seem to make a good deal of sense. Rational gamblers take fewer risks if the odds are worsened; therefore, simple adjustments to enforcement parameters have the desired effect. Rich gamblers (evaders) stake more than those of modest means—the reckless more than the cautious. And the predictions of the elementary model are borne out by the available evidence on tax audits, to some extent.[28] However, there does appear to be an important discrepancy: The evidence suggests that evasion *rises* with the tax rate, in contrast to the results of the basic model. This apparent conflict does not disappear if the basic model is elaborated to encompass more complex tax and enforcement structures,[29] although it may be resolved in models that allow for heterogeneous taxpayers and incorporate public goods.

The underlying idea of the theoretical model—that people act out of semi-enlightened self-interest rather than out of strong personal conviction—seems to have a powerful appeal: Most tax evaders surely do it for the money rather than for fun or perversity. However, in the light of the important discrepancy we have just noted and of the apparent diversity of tax evaders' behavior, it may well be that the approach examined in this chapter is rather incomplete. The simple individualistic model of tax evasion in the hope of monetary gain needs to be modified to allow for the influence of other factors in the community as a whole. Accordingly, chapters 5 and 6 will elaborate on the elementary theory in two directions: by considering more carefully the constraints on evasion imposed by the structure of production and market transactions, and by taking into account the structure of social relationships.

5   Production and the Market

When a felon's not engaged in his employment,
Or maturing his felonious little plans,
His capacity for innocent enjoyment
Is just as great as any honest man's
W. S. Gilbert, *The Pirates of Penzance*

Popular usage of the term "black economy" conjures up some powerful images. It suggests a world apart, where the rules and customs of ordinary social and commercial life are modified or suspended. For some this means a world of cheerful anarchic efficiency, peopled by cheap plumbers, swift-footed street-traders, and Honest Ron the car dealer. For others it conveys the idea of a few unsavory fringe activities nurtured by anomalies in the regular universe. At the very least the term seems to connote a separate sector with distinct economic characteristics. Such a separate sector presumably deserves separate study.

In this chapter we look at the black economy as a productive entity. We examine the *economic* content of some basic questions that arise from the notion of a "shadow world" and the people who inhabit it: What makes their activity special? Are they are really "not as other men"? Or is it just that they segregate themselves into different economic compartments? If so, how does this segregation come about? And how does the black economy respond to changes in the fiscal environment?

In order to investigate these issues, we need to reexamine the analysis of the gambling taxpayer which we developed in chapter 4. One of the principal assumptions in the basic model set out there was that a person's income is exogenously given. This patently will not do if we are trying to understand the economic workings of the black economy as a distinct sector. It ignores the essential phenomenon of the black economy as a begetter of productive employment, and it neglects the interesting possibility that the presence of this sector may open up opportunities for economic activities that would not otherwise exist.

Accordingly, the next three sections develop the story of evasion behavior from that of the simple gambler to that of the moonlighter.

Endogenous Incomes

If we are to make progress with the ideas raised in the preceding paragraphs, then clearly our first task should be to model the income-creating process within an economy in which people evade taxes.

We proceed by extending the basic model of chapter 4 to include personal decisions about factor supply. In order to obtain some more interesting results in this extended model, we replace the simple proportionate tax system with a system in which there is a constant marginal tax rate t and in which a lump-sum grant B is received by the individual from the government. If B is positive, this system is equivalent to a linear progressive income tax combined with a negative income tax.[1] Some elements of the model remain essentially unchanged; for example, once again we have the standard budget constraint, which determines consumption $\mathbf{c}$ as a random variable:

$$\mathbf{c} = B + [1 - t]y + \mathbf{r}te \tag{5.1}$$

(where **r** is the random rate of return to evasion, specified in equation 4.2). However, the variables y and e now require more careful specification and some reinterpretation in the context of the black economy.

The important departure, of course, is that income is endogenous. We shall suppose that it is in fact determined by the amount of labor a person supplies. This is not a very restrictive assumption, because the type of analysis that we shall develop could also be used with reference to other productive factors—for example, the supply of savings. This concentration on employment and self-employment has the additional advantage of focusing on a striking feature of the black economy in widely differing types of social system: the presence, simultaneously, of two sorts of labor over quite a broad range of activities.

To fix ideas let us imagine two sectors corresponding to these two sorts of labor, one legal and one illegal. In some cases the distinction between the sectors is no more than a convenient fiction, since the actual physical labor supplied in the two sectors is of identical form and the (gross) wage rates are identical; work in the illegal sector would then be identical in every respect to work in the legal sector, except for the fact that the income it generates is not reported to the authorities for tax purposes. In other cases there really are two sectors, with different equilibrium wage rates as though for different types of labor; the circumstances under which this is likely to arise are discussed in the next section.[2]

Denote the time that a worker supplies to the regular sector by h_0 and time he supplies to the illegal sector by h_1, where the total time available per period is normalized at unity. Let w_0 and w_1 be the wage rates in the legal and the illegal sector, respectively; for convenience, define $\mathbf{h} := (h_0, h_1)$ and $\mathbf{w} := (w_0, w_1)$. If all people were identical and the two sectors really were distinct, then we might expect to find $w_0 > w_1$, but if there were no substantive economic difference between the sectors we would have $w_0 = w_1$. However, we shall be considering a variety of possible occupations, and a heterogeneous community of individuals who differ according to their market opportunities ($\mathbf{w}$) and their list of personal attributes (a). In such a community we expect to find some ($\mathbf{w}, a$) types for whom $w_0 > w_1$ in their chosen occupation and some other types for whom the reverse holds.

For any person of a particular ($\mathbf{w}, a$) type, we may now write the two key endogenous variables:

$$e = w_1 h_1 \tag{5.2}$$

and

$$y = w_0 h_0 + e. \tag{5.3}$$

In other words, e now represents the income generated in the illegal sector, which is not reported to the authorities, and y represents total income from both legal and illegal sectors. We suppose once again that the whole of y is in fact liable to tax.

We need to modify the specification of taxpayers' preferences to allow for the supply of labor. Suppose that, irrespective of whether labor is supplied to sector 0 or to sector 1, it is perceived to be uniformly irksome. Individual utility is now given by $\mathbf{E}u^a(\mathbf{c}, \ell)$, where the second argument represents leisure and is defined as $\ell := 1 - h_0 - h_1$. As in chapter 4, $\mathbf{E}$ denotes the expectations operator and u^a is a strictly concave function. We shall assume that both consumption and leisure are "normal goods"—the demand for them rises as the person's budget increases. Now, maximizing $\mathbf{E}u^a$ with respect to $\mathbf{h}$, subject to the constraints $\mathbf{h} \geq \mathbf{0}$, $\ell \geq 0$, and 5.1–5.3, we find that the first-order conditions[3] are

$$[1 - t] w_0 \mathbf{E}u_c^a - \mathbf{E}u_\ell^a \leq 0 \tag{5.4}$$

for the legal sector and

$$[1 - t] w_1 \mathbf{E}u_c^a - \mathbf{E}u_\ell^a + t w_1 \mathbf{E}(u_c^a \mathbf{r}) \leq 0 \tag{5.5}$$

for the illegal sector,[4] where in each case the arguments $(\mathbf{c}, \ell)$ of the u derivatives have been suppressed. Clearly 5.4 is the standard first-order condition for the neoclassical labor-supply problem; 5.5 has a very similar structure but with an extra term tacked on that corresponds to the left-hand side of 4.3.

Writing out the arguments $(\mathbf{c}, \ell)$ in full and substituting from equations 5.1–5.3, we see that conditions 5.4 and 5.5 can be expressed in terms of the endogenous variables $\mathbf{h}$ and the parameters characterizing the individual's type and the tax-enforcement system. Accordingly, we can use those conditions to extract the labor-supply functions:

$$\mathbf{h} = \mathbf{h}(\tau, \mathbf{w}, a) \tag{5.6}$$

where the tax-enforcement parameters are again represented by $\tau = (p, s, t, B)$. If we examine the structure of this system, though, we find that it is rather more complicated than the corresponding expression for $e(\tau, y, a)$ in chapter 4. In principle, the amount of labor supplied to each sector (legal or illegal) depends on the wage rate in that sector *and* on that in the other sector, as well as on tax-enforcement parameters. Thus, in considering the effect of any parameter on evasion activity one has to consider what happens on both the legal/illegal work margin and the consumption/leisure margin simultaneously—and disentangling the two may be difficult. It is not too hard to think up examples, consistent with the standard assumptions A1–A5, that produce some seemingly odd results. For instance, an increase in the penalty surcharge s could *increase* evasion—an increase in s reduces the expected net (post-tax-and-investigation) wage in the illegal sector, and if the individual's supply curve is backward-bending then it is conceivable that such an adjustment in the reward to labor will result in more labor being supplied to either sector or both sectors.[5]

Of course the problem is that, by extending the simple tax-evasion model to include a productive factor, we have combined a portfolio-allocation problem with a conventional labor-supply model. Fused together, these can give ambiguous answers or even, as we have seen, apparently perverse results. To see the reason for the ambiguity, take the following simple example: Suppose the tax system is made more progressive by increasing the parameters t and B, and consider an individual for whom the expected total tax payment remains unchanged (in other words, one who is "compensated" in terms of tax). From standard textbook arguments we could deduce two things about the person's behavioral responses: (i) that his demand for risky assets should increase and (ii) that the labor he supplies should decrease.[6] Now, participating in the black economy clearly involves both taking risks and working; so, for this person under the postulated tax change, effect i suggests that he allocate more of his time to the chancy "black economy" and effect ii suggests that he allocate less.

To obtain more specific insights, it is useful to impose a bit more structure on the choice problem. In the next two sections we shall look at two alternative ways of doing so, which correspond to two different types of labor activity in the illegal sector.

Self-Declaration

We begin with those of the self-employed who operate simultaneously in both the legal and the illegal sector. The actual work done in each case may be identical; what is essentially different between the two sectors is the type of contract made between the supplier and the hirer of labor. It is a situation that is probably quite familiar—for example, a plumber may offer you an "invoiced price" and a lower "cash price" for the same job. The economic elements of the problem that concern us here are that the worker has free choice about how much work to do in the legal sector and that tax is assessed on the basis of the worker's declaration.

To analyze this we shall assume that preferences have the standard properties expressed by assumptions A1–A5. We will also require the utility function to be structured in such a way that the individual's decision about the labor supply in the black economy can effectively be separated into two stages[7]: *stage 1*, in which the individual decides how to divide the total time available between leisure and work (of any sort), and *stage 2*, in which the individual decides upon the division between legal and evasion activities of the total labor supply.

This simplified structure of the self-declaration decision problem implies that the formal model is such that the demand for leisure (or, equivalently, one minus total work supplied) can be written

$$\ell = \ell(w_0, t, B, a). \tag{5.7}$$

The amount of work in the black economy can then be implicitly defined by the type of "evasion function" that we used in chapter 4. In the special case where the (gross) wage rates are equal in the legal and illegal sectors, we may then write

$$h_1 = e(\tau, w_0[1 - \ell], a)/w_0 \tag{5.8}$$

where ℓ is given by equation 5.7. The two counteracting effects noted above can now be sorted out rather conveniently, since equation 5.7 is the "pure labor supply" part and equation 5.8 gives the "portfolio" part of the combined impact of the tax-enforcement system. This makes it much easier to analyze both the variations in behavior across individuals of different types and the change in behavior as one or more of the tax-enforcement parameters τ is changed.

Consider first what happens across groups of people characterized by (w, a) type. It is obvious from the analysis of chapter 4 that those with higher risk aversion will devote less of their time to the black economy. It is also true that for a given level of w_0, those with relatively greater potential market rewards in the illegal sector (higher w_1) and low relative risk aversion will

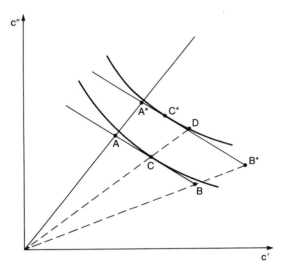

Figure 5.1
Effect of an increase in disposable income.

devote more of their time to the illegal sector.[8] But what happens if we compare two individuals who have the same attributes a, but one of whom has a higher potential wage than the other in both the illegal sector and the legal sector? Take the case where $w_0 = w_1$ and examine figure 5.1. Since leisure and consumption are assumed to be normal goods, the higher wage rate increases total taxable income, $[1 - \ell]w_0$, and so the budget constraint shifts outward as shown; hence, the standard assumptions are sufficient to ensure that the higher-wage person conceals more income from the tax authority. Nevertheless, he may actually *participate less* in the black economy: If the labor-supply curve is locally "backward-bending" (figure 5.2), then the budget constraint A^*B^* in figure 5.1 actually corresponds to a case of *fewer* total work hours than the budget constraint AB; if preferences also exhibit increasing relative risk aversion,[9] then the new equilibrium, C^*, must lie to the left of D; so hours spent in the illegal sector are actually a smaller proportion of an already

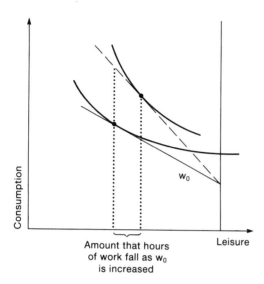

Figure 5.2
Effect of an increase in the wage rate.

smaller total. Thus, in comparing participation in the black economy by persons of different types, we clearly have to be careful whether we are discussing *income concealed* or *hours worked* as a measure of illicit activity.

Now let us see what happens to black-economy activity as the tax regime is altered. Clearly the "separable decisions" assumption simplifies matters considerably, in that the parameters p and s do not enter equation 5.7; thus, using the results of chapter 4,[10] we see immediately that increasing the probability of detection or the penalty for convicted evaders unambiguously switches activity from the illegal sector to the legal sector. Other changes in the regime will affect both the overall supply of effort, given by equation 5.7, and the allocation between sectors, given by equation 5.8. A rise in B, the lump-sum benefit, clearly increases the demand for leisure, but at the same time it also tends to increase work in the black economy; the reason for this is that the rise in B shifts the budget constraint AB in figure 5.1 outward, and so assumption A5 implies that people are willing to take more risks. A rise in t will increase the proportion of time spent in the illegal sector out of any *given* total of work hours for those $(\mathbf{w}, a)$-type individuals who display increasing relative risk aversion; thus, if the labor-supply schedule is vertical or backward-bending, it is clear that a rise in the marginal tax rate will increase illegal activity absolutely.[11]

These results for a person of one particular $(\mathbf{w}, a)$ type have some interesting implications for the economy as a whole, under the restrictions that we have considered. Making the tax system more progressive clearly increases the illegal sector as a share of the total labor supply, and if each person's labor-supply curve is vertical or backward-bending then activity in the black economy increases in absolute terms. What happens to activity in the legal sector depends crucially on $F(\mathbf{w}, a)$, the distribution of wage rates and tastes within the community: For low-wage individuals (who experience a gain in disposable income when the tax system is made more progressive), legal work h_0 will fall; for high-wage individuals it will rise.

Moonlighters and Ghosts

The simplicity of the model we have just analyzed obviously derives from the effective separation of the labor-supply and tax-evasion decisions. It relies heavily on an elementary extension of chapter 4's "roulette model" of the tax evader; thus, it misses the point as far as a lot of illegal work is concerned. Such an analysis takes little account of the institutional constraints that may have fostered the growth of the black economy in the first place and that shape the way in which it operates. For example, we assumed that the supply of hours to each sector of the labor market could be freely varied—an option that is just not open to many an ordinary worker who wants to turn a dishonest penny. In this section we will attempt to deal with important cases of activity in illegal labor markets that will not fit into the framework that we developed in the preceding section.

The first of these cases concerns employees (rather than self-employed individuals), who usually experience significant restrictions on the flexibility of the hours that they work, at least in the short run. If we couple this observation with the fact that tax enforcement is often almost automatic for certain types of regular paid employment,[12] we can see that if one is to make a dollar or two out of the taxman it will not be through one's regular work contract.[13] The usual solution is to take a second, irregular job. For such persons—the moonlighters—legal and illegal work are seen as distinct, nonsubstitutable activities, at least in the short run.

Secondly there is the black-economy specialist—typically a self-employed worker who does not work at all in the legal sector (perhaps because he finds himself unemployed, or because the returns in the black economy are especially attractive).

In modeling the system, it is clearly no longer reasonable to use the "separable decisions" assumption. But there is an interesting alternative way of simplifying the problem. Let us take a particularly straightforward (but realistic) case in which, as far as a person's legal work is concerned, the choice is simply whether or not to participate in a job where the hours are preset at some value $\overline{h}_0$. This choice will be determined by the wage rates $\mathbf{w}$ confronting this particular worker, by his personal attributes a, and by the tax-enforcement parameters τ. Write the set of tax-enforcement parameter values within which the person will accept the opportunity of legal work as $A(\mathbf{w}, a)$.[14] Then, in this special case, the function determining h_0 in equation 5.6 can be written as

$$h_0 = \begin{cases} \overline{h}_0 & \text{if } \tau \in A(\mathbf{w}, a) \\ 0 & \text{otherwise.} \end{cases} \tag{5.9}$$

For either of the two regimes indicated in equation 5.9, the problem of determining hours worked in the illegal sector then reduces to the same—considerably simplified—form. Within each of the two regimes, income generated in the legal sector is fixed, at either $w_0 \overline{h}_0$ or 0. So the individual's optimization problem now becomes one of chosing h_1 to maximize $\mathbf{E} u^a(\mathbf{c}, 1 - h_0 - h_1)$ subject to

$$\mathbf{c} = y_0 + [1 - t]w_1 h_1 + \mathbf{r} t w_1 h_1 \qquad (5.10)$$

where equation 5.9 holds and where

$$y_0 = \begin{cases} B + [1 - t]w_0 \overline{h}_0 & \text{if } \tau \in A(\mathbf{w}, a) \\ B & \text{otherwise.} \end{cases} \qquad (5.11)$$

The problem of labor supply and labor allocation under uncertainty has thus been simplified by keeping h_0 fixed within each of the two cases, so that the only *effective* variable is h_1.[15]

Before we examine the solution to this optimization problem, we need to talk about "ghosts"[16]—individuals of whom no official record exists. The economic incentive to become or to remain a ghost is clear: If there is no official record of you in one type of activity (for example, in the claiming of welfare benefits), then there may be a very small probability of having your misbehavior detected in some other activity (for example, working in the black economy).

Ghosts enter our simplified model in two ways: First, the probability of detection may be much lower for them than for true moonlighters or for those who have a mixed portfolio of legal and illegal self-employed work, since the tax authority has yet to discover their very existence. Second, one's budget constraint may change abruptly as one moves from the twilight world to a situation in which one is at least known to the authorities, since this may affect one's ability to claim the lump-sum benefit B, depending on the way in which the system of taxes benefits is administered. Thus, for ghosts the second part of equation 5.11 may read $y_0 = 0$ rather than $y_0 = B$. The precise definition of a ghost does not affect the workings of the underlying model, although it may modify the interpretation of the impact of tax-enforcement parameters.

Now let us look at the characteristics of the solution to this modified optimization problem. As we have seen, it takes the form of a pair of expressions for $\mathbf{h}$, with h_0 given by the hours restriction (equation 5.9) and with h_1 derived by solving equation 5.5 for the given value of h_0. Define a function L to simplify the left-hand side of equation 5.5:

$$L := [1 - t]w_1 u_c^a - u_\ell^a + tw_1 u_c^a \mathbf{r}. \tag{5.12}$$

We can then see that the condition for an interior solution can conveniently be rewritten as

$$\mathbf{E}L(\mathbf{c}, \ell) = 0. \tag{5.13}$$

This condition gives us the insights that we seek into the behavior of moonlighters and ghosts.

Again it is interesting to ask how the pattern of behavior is likely to vary across persons belonging to different $(\mathbf{w}, a)$ types, and what happens to this behavior if the tax-enforcement parameters are changed.

Let us begin with the contrasts in behavior between individuals who differ as to their market opportunities in the legal sector (y_0) and in the illegal sector (w_1), or who differ in personal attributes (a). Differentiating the first-order condition (see equation 5.5 or 5.13) with respect to y_0, we can derive the following:

$$\frac{\partial h_1}{\partial y_0} = \frac{\mathbf{E}(u_{cc}^a[1 - t + t\mathbf{r}])w_1 - \mathbf{E}u_{c\ell}^a}{D}. \tag{5.14}$$

This tells us quite a lot. It can be shown that the numerator of the right-hand side of equation 5.14 is negative,[17] so that $\partial h_1 / \partial y_0$ is negative. Hence it is clear that, for a given profile of attributes a, those who are better off in the legal sector work less in the illegal sector. This is true if we are comparing high (legal) earners with low earners, or if we are comparing the employed with the (voluntarily or involuntarily) unemployed. But what of those—say, bank clerks with a flair for painting and decorating—who have a disproportionately high market wage in the black economy? Again we differentiate the first-order condition, this time with respect to w_1. After some simplification, we obtain

$$\frac{\partial h_1}{\partial w_1} = \frac{\partial h_1}{\partial y_0} h_1 [1 - t + \overline{r}t] + h_1 t \frac{\text{cov}(L_c, \mathbf{r})}{D}, \tag{5.15}$$

where the "cov" denotes covariance. To interpret this equation, notice that the first term on the right-hand side of equation 5.15 is negative—see equation 5.14. However, the covariance term is of indeterminate sign,[18] and so the effect of higher market rewards for work in the black economy is ambiguous. Interestingly, the relationship between evasion and risk aversion is also ambiguous (why this is so will emerge in the next paragraph), and so (in contrast with what we had in chapter 4) we do not have a particularly simple relationship between a person's $(\mathbf{w}, a)$ parameters and his activity in the black economy.

Let us turn to the tax-enforcement parameters. Recall that the parameters p and s had an unambiguous impact on the black economy in previous models. This is no longer the case. Within either of the two regimes cited in equation 5.9 we now find

$$\frac{\partial h_1}{\partial p} = \frac{L(c'', \ell) - L(c', \ell)}{D} \tag{5.16}$$

and

$$\frac{\partial h_1}{\partial s} = -ptw_1 \frac{u_c^a(c'', \ell) + h_1 L_c(c'', \ell)}{D}. \tag{5.17}$$

To interpret these conditions, notice that a necessary and sufficient condition for a backward-bending supply curve is that

$L(c', \ell)$ be a decreasing function of w_1. It is immediate that both equation 5.16 and equation 5.17 are positive or negative according as L is decreasing or increasing in w_1.[19] Thus, making the penalties for evasion more probable or more severe reduces moonlighting if (and *only* if) the labor-supply schedule is forward-rising. Equations 5.16 and 5.17 further show that the impact of a "mean-preserving spread" of the returns to evasion[20] *also* depends on the shape of the labor-supply curve. It is for this reason that when we now compare two people with the same market opportunities, the one with the lower risk aversion may not be the one who is more active in the black economy: If the labor-supply curve happens to be backward-bending, then mildly risk-averse people may work less, and evade less, than their highly risk-averse peers.

The impact of an increase in the lump-sum grant is easily determined. Since a rise in B simply increase y_0 (for moonlighters and some ghosts), this must discourage evasion within either regime of the model described by equations 5.9–5.11.[21] In fact, *any* tax change that increases take-home pay (while leaving unchanged the probability of detection and the absolute penalty for evasion, *st*) will have this effect. So it appears that an increase in progressivity (raising both B and t) would *reduce* illegal activity among the poor and encourage illegal activity among the well-off.[22]

All of this, of course, relies on a piece-by-piece approach to the analysis of workers' behavior. Before we try to assemble the pieces from the models in this and the previous section, let us take another look at what may be learned from the available evidence on evasion behavior.

Empirical Evidence

Recall the fundamental problem posed by empirical work in this area: The very nature of the subject is such that people have an incentive to conceal information. Few countries' tax administrations attempt—let alone release for public use—official investigations into evasion such as the Tax Compliance Measurement Program; and even so, thorough audit programs such as the TCMP tell us little about the portion of the black-economy activity that is attributable to ghosts rather than moonlighters. Let us look at two reasonable alternative approaches.

The first way of getting around the data-deficiency problem is to adopt a two-stage procedure. *Step A*: Identify the groups of the community under investigation that are likely to be closely associated with the black economy. *Step B*: Use readily available information on the economy in general (for example, the detailed evidence on the expenditure patterns of different types of households) to spotlight what appears to be going on in the problem groups.

This approach has been used by the Institute for Fiscal Studies, with the United Kingdom's Family Expenditure Survey (FES) as a data source.[23] A reasonable conjecture for step A might be that the problem group (in the tax authority's eyes) consists of the self-employed; as has been argued above, those in regular, paid employment will have taxes automatically deducted at the source. However, this is only conjecture. It would be interesting to see if there is any hard evidence that, in line with the models we have developed, self-employed status is associated with black-economy activity (and, if so, whether this is quantitatively significant). In fact there is a direct way of confirming this conjecture: Use the FES to identify those households whose expenditures are suspiciously high in relation to their incomes. Some 10–15 percent of the 1977 sample fell into this category, depending on the precise definition of "suspiciously high."[24] Of these households, 22 percent were headed by a self-employed person—more than three times the representation of the self-employed in the sample as a whole.[25]

Step B involves a more detailed analysis of household budgets. Figure 5.3 illustrates three different hypothesized relation-

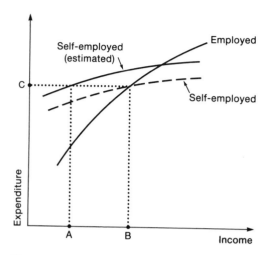

Figure 5.3
Estimating concealed income from expenditure patterns. A: Average reported income of self-employed. B: Inferred income of self-employed. C: Average observed expenditure of self-employed.

ships between expenditure and income. Notice that the estimated relationship for the self-employed has a different shape from that of the rest of the community because of the more volatile nature of this group's income compared with the steadier income of employees. Observe also that, in the neighborhood of the self-employed group's *reported* mean income, expenditure of households headed by the self-employed is greater than that of households headed by employees: Self-employed-headed households spend more than employee-headed households with similar reported income levels, a pattern that is exhibited over various categories of goods.[26] Either there is some quirk in the tastes of the self-employed so that *as a group* they have abnormally high expenditure in each of these categories, or the estimated relationship between observed expenditure and reported income is misleading.

The evidence on expenditure suggests that the self-employed are indeed concealing a substantial part of their income. If so, then for this group each expenditure level (the vertical axis in figure 5.3) really corresponds to a higher level of income than that indicated by the "self-employed (estimated)" curve. The true relationship between expenditure and income for the self-employed is presumably that illustrated by the broken line in figure 5.3, so that the expenditure (point C) corresponding to their "true" average income (point B) would be the same as the expenditure for the employed at that level of income. If so, then the average income generated by the self-employed in the black economy is given by the gap AB. This gap has been estimated at between 10 and 20 percent of the total income of the self-employed.

Let us now look at a second way of dealing with the lack of data: the use of a purpose-designed private survey. This more direct approach was attempted in Norway in 1980 and 1983.[27] Its main advantage is that one can put into the questionnaire detailed questions about hours worked and attitudes which would not normally be covered by the kind of data sources we have discussed earlier, and then estimate a specific functional form of the labor-supply equations 5.6. This approach appears to confirm the conventional effects of tax-enforcement parameters on evasion.[28] Furthermore, black-market labor activity is found to be greater among craftsmen, the middle-aged, and those with nonworking spouses; expected hours of work in the black economy *decrease* with income[29]; and men are more likely to be involved in the black economy than women.

The principal worry that one has about both of the approaches discussed in this section concerns the quality of the data. Perhaps the really big operators in the black economy are among the nonresponding 30 percent in both the Norwegian surveys and the FES. Nevertheless, it is remarkable that the interview data exist at all. Perhaps the climate of opinion in Scandinavia is such that people are prepared to respond more readily and more truthfully to questionnaire surveys than people in the rest of the world. In that case, it may also be that evasion behavior itself is strongly influenced by such a climate of opinion; that is something we shall look at more closely in the next chapter.

A Segregated Economy?

In the light of the models we have examined and the bits and pieces of evidence at hand, let us try assembling an analysis of what happens in the economy as a whole. We begin with the deferred task of piecing together the various component models of illegal work that apply under different economic circumstances.

Consider the behavior of a dishonest worker as we vary the tax-enforcement parameters. Figures 5.4 and 5.5 depict two examples of, respectively, the relationship between evasion penalties and the work activity of the type of self-employed

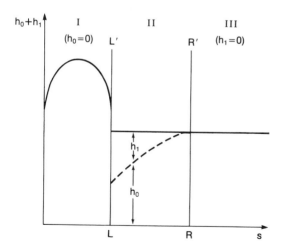

Figure 5.4
Labor supply and the evasion surcharge: separable decisions.

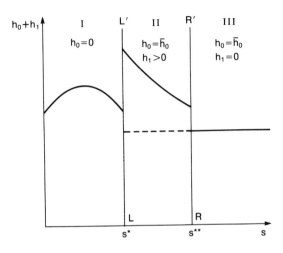

Figure 5.5
Labor supply and the evasion surcharge: fixed legal work hours.

person discussed in the section on self-declaration and the moonlighter discussed in the section on moonlighters and ghosts. Both figures can be easily interpreted by reading from right to left. Figure 5.5 shows the regime switch of the model of equations 5.9–5.11: If s is very large, then the person is persuaded to be completely honest ($h_0 > 0$, $h_1 = 0$); if s is reduced below s^{**}, then some illegal work is done ($h_1 > 0$) but the regular job is carried on, as before; if s is reduced further still, below s^*, the returns to illegal work become so attractive that the person specializes completely in such work ($h_0 = 0$). Clearly the story is similar in figure 5.4 in the first and last phases, but in the middle phase the worker adjusts his behavior by reallocating the proportion of time spent in each activity out of a given number of hours.

Figures 5.4 and 5.5 depict a discontinuity in the supply of work to the illegal sector where the curve crosses the two lines LL' and RR'. Why might there be such a discontinuity? Take the left line, LL'. As we move from right to left across this line, we pass from a situation in which the authorities have a record of a person's activities (he is doing *some* legal work) to one in which it is possible that they have no information at all. The reason for the discontinuity at RR', the right line, is easily seen for those workers whose legal work hours are fixed, since the search costs of starting a second job can be considerable. Those who are self-employed (figure 5.4) may face a similar fixed cost (such as keeping up a duplicate account book), which would be sufficient to deter many from evasion.

In some cases, figures 5.4 and 5.5 could perhaps be simplified yet further. The lines LL' and RR' may coincide, the middle phase dropping out altogether. If so, then we have a situation where each person is confronted by evasion opportunities on an "all or nothing" basis: He works either in the 0 sector or in the 1 sector, but not in both.[30] There are several reasons why this may come about, which are related to the type of taxes that are being evaded—"direct" taxes, based on income, or "indirect" taxes (such as sales and value-added taxes)—and to the methods of enforcement.

Apart from the obvious fixed costs of becoming a "ghost" (such as building your network of contacts), the way in which the authorities gather and collate information may also make it more advantageous for the dishonest worker to remain *wholly* concealed rather than to hold a "mixed portfolio" of jobs by working simultaneously in each economy, as was noted above. The characteristics of goods may also contribute to such segregation. Goods and services whose quality is important and is unobservable at the time of the transaction (e.g. dentistry), or for which reputation of the supplier is an essential component (banking, legal services), are unlikely to be traded in the black economy; therefore, it will be relatively difficult to evade indirect taxes based on the transactions in such goods.[31]

Would the disappearance of phase II mean that the economy is segregated? Certainly the separation of the labor market into two groups (I and III) gives the appearance that there is a distinct, segregated "second economy" that operates in tandem with the official economy. However, in contrast with racial or sexual discrimination, this segregation is primarily by *category of goods* rather than by personal attributes, although personal attributes will have a part to play: Those who select the illegal sector will, on the whole, be the less risk-averse and will have a comparative advantage in the production of goods and services associated with the black economy. In this limited sense, those who work in the black economy are "not as other men"; however, a truly segregated economy would require little or no mobility of people between the sectors across the boundaries in figures 5.4 and 5.5.

The Black Economy and the Market

The structure of the productive black economy is bound to affect the workings of the economy as a whole. Two particularly important consequences of the illegal sector need to be mentioned.

First, if there is effective segregation of the sectors in the manner discussed in the preceding section, then we ought to take account of how this affects *relative prices* in equilibrium.[32] The three-sector model of the economic system that we developed in chapter 4 is obviously rudimentary and rather incomplete. If we extend it by explicitly allowing for two distinct types of private-sector commodities (indexed by the sector labels 0 and 1), then as the government alters its taxation or expenditure policies we have to take into account the effects of these upon the goods-price ratio P_0/P_1. For example, suppose the aggregate production relationships in the economy can be well represented by a technology with constant returns to scale, and that both sectors are competitively organized. The equilibrium of the model can then be represented as in figure 5.6, where the preference contours (those of a hypothetical "representative" member of the community) allow for the de-

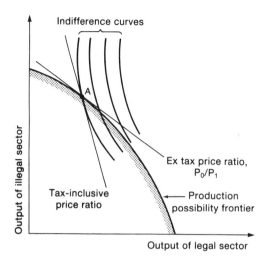

Output of illegal sector

Output of legal sector

Indifference curves

A

Ex tax price ratio,
P_0/P_1

Tax-inclusive
price ratio

Production
possibility frontier

Figure 5.6
Allocation of output between legal and illegal sectors.

mand for the outputs of sector 0 and sector 1 by the govern-ment.[33] Consider what happens as the public sector is ex-panded by increasing direct taxation.[34] There will be a shift in the composition of the final demand for goods, and it is likely that this will be biased in favor of sector-0 goods.[35] This can be represented by a small clockwise rotation of the indifference curves in figure 5.6: The demand for sector-0 (legal) goods rises; the price ratio P_0/P_1 rises and with it the ratio w_0/w_1. Clearly a similar exercise could be worked out for variations in other policy parameters, although the story would probably be more complicated. In each case equilibrium in the labor market would be maintained by "migration" between the two sectors, but if there were substantial migrational costs (the problem of acquiring a respectable curriculum vitae if moving from 1 to 0, or perhaps setup costs if moving from 0 to 1) then changes in the size of the public sector might be accompanied by transi-tional unemployment.

The second consequence of the illegal sector's presence is that it can confer *market power*. This power is often, but not always, to the advantage of the seller.[36] Because of the covert nature of the transaction, it is often difficult for the buyer to compare prices, to search for alternative suppliers, or to seek redress for poor service. Because this informational setup naturally leads to situations of local monopoly or quasi-monopoly, it is instructive to examine the impact of the tax-enforcement parameters τ on the seller's optimal policy under those circumstances. If we take a model of partial equilibrium with a monopolist faced by a single determinate downward-sloping demand curve, the argument is easy: Write the profit of a firm selling output Q as $\Pi(Q)$, which under perfect honesty equals

Sales revenue − Cost − Taxes.

(Each of the three items in this expression will usually depend on Q.) If the firm is liable to pay the fines for proven breaches of tax law, if the penalties are levied on the amount of evaded tax, and if the firm's objectives can be represented as a simple expected utility-of-profit function, then the optimization problem is simply "choose Q and et to maximize $\mathbf{E}u(\Pi(Q) + et\mathbf{r})$," where, as before, et denotes evaded taxes and $\mathbf{r}$ is the usual rate of return to evasion; in this formulation it does not matter what particular base has been used for the tax (profits, sales, turnover, . . .). It is then immediate that the optimal choice of Q, and hence the optimal monopolistic price, is *independent of the rate of return* $\mathbf{r}$, although it will usually be affected by the tax rate.[37]

However, this result should not be taken as implying that the enforcement system has no impact on the quasi-monopolistic power (the markup of price over marginal cost) attainable in the black economy. If we allow for migration to and from the black economy, it is clear that the tax-enforcement parameters τ may also affect such markups by altering the number of firms in the black economy, hence altering the elasticity of demand that faces each one of them. Moreover, where the seller of the good or service operates simultaneously in both the legal and the illegal sector there may be an opportunity for price discrimination and the above result breaks down.[38]

Conclusions

Opening up the issue of the black economy as a productive entity inevitably makes things much more complicated. Not only do we find some new twists to the "tax evader as gambler" model; we also encounter new economic issues.

From the point of view of the individual workers, there is scope for substitution of time between different types of between-labor activities as well as scope for substitution between income-generating work and leisure; the type of labor contracts in force and the system of tax collection can dramatically affect the economic constraints that confront them. Market structure is also important; the presence of a distinct illegal sector will affect the response of the economy to tax parameters through the price mechanism and the structure of factor rewards,[39] and market segmentation will provide opportunities for exploitation in captive illegal submarkets.

The diversity of form that emerges from our discussion suggests that the institutional structure of a particular economy has a particularly important role to play. It will strongly influence the opportunities for black-economy activity in both the factor market and the goods market, and therefore the degree of control that the government can hope to achieve.

6   Morality and Community

A lie is an abomination unto the Lord, and a very present help in trouble.
Adlai Stevenson

The Social Context

Thus far we have been rather narrow-minded about tax evaders. The formal analysis of chapters 4 and 5 implicitly assumed that everyone other than the tax authority acted as an isolated individual playing a "game against nature." This individualistic approach is unsatisfactory in several respects. It neglects the potential for strategic behavior by individual citizens, groups of citizens, and the authorities; it overlooks the possibility that participation in evasion may be driven by perceived injustices or inequities in the tax system; and it ignores the influence of the prevailing social climate upon each person's willingness to take a chance and break the law. No tax evader is an island, entire of itself.

In this chapter we will look more closely at the structure of social relationships within an economic analysis of tax evasion—-at conflicts of interest among the different agents (evaders, the tax authority, and other taxpayers) and the areas of common concern to those agents. Our objectives are to clarify the way in which this structure affects the workings of our model of the black economy and to compare the results with the insights afforded by the more limited "tax evader as gambler" approach that we have pursued hitherto.

It is, of course, easy to highlight the limitations of the individualistic model and to refer in vague terms to the importance of including in one's model factors arising from the social context. However, to make substantial headway in overcoming such limitations we must address some mundane but fundamental questions: What is meant by "the social context"? Why should one wish to complicate everything by attempting to build such a concept into a formal model? To provide sensible answers to these questions, it is perhaps a good idea to look for clues among the scanty evidence on evasion behavior.

Empirical Evidence: Another Look

In fact we do not have to look very far. Evidence from the IRS's Tax Compliance Measurement Program suggest that whether or not a taxpayer is compliant with tax demands is significantly affected by the social grouping in which the taxpayer finds himself, and also by the type of income being declared (which may amount to much the same thing). Educated people appear to have a weaker predisposition to compliance; so do the young as compared with the old and the self-employed as compared with the employees—in many respects we find that evasion behavior seems to differ markedly among groups within the population.[1] When we compare countries, a similar story comes through: The citizens of some countries have a record of probity in the paying of taxes, whereas those of other nations have a reputation for cavalier noncompliance. These systematic differences among countries and among groups within one country cannot be dismissed as innate differences in taste or temperament. Inconvenient though it might appear for neat, individualistic models of economic behavior, people do seem to take into account the "climate" within the group or groups to which they belong.

To be more specific about this idea of "climate" it might be useful to ask people directly about tax evasion. A blunt approach, such as a survey of actual evaders, is not necessary[2]; a broader-based survey of taxpayers' attitudes may be sufficiently direct and realistic.[3] Such surveys have attempted to formalize such vague notions as taxpayers' perception of the structure of taxation, their views as to its purpose, their views on the opportunities for avoidance, and the seriousness of the crime of evasion. The circumstances of taxpayers—for example, their age group and the opportunities they have for evasion—once again emerge as important factors that predispose them to evasion. And, of more immediate concern, so too do certain perceptions about the community—for example, the supposed inequity of the tax system, and the perceived ineffectiveness or coerciveness of the tax administration. However, the evidence on the effect of tax rates and of personal income appears to be ambiguous.

To some extent these findings are borne out by evidence from a rather different source: the results of experiments to determine tax evaders' motivation. This approach is a variant of the laboratory exercises that have been used for years to examine behavior in other risky situations, such as gambling and business simulations. Consider what might be learned from such an approach. The uncharitable view of this sort of thing is "if the data sets we need don't exist, then let's invent them." Nevertheless, in view of the scarcity and unreliability of "hard" real-world data, such experiments may give some broad insights into the determinants of evasion behavior. For example, if it emerges that certain hypotheses are consistently rejected in a simulation, it may be reasonable to conclude that they would also be rejected by real data, were such data ever to come to light.

It is clear that a substantial burden rests on the design of the experiment[4] and that, as some of the practitioners of this approach have pointed out, some key results may be highly sensitive to the particular experimental design.[5] It is also clear that one has to be extremely cautious in extrapolating from the way people respond in a micro-computer simulation or a laboratory exercise to what people actually do at home or at work.[6] Despite these reservations, it is useful to see what may be learned from the substantial literature on this approach. Perhaps the most significant general conclusions that may be drawn from this are that how one goes about the difficult task of measuring attitudes is of great importance and that the choice between compliance and evasion is far more complex than just another form of gambling.[7] These conclusions are, possibly, what we would have guessed *a priori*, but the details of some of the principal findings are quite illuminating:

• Some individuals choose not to evade, apparently on moral grounds (Baldry 1986, 1987).

• The probability of an audit may have its principal impact on whether or not the person evades at all rather than on the actual amount of tax paid (Spicer and Thomas 1982).

• Social devices that appeal to conscience and civic responsibility may be more effective than legal sanctions (Schwartz and Orleans 1967).

• The probability of an audit appears to be more effective a deterrent for those who have already been audited than for others (Spicer and Hero 1985, Webley 1987).[8]

• The structure of taxes appears to have an influence on people's willingness to evade, over and above any income or wealth effects that may be induced (Baldry 1986).[9]

How much does this help us on the main issues of whether potential tax evaders take into account what other people are doing and such things as social injustice? The first of these findings suggests that values derived from the community could be important, although in certain cases the finding could be explained in part by quite mundane influences, such as a simple perceived transaction cost to evasion—inertia might be mistaken for morality. The second finding could be consistent with either the "community values" or the "transactions cost" explanation. The third finding speaks for itself. The last two points illustrate again the importance of perceptions in influencing behavior.

However, despite the apparent importance of the tax structure, the simulation evidence on the impact of perceived inequity is ambiguous.[10] The fact that some studies find that such perceived inequity is unimportant as a determinant of evasion appears to be at variance with the results that emerge from the attitude surveys. There are two plausible explanations for this: that simulation subjects do not perceive inequities in tax treatment with the same infuriating clarity as if it involved their real income and the real people next door, or that "inequitable taxation" is cited by survey respondents as a factor in the evasion they are prepared to report to the interviewer but that in fact it bears little relationship to actual amounts of evaded tax.[11]

Equipped with this skimpy but suggestive evidence, let us look at how features such as inequity, morality, and the influence of the community can be fitted into the theoretical model.

Inequity and Externality

The concept of inequity can be introduced with no trouble at all. Define ι as the index of inequity. Write the utility function as $Eu^a(c, z, \iota)$ and the evasion function as $e(\tau, y, a, \iota)$. For the moment, let us pass over the more demanding task of trying to pinpoint what ι is actually supposed to be and move straight on to a reexamination of the behavior of rational tax evaders. Let us take on board, once again, assumptions A1–A5 about personal preferences and the tax-enforcement system, and suppose that the individual is "small" relative to the community, so that no action of his can directly affect the magnitude of ι. Now, if we differentiate the first-order condition—equation 4.7, suitably modified to accommodate ι—we obtain[12]

$$e_\iota(\tau, y, a, \iota) = \mathbf{E}(u_{c\iota}^a \mathbf{r})/Dt. \tag{6.1}$$

A simple but apparently odd result immediately follows from the equation: Suppose people's perception of "inequity" ι (measured as their marginal evaluation of ι in terms of the consumption good) is independent of their personal consumption; then the evasion of a (y, a)-type person increases with perceived inequity if and only if "inequity" appears as a *good* in that individual's utility function.[13] So no matter how ι is defined (as a conventional inequality of reported personal incomes, as the inequality of estimated "true" incomes, or as some function of the tax rates), if the partial derivative u_ι^a is negative (the natural assumption to make) any rise in ι will actually *reduce* evasion by each person.

We set out with the idea that perceived social inequity encourages evasion, and yet the standard economic model seems to show the opposite. What has gone wrong? Nothing, in fact. The result illustrates a general phenomenon: the effect of an *externality* on the optimal decision in the face of the risk of punishment. In this case we happen to have labeled the externality "inequity," but by assumption we have ruled out any perceived impact of the person's own evasion on the magnitude of ι. Thus, the result we have obtained simply says: "If someone induces a favorable externality, everybody feels better off and evades more; if the externality is unfavorable the reverse happens."

However, if the individual's own actions can directly and substantially affect perceived inequity, we clearly get quite a different story. For example, imagine the situation in which, for each person of the (y, a) class, we may write

$$\iota = x(y) - \mathbf{Ec} \tag{6.2}$$

where $x(y)$ denotes the mean of the population group consisting of those people who are observed to have greater incomes than the person in question.[14] Observe that if $x(y)/y$ were to rise everywhere, income inequality would rise. It is clear that such an increase in income inequality would increase the perceived inequity, ι; it is also clear that if $e < y$ the individual can do something about "inequity" by taking the law into his own hands, increasing e, and thus increasing his expected disposable income, $\mathbf{Ec}$. Since $\iota_e = -\bar{r}t$, the first-order condition 4.7 can now be rewritten as[15]

$$\mathbf{E}(u_c^a \mathbf{r}) - \bar{r}\, \mathbf{E}(u_\iota^a) = 0. \tag{6.3}$$

The impact of an exogenously imposed increase in inequity can be modeled by an increase in x. Thus, differentiating equation 6.3 with respect to x and simplifying, we have

$$e_x(\tau, y, a, \iota) = [\mathbf{E}(u_{c\iota}^a \mathbf{r}) - \bar{r}\mathbf{E}u_{\iota\iota}^a]/Dt. \tag{6.4}$$

The first term on the right-hand side of equation 6.4 is obviously the same as before (see equation 6.1), and under the usual assumptions it must be negative; however, the second term is clearly positive, because the strict concavity of cardinal utility requires that $u_{\iota\iota}^a < 0$. We see immediately that if the person can do something directly about his own feelings of inequity, and if he is sufficiently sensitive to inequity ($u_{\iota\iota}^a/u_\iota^a$ is large), then greater inequality of income will induce greater evasion.

The analysis shows clearly that one has to specify fairly carefully what one means by the inequity or injustice that is often cited as a motive for evading taxes. It is not enough just to write down some nasty externality that depends on income inequality or on the tax function. How the person perceives *his own role* in modifying that externality is of central importance. We shall see a similar point emerge in the analysis of "social conscience."

Social Conscience and Epidemics

The notion of "inequity" that we have discussed thus far is personalized and rather selfish. However, it is often argued that a more detached—and principled—system of social conscience is at work, ensuring that taxpayers do not succumb to the temptations of the black economy. Let us see how this might affect the analysis of individual behavior.

If we are to assign a role to "social conscience" in influencing economic behavior, then we had better specify a lever by which that influence is exerted. Virtue for its own sake is laudable, but it is unexciting in terms of economic content.[16] Instead we shall suppose that the individual taxpayer is no more inclined to innate goodness than he was in chapter 4; but he does respond to penalties, and just as the state can impose legal penalties in the form of surcharges and fines, society can impose on the exposed malefactor the penalty of disgrace. It is the potential stigma that such exposure would produce that acts as the lever.

However, if the concept of "stigma" is to be given an operational role, we need to be more precise about what the social or economic phenomenon is actually supposed to be. It presumably involves a fairly complex interaction between a person's evaluation of the consequences of his own decisions and how he thinks such decisions would be viewed by others in the light of what they are doing[17]—in other words, his perception of other people's perception of his own actions. One of the simplest methods by which to analyze the possible interaction between the individual taxpayer and the rest of the community is to allow for the possibility that evasion in the community at large may generate a consumption externality that affects the welfare of each of its citizens.[18]

This approach is prompted both by the notion of stigma outlined above and by the observation that a person's propensity to dodge taxes seems to be strongly affected by the number of other people who are already doing the same. Let us again use the apparatus of chapter 4, whereby individual citizens were characterized by their income (y) and their personal attributes (a). The principal departure here is that, whereas in our earlier approach all personal attributes and attitudes were taken to be exogenous to the model, we will now consider the possibility that some components of them are determined by the behavior of others. Accordingly, we reinterpret a as being the list of *exogenous* personal attributes, possibly including innate risk aversion, taste for public goods, and the like. Once again let $e(\tau, y, a)$ be the amount of evasion (concealed income) for a (y, a)-type individual, where, of course, $0 \leq e(\tau, y, a) \leq y$.

Inspection of the basic model in chapter 4 suggests that we might conveniently deal with the person's subjective evaluation of society's view of his evasion by rewriting the individual taxpayer's objective function $\mathbf{E}u^a(\mathbf{c}, z)$ as a function with a third argument: the decision variable e. This, of itself, does not move the analysis much further forward; one would simply find that the solution $e(\tau, y, a)$ now takes account of the "taste for evasion" aspect of personal attributes (represented by the third argument of the utility function) as well as of risk aversion and taste for public goods (which we have already discussed). However, suppose that the value of the individual taxpayer's objective function is determined by the evasion activity engaged in by *everybody else*. We may then write this function as $\mathbf{E}u^a(\mathbf{c}, z, E)$, where, as before, E denotes the aggregate amount of evasion, or the size of the black economy, and is equal to $\int e(\tau, y, a) \, dF(y, a)$. Appropriate specification of the form of the cardinal utility function u^a may then enable us to capture the phenomenon of social interaction as a feature of the equilibrium of the model, as we shall see.

In order to do this, in fact, it is easier to work with a slightly modified form of the utility function. Substituting for $\mathbf{c}$ and z from equations 4.1 and 4.6, we may write the utility realized by a person with innate attributes a as a function of his own evasion e and of the size of the underground economy E thus[19]:

$V^a(e, E) := \mathbf{E}u^a(\mathbf{c}, z, E).$

Clearly $V^a(e, E)$ will also depend on income y and on the tax-enforcement parameters τ, which have been suppressed for notational convenience. There are actually several reasons why it makes sense to introduce E into the utility function in this way. One reason (already mentioned) is the social stigma that might afflict a person if his wrongdoing were to be exposed. This might be very great if he perceives himself to be in a tiny minority; but if it is part of the local folklore that *everybody* evades taxes, such a person might find himself less severely conscience-stricken. Other social mechansims may produce a similar effect. For example, learning from one's fellow evaders may be a particularly important component in determining a tax evader's behavior.[20] Or the tedious search costs of finding a "bent" accountant might very well be reduced as the black economy grows: If everyone else is at it, then there is presumably a thriving and readily accessible cottage industry in the expert falsification of tax returns. Because of the reduction in costs, the realized utility level of the practising tax evader will rise with E.[21]

Let us take the "stigma *cum* social norm" story and examine the objective function $V^a(e, E)$ in more detail. The signs of the first and second derivatives of V^a clearly depend on one's view of the nature of the externality within the model. If people tend to feel bad about evasion in the light of their perception of other people's perception of themselves, presumably we have $V^a_e(e, 0) < 0$; for the same reason, the restriction $V^a_{eE} > 0$ may seem reasonable: Evasion becomes less soul-searing the more that other people do it. Other restrictions are harder to justify *a priori*, but one fairly mild further condition that produces interesting results is that $V^a_E(e, E) > 0$.[22]

The important elements of this model are illustrated in figure 6.1, where aggregate evasion is plotted along the horizontal axis and the realized utility level of a (y, a)-type is plotted along

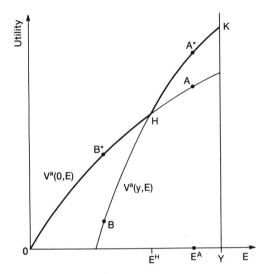

Figure 6.1
Evasion equilibrium with social stigma.

the vertical axis. In order to simplify the discussion, let us, for the moment, take e to be a dichotomous variable that may be equal to either 0 or y. For each of these two values, sketch $V^a(e, E)$ as a function of E. Observe that, in line with our assumptions, $V^a(0, E)$ and $V^a(y, E)$ are both upward-sloping (the curves OB^*HA and BHA^*K, respectively), and that $V^a(0, E)$ at first lies above $V^a(y, E)$ and then lies below it, for large E. Clearly the portion of the diagram that lies to the left of $E = 0$ and to the right of $E = Y$ is irrelevant. The position of the two curves depends on the person's (y, a) type: Those with higher incomes will have their $V^a(y, E)$ schedule shifted upward relative to their $V^a(0, E)$ schedule; those who are relatively risk-averse will have a steeper $V^a(y, E)$ schedule.

Now let us consider the question of equilibrium in this sort of model. To start with, imagine the situation of a person who is completely honest in an economy where there is a huge amount of evasion. He is at a point such as A in figure 6.1. Clearly A is not an equilibrium for him, since at this value of E he finds $V^a(y, E) > V^a(0, E)$: His utility will increase if he switches e from 0 to y so that he then attains point A^*. A similar argument applies in the opposite direction for a tax evader in an economy where E is in fact quite small: An increase in utility is achieved by switching from B (on the $e = y$ schedule) to B^* (on the $e = 0$ schedule). Since e is restricted to be a dichotomous variable, it is clear that the locus that gives optimal e as a function of E is made up of segments of the two schedules, as shown by the heavy, kinked curve OB^*HA^*K. But which point or points on this locus represent an equilibrium for the economy *as a whole*? The crossover point H appears to be a candidate for such an equilibrium, for here the individual has no incentive to switch his evasion decision in either direction. But in fact H is not very interesting. Imagine an economy in which there are really quite a lot of people of this particular (y, a) type. Let them all be at H—some with $e(\tau, y, a) = 0$ and some with $e(\tau, y, a) = y$. Now consider what happens if there is a small increase in the overall size of the black economy E away from E^H. This could arise from a tiny change elsewhere in the system, or just from one of the little (y, a)-type people changing his mind and switching from $e = 0$ to $e = y$ (he is, after all, indifferent between the two at H). Immediately *all* the (y, a)-type people who had been perfectly honest now switch, since

$$V^a(y, E^H + dE) > V^a(0, E^H + dE);$$

this causes E to rise yet further. A similar argument applies for downward perturbations of E. Clearly, then, the point H is unstable.

By this argument it is also clear that the system will, under these circumstances, possess multiple locally stable equilibria. Take as an example the special case where the whole population is of the same type. Then any point such as A^* cannot be an equilibrium for the system: Since $E^A < Y$, not all taxpayers can have chosen the evasion ($e = y$) option at A^*; but since we have assumed everyone is identical in tastes and in income, this means that those who have chosen the alternative ($e = 0$) option would have to be at A, which is suboptimal for them. A similar argument rules out points such as B^* as equilibria for the system. Thus, in a homogenous population, *everybody* is either at point O (economy-wide honesty) or at point K (total defiance of the tax authority). Moreover, small perturbations will not shift other taxpayers away from O or K once either of these equilibria has been attained. The weight of social convention ensures stability.

Of course we should not observe such extreme outcomes in an economy with heterogeneous taxpayers, although we do expect to find similar "clumping" behavior in equilibrium (because the evasion behavior of others acts as an externality). The precise story to be told depends on $F(y, a)$, the joint distribution of income and personal attributes, and on the way in which reference groups are formed in the community.[23] It will be complicated further by the fact that each individual can choose the amount of evasion from the *entire range* of values $[0, y]$ and not just the two endpoints.

More generally, we shall find that the analysis of the perceived black economy as a consumption externality suggests two important behavioral features in an economic model of tax evasion: that the individual decision about evasion is a two stage process and that it is quite possible to find, in the aggregate, "epidemics" of evasion.

Take the point about individual decisions. The two stage process is as follows. *Stage 1*: The person answers the question "Am I going to be essentially honest or not?" *Stage 2*: If the answer to the question in stage 1 is that the person is prepared to be dishonest, the person then asks himself "How much shall I do it?" The first stage may involve the possibility of a loss of reputation in the community, and this may not be related to the monetary amount of the wrongdoing. However, once one is prepared to risk public opprobrium if one is found out, one can proceed to calculate the size of the gamble one is prepared to take with the taxman's watchdogs.

Now consider the point about epidemics. In figure 6.1 we can see that marginal shifts of tax-enforcement parameters could have, in the aggregate, quite dramatic effects. Imagine a situation where the combination of the state's tax-enforcement parameters τ and the closely observed behavior of his peer group forced each taxpayer to be honest: an equilibrium at O. Now suppose there is a new era in which the tax enforcers become progressively more slack, and everybody well knows it. The curve $V^a(y, E)$ then shifts upward. For a while nothing happens. Evasion has become actuarially more profitable, but the weight of social convention restrains everyone from taking advantage of the fact. However, there eventually comes a watershed—opting out has become so lucrative that any one person is prepared to do it, even if no one else does. From that moment evasion spreads rapidly throughout the community, so that the new equilibrium is established at a point such as K. Once one taxpayer catches the "evasion bug," all the rest quickly do so too.[24] It is easy to see that the reverse argument also applies: Once the system has tipped over to a full-evasion equilibrium, marginal reversals of the policy parameters τ will not immediately recoup the lost ground of honesty. Substantial effort by the state would be required before the social convention of tax dodging could be eliminated. (This insight may be put to use by a tax-enforcement agency in targeting certain groups in order to foster a culture of honesty.)

What drives the whole thing, of course, is the ultimate flexibility of moral codes in the face of communal behavior. As the epigraph at the head of this chapter suggests, truth-telling in this and other contexts may be more a matter of public convention than a matter of personal conviction.

We now turn to another way in which social convention may come to bear upon individual actions: through the channel of the public supply of goods and services.

Public Goods and Tax Evasion

In chapter 3 we saw that tax evasion has its roots in a central problem of public economics: the lack of a *quid pro quo* in the relationship between the state and each of its citizens. One aspect of this is the unwillingness of people to reveal their true "willingness to pay" for the services that the government provides. Recall that this unwillingness may be seen as the (myopic) optimal strategy in a game where each citizen adopts the Cournot conjecture: that the amount of evasion undertaken by others will remain unchanged by any decision that he makes. It is time to reexamine this conjecture.

As was suggested in chapter 3, the apparent reasonableness of the Cournot conjecture depends on the size of the community. In the light of the assumption made in chapter 4 that the economy consists of an infinite number of infinitesimal taxpayers, the conjecture seems understandable enough; however, in a small community a considerable amount of copycat behavior might be presumed to take place. Because each of the participants in the game of tax evasion is aware of this, such copycat behavior might have a significant restraining influence on the antisocial behavior of each person. It is rather like a classroom of innately mischievous children, each of whom, though longing to start messing about, realizes that his doing so will induce his classmates to follow suit, with adverse consequences for the whole little community. In this section we shall specifically take account of how this perceived conformity of behavior affects the provision of publicly supplied goods.

Imagine a community of n identical[25] individuals, each of whom has a utility function that satisfies the standard assumptions listed in chapter 4; n is large enough to ensure that p can be taken as the proportion of the population that is investigated. We shall now extend the analysis of the public sector (introduced in chapter 4) to encompass the whole spectrum of publicly supplied goods and services—not just "public goods" in the conventional, strict sense of the term. We will consider a basket of goods that could be provided by the public sector.

In this analysis we shall find that the number of persons in the community is important in two ways: It can affect the extent of the service delivered to each person from any given provision by the government, depending on whether the consumers of such a service are rivals or shared users; and it can affect each person's perception of his own "importance" in the community, in the sense that a person judges the impact of his own actions upon others, to some extent, by how many of "the others" there are.

In order to capture the importance of numbers, we shall modify the analysis of chapter 4 in two ways.

First, we shall make the physical relationship between the required sacrifice of private goods and the production of units of the public service depend on n as expressed in assumption A6′.

A6′   For any given population of size n, the private consumption good can be transformed by the government into the publicly supplied good at a constant marginal rate of transformation $\psi(n)$ where ψ is a nondecreasing function of n and satisfies the conditions $1 < \psi(n) \le n$, $\lim_{n \to \infty} 1/\psi(n) = 0$, and $\lim_{n \to \infty} \psi(n)/n = \bar{\psi} > 0$.

This modified assumption shows that as more people are added to the community the amount of publicly supplied goods available for each of the identical persons either falls or remains the same, and as the community becomes very large the model converges on that of chapter 4. The government's budget constraint is now modified so as to read

$$z = \frac{tY - \bar{r}tE - \Phi}{\psi(n)} \qquad (6.5)$$

where $Y = ny$ and $E = ne$. Notice from equation 6.5 that $\psi(n)$ can be interpreted as the degree of *rivalness* of the publicly supplied good. The extreme value $\psi(n) = n$ may be taken to correspond to the case of completely rival goods (the net public proceeds are divided up equally among the n people), and $\psi(n) = 1$ may be taken to correspond to the case of absolutely nonrival goods. (For a given volume of net public proceeds, the addition of one extra person makes no difference to the public per-capita supply of goods and services.)

Now let us think about the second way in which n affects the analysis. As we have just remarked, the size of the community may have some bearing on the conjecture that each taxpayer makes about the reactions of others to his behavior. Let us capture this by supposing that $\overline{e}$—the evasion of any other typical taxpayer—is given by

$$\overline{e} = e_0 + q(n)e \tag{6.6}$$

where $q(n)$ is an *index of conformity* that satisfies $0 \leq q(n) \leq 1$ and is nonincreasing in n.[26] If, in fact, $q(n)$ becomes zero as n gets large, then we are back to the Cournot case again. The case $q(n) = 1$—"perfect conformity"—is a situation of ultra-rationality where each individual assumes that his own behavior will be immediately and exactly matched by that of everybody else. The pair $(\psi(n), q(n))$ characterizes the basket of goods for a community of size n; it is a simple description of "how public" the z goods are.

Now, substituting equation 6.6 into equation 6.5, we can immediately find the conjectured response of publicly supplied goods to one's own evasion e as follows:

$$z = \frac{tY - \overline{r}\,t(n-1)e_0 - [r + [n-1]\overline{r}\,q(n)]te - \Phi}{\psi(n)}. \tag{6.7}$$

Using equation 6.7 and the individual's budget constraint (equation 4.1), we find that the first-order condition for an interior maximum of $u(\mathbf{c}, z)$ becomes

$$\mathbf{E}([u_c\mathbf{r} - [\mathbf{r} + [n-1]\overline{r}\,q(n)]u_z/\psi(n)]) = 0 \tag{6.8}$$

where the arguments of the u derivatives are, in each case, (c, z). Once again it is straightforward to write down the appropriate modifications to equation 6.8 for the two possible corner solutions. Comparing equations 6.8 and 4.7, we notice that the individual now allows for the *direct* impact of his own evasion and the *indirect* impact of the copycat evasion by others upon the provision of publicly supplied goods.

The conformity index $q(n)$ can also be seen as an index of "excludability" of the goods that are being supplied within the basket. To see this, imagine the situation that would arise if it were possible to sell a proportion of the z goods to the members of the community but impossible to enforce the tax. The proceeds from the sale of the excludable portion of the publicly supplied goods could then be used by the government to finance the production of the *whole* amount of publicly supplied goods z, and an individual consumer would achieve an optimum at the point where

$$u_c(c, z) - \frac{1}{\rho} u_z(c, z) = 0 \qquad (6.9)$$

where ρ is the price charged for the saleable publicly provided good.[27] Observe that, if there is no enforcement of the tax, r is determinate and equal to 1, and that for large n equation 6.9 becomes

$$u_c - \frac{q(n)}{\psi(n)} u_z = 0;$$

it is clear that this condition is identical to equation 6.9 if ρ is set equal to $\psi(n)/q(n)$, at which price the excludable good forms exactly a proportion $q(n)$ of total publicly supplied goods, z. On this interpretation, $q(n) = 0$ gives the case of totally non-excludable goods and $q(n) = 1$ the case where all publicly supplied goods are excludable.

Now examine what happens as the "basket" characterized by the parameter pair $(\psi(n), q(n))$ is modified. Such a modification can be interpreted as a change in the mix of the physical characteristics of the publicly supplied good, or (in the case of $q(n)$) as a change in the system of beliefs governing the behavior of the individuals in the community. Note that, because $\psi(n)$ and $q(n)$ have opposite effects on the imputed price of excludable publicly supplied goods ρ, we should expect opposite effects on individuals' willingness to evade.

Take first the case of an increase in $\bar{\psi}$. Differentiating equation 6.8 and letting n tend to infinity, we find

$$e_{\bar{\psi}} = \left[\mathbf{E}(u_{cz}\mathbf{r}) - \frac{\bar{q}}{\psi} \mathbf{E}(u_{zz})\bar{r} \right] \frac{z_{\bar{\psi}}}{t\hat{D}} + \frac{\overline{qr}\mathbf{E}u_z}{t\hat{D}\bar{\psi}^2} \qquad (6.10)$$

where $\hat{D}$ is the analogue of D (defined above), $\bar{q}$ is the limit of $q(n)$, and $z_{\bar{\psi}}$ may be evaluated from equation 6.5. There are two offsetting effects on the right-hand side of equation 6.10: The first term gives the direct impact on evasion via an increase in $\bar{\psi}$, and under the Ziff assumption and A5 it is negative; the second term gives the indirect impact via the conformity effect (or the imputed price of excludable goods) and is positive; the net effect depends on the extent of conformity $q(n)$. Now imagine a pure increase in conformity, which can be taken as a simultaneous increase in $q(n)$ and a change in e_0 such that $\bar{e}$ in equation 6.6 remains unaltered. This yields

$$e_q = \frac{-\bar{r}[n-1]\mathbf{E}u_z}{\hat{D}\psi(n)t} \qquad (6.11)$$

which is negative. Thus, an increase in conformity, by itself, necessarily reduces the equilibrium level of evasion. For this reason, as n increases we expect the size of the black economy either to remain the same or to increase, because conformity may eventually weaken as the population grows.

In contrast with the epidemic model, however, conformity cannot be relied upon to buttress honesty and thus to enforce efficiency. Recall that the condition for efficiency requires $nu_z/u_c = \psi(n)$.[28] Suppose that the provision of publicly supplied goods is such that this condition is satisfied. Then, in the neighborhood of $e = 0$, the following holds:

$$\frac{\partial \mathrm{E}u}{\partial e} = \frac{t\bar{r}[n - 1][1 - q(n)]}{n}. \tag{6.12}$$

This is clearly positive if the expected rate of return is positive and conformity is less than perfect. So, unless conformity is complete, a better-than-fair gamble will still induce people to evade taxes.

Taxpayers' and Tax Collectors' Games

There is one final area of the relationship between the taxpayer and those around him that needs to be discussed. It plays an important part in the design of policy, as we shall see in chapter 8.

To identify this area let us glance briefly back at the basic model of a tax evader's behavior in chapter 4. In the course of developing this model we noted that its structure is almost identical to that of portfolio selection. The "almost" is important because the close analogy between the two problems fails in one respect: the nature of the risk involved. The investor is usually assumed to face a known distribution of the rate of return that is determined by market conditions, but in the case of the confrontation between the taxpayer and the tax authority the "rate of return" to tax dodging lies in the hands of the tax authority. Subject to the cost of investigation and to the constraints on punishment imposed elsewhere in the legal system, the distribution of r can be whatever the tax authority dictates it to be. It could change abruptly over time, or it could differ dramatically between taxpayers. How should this affect our view of the appropriate way of modeling tax evasion?

We can modify the basic model by allowing a variable probability of detection,[29] but by itself this will do little to modify the essential character of the model or to yield fresh insights. A more promising approach, and one that takes explicit account of the individual taxpayer's sometimes complex relationships with the rest of the community, is to drop the assumption that uncertainty is exogenous—that the risk involved can be viewed as rather like the spin of a coin or the drawing of a lottery ticket. Dropping this assumption introduces the interesting possibility of *strategic behavior* by the parties concerned. Perhaps the most familiar examples of strategic behavior are drawn from the field of industrial organization (the analysis of oligopoly, bilateral monopoly, and other market structures). The situation that confronts a particular economic agent in such cases can be seen as one of *endogenous* uncertainty: The intimacy of the conflict and the will to win may encourage each player to use his private information to keep his opponent guessing. It is the uncertainty of the chessboard rather than that of the dice. Issues similar to those that arise in the context of conflict and cooperation among firms in the marketplace may also be relevant to conflict and cooperation among the "players" in the game of trying to cheat the tax authority of the resources the government requires. We have already had a glimpse of one aspect of these issues in our discussion of the provision of public goods, but here we will concentrate on the cat-and-mouse games played between the gatherers and the payers of tax.

As a first attempt at analyzing the strategic interactions involved, let us imagine a very simple formulation of the confrontation between the taxpayer and the tax authority as an economic game.[30] Within this game the payoffs to the tax authority are measured by ΔR, the addition (if any) to government revenue, net of investigation costs; the payoffs to the taxpayer are measured by his disposable income, c. Once again the tax rate is t and the surcharge rate on detected evasion is s. If the tax authority decides to investigate this particular individual, it incurs a fixed cost, φ. Let us suppose that the two players each have exactly two pure strategies: For the taxpayer,

Table 6.1
A simple game of taxpayer versus tax collector. Each entry in the matrix
gives the payoff $(c, \Delta R)$ to the two players.

| | | Tax authority | |
		"Investigate"	"Not investigate"
Taxpayer	"Cheat"	$([1 - t - st]y, [1 + s]ty - \varphi)$	$(y, 0)$
	"Not cheat"	$([1 - t]y, ty - \varphi)$	$([1 - t]y, ty)$

the decision is whether or not to participate in the black economy; for the tax authority, it is whether or not to investigate.
The payoff matrix is illustrated in table 6.1.

We see immediately that no equilibrium in *pure* strategies
exists. If the taxpayer played the "not cheat" move, the tax
authority would do better for itself by playing "not investigate," but if the tax collector were *known* to be playing the
"not investigate" move, the collector would want to switch to
"cheat," and so on. However, if the monetary values stipulated
here measure the value of the particular outcomes to the players,
there is a Nash equilibrium in *mixed* strategies: The tax authority plays the "investigate" move with probability $p = 1/[1 + s]$
(and, of course plays the "not investigate" move with probability $s/[1 + s]$), so that $\bar{r} = 0$; the taxpayer plays the "cheat"
move with probability $\pi = \varphi/[yt[1 + s]]$, so that the probability of evasion increases with the marginal cost of investigation per dollar of income and decreases with the penalty. If
the game is repeated, it becomes evident that the expected
tax evaded is zero; the expected payments by the taxpayer
actually equal the official tax burden.

However, so simple a model is only a beginning. To take the
conflict approach a stage further, we need to bring in many
players. And once we move away from the paradigm of a pair
of chess players, we need to look into the asymmetry that
presumably exists between the two sides of the game. Rather

than the type of symmetry of information and of behavior that we assumed in the simple example above, we might reasonably suppose that the government, via its agent the tax authority, acts as a "leader,"[31] and that the taxpayers act as recalcitrant followers.

This fundamental asymmetry suggests several possibilities for fruitful development. The tax authority may use information that it acquires about the population liable to tax in order to "tailor" the distribution for different classes of taxpayers. This information could consist of tax returns, in the case where the taxpayer actually files a return; or, in the case of ghosts (and some taxpayers), it may involve the use of more subtle information concerning lifestyle, business advertising, and contacts. Shrewd taxpayers (and, presumably, the more enlightened of the ghosts) will be alert to this information-gathering by the other side, recognize what it implies for the consequences of their own actions, and respond accordingly. Indeed, in some cases it is in the tax authority's interest to make sure that the individual is well aware that his behavior can affect the distribution of the rate of return to risk-taking, r. Indeed, by adopting a particular announced investigation rule contingent upon the information provided by taxpayers' behavior, the tax authority might actually be able to enforce truthful reporting at a relatively low cost.[32]

Whether this would be a good idea depends on the objectives that are presumed to be pursued by the tax collector's master, the government. That topic will be addressed in the next chapter.

An Assessment

Introducing into the analysis the various human relationships within the community makes the tax-evasion model much more complex, and rightly so.

One simple lesson to be drawn is that it is not enough just to stick a variable representing inequity, social conscience, or the desire for conformity into the taxpayer's objective function. In order to model the role of social influences, it is important to include a *mechanism* that clearly links the individual's behavior with the social factor in question. We have seen this in terms of individuals mitigating the "inequity" that they feel by feathering their own nests, and in terms of the dynamic of the "social conscience" linked to the mass of individual behavior by a flip-flop mechanism, and in terms of individuals' perception of the conformity of other individuals' behavior to their own.

We have also seen—in addition to the segmentation arguments of chapter 5—a further explanation of why evasion behavior may be seen as an amalgam of two separate decisions: whether to join the ranks of the underground, and (once one has made up one's mind to join) how much of a risk one is prepared to take.

We can draw from these observations some potentially useful lessons for policymakers. In view of the possible role of social convention and the drastic implications of the breakdown of a convention of tax compliance, it may not be possible to do much about antisocial behavior by a gradualist approach. On the other hand, conformity—tying others' actions to one's own—acts as a bulwark against tax evasion and against joining the black economy. However, before we look at the implications for policy in more detail we need to look at the principles upon which such policy may be based.

7   Policy Agenda

It had been found expedient to merge the functions of national defence and inland revenue in an office then in the capable hands of General Gollancz Jackson; his forces were in two main companies, the Ishmaelite Mule Taxgathering Force and the Rifle Excisemen with a small artillery Death Duty Corps for use against the heirs of powerful noblemen; it was their job to raise the funds whose enlightened expenditure did so much to enhance President Jackson's prestige among the rare foreign visitors to his capital. Towards the end of each financial year the General's flying columns would lumber out into the surrounding country on the heels of the fugitive population and returned in time for budget day, laden with the spoils of the less nimble....
Evelyn Waugh, *Scoop*

What Is To Be Done?

Tax evasion, welfare fraud, and the underground economy are all good standby topics for barroom policymakers. You do not have to go very far to discover champions of the Social Good who will demand condign punishment for those offenses against the state that happen to catch the public eye. Unfortunately, their prescriptions often amount to little more than "Whatever they're doing, stop it at once." This is hardly a sensible foundation on which to construct economic policy.

One problem is that discussions on these subjects tend to be clouded by emotive terminology. There is a plethora of general pejorative terms which suggest social undesirability if not innate evil, such as the "black economy" (= "black deeds"?), "evasion" (= "shiftiness"?), and "underground activity" (= "under the counter" or "under the bed"?). It would not be surprising to find that people's views on policy become colored by such language, and hence, insofar as policymakers are responsive to opinion, that the language influences the strategy and the tactics of enforcement. It is perhaps advisable to query how strong that influence should be.

Introspection, at best a shaky guide to analyzing economic behavior, can be quite misleading when it comes to the design of economic policy. Perhaps we all want to impose our own opinions on Life, the Universe, and Everything, and perhaps it is just as well that most of us will never get the chance to do so. Personally I think that people (including me) should be honest at all times. Maybe you do too. But neither your opinion nor mine may count for very much in the political process that actually establishes the goals which the government seeks to pursue. The widely differing tastes and standards within the community will play an important part in determining what, if anything, should be done about the various forms of cheating the government, as on other social issues. Tax evaders are citizens too; and even those who are not evaders may take the view that, within the current political constraints, many productive economic activities can take place only if the black economy is allowed to thrive. Moreover, as we saw in chapter 6, views of what is "acceptable behavior" may be malleable. The morality of the majority may be strongly influenced by what is perceived to be going on anyway, so that the upright opinions which you and I might share could be outweighed by the tide of sentiment in favor of established practice.

Under such circumstances it is hardly self-evident that honesty is bound to be "desirable" from the viewpoint of the government. Moreover, even if honesty is desirable, it is not self-evident that people should be compelled to be honest, or how they should be compelled. So our immediate task is to address the following questions, which are central to the normative economics of tax evasion: Should the tax authority attempt to force complete truthfulness on the citizens? If not, how far should it go in pursuit of "missing" income? And, apart from the intrinsic desirability of honesty, are there other criteria on which action against tax evasion may appropriately be based?

In order to make headway, we need to consider the desirability of various combinations of policy instruments within a coherent framework of economic analysis. There is, after all, an extensive literature on welfare economics, which may be brought to bear on the design of tax policy. To the popular cry of "Something ought to be done" the economist ought to reply "Why?" and "What?" In this chapter we will tackle primarily the "Why?" part of the problem. In the next, we will look more closely at the question of "What?"

How to Stamp Out Evasion

Let us go back to the basic model of the tax evader onto which we grafted various refinements of labor-supply decisions and social factors. This is the "evader as gambler" model set out in chapter 4.

Given the budget constraint

$$\mathbf{c} = [1 - t]y + \mathbf{r}te \tag{7.1}$$

where $\mathbf{r}$ is the rate of return to evasion (a random variable with a known distribution), the person chooses evasion e so as to maximize expected utility $\mathbf{E}u(\mathbf{c})$. The necessary condition for an optimum is that e should be chosen such that

$$\mathbf{E}(u_c(\mathbf{c})\mathbf{r}) \begin{cases} \leq 0 \text{ if } e = 0 & (7.2a) \\ \geq 0 \text{ if } e = y & (7.2b) \\ = 0 \text{ if } 0 < e < y & (7.2c) \end{cases}$$

and, since u is assumed to be strictly concave, this condition is also sufficient.

It is obvious that, if evasion is to be eliminated, the tax authority is "home and dry" if it can force people to an equilibrium such as 7.2a. To achieve this, the tax authority merely has to make sure that $\bar{r}$, the expected value of r, is negative or zero.[1] Now, if (as in preceding chapters) we assume that

$$r = \begin{cases} 1 & \text{with probability } 1 - p \\ -s & \text{with probability } p \end{cases} \tag{7.3}$$

then we know that $\bar{r} = 1 - p - ps$. It is then immediate that the boundary between cases 7.2a and 7.2c is given by values of the surcharge and the probability of detection such that

$$s = \frac{1 - p}{p}. \tag{7.4}$$

If, for a given value of p, the level of the surcharge is at least as great as that given in equation 7.4, then the rational taxpayer chooses to be at the equilibrium 7.2a. Hence, all the tax authority has to do (so it seems) is arrange things so that the expected return to evasion $\bar{r}$ is never positive—that is, make sure that the surcharge s is set at or above that given in equation 7.4— and the problem of tax evasion is solved.[2]

It is also obvious that I do not consider this "solution" very appealing. Why not? There are five main reasons:

• It is the *government* that sets the legal penalties for crime, and in particular the surcharge for evasion. The determination of s may be outside the tax authority's immediate control. Granted that the left-hand side of equation 7.4 is fixed, the tax authority might not be able to increase p sufficiently to ensure that $\bar{r}$ is actually zero or negative— there are, after all, substantial resource costs to increasing the probability of detection and conviction. So the enforcement of zero evasion may not be a feasible policy.

• People might benefit in terms of their expected utility if, for a given s, the authorities were a little lenient, reduced p below the level that would satisfy equation 7.4, and returned the savings in public administration costs to the private sector.

• The condition given as equation 7.4 depends on the assumption of risk-averse or risk-neutral von Neumann-Morgenstern preferences and the correct perception by the taxpayer of the values of the parameters p and s. What may be a convenient paradigm for positive economics —an "as if" assumption in a toy-town model that yields insights on behavior—may be a dangerous basis for policy prescription.

• Enormous fines do not, somehow, seem to be just. Yet the system of tax legislation and its enforcement should, presumably, incorporate the same principles of social justice that underlie other areas of economic policymaking. So, if enormous fines are indeed unjust, then it seems to be an abuse of language to claim that the suggested "solution" is actually optimal in any reasonable sense.

• The "solution" neglects the point that taxable income should be treated as endogenous to the economic system (discussed in chapter 5). Choking off tax evasion may also mean choking off national income.

The following sections tackle these five objections, one at a time. We start by looking more closely at the basic ingredients of the normative problem.

Objectives and Constraints

If we were to try to jot down a list of criteria as a guide to economic policymakers, it is quite likely that "efficiency" and "equity" would come at the top of the list. A more detailed list would probably subdivide "efficiency" into allocative and administrative efficiency, and also resolve "equity" into vertical and horizontal components.

All of these familiar concepts belong on the agenda of tax-enforcement policy. However, not all of them have received adequate attention in the literature on tax evasion and enforcement. There are two main reasons for this patchy treatment.

The first of these two reasons is that the problem of policy design actually contains several separate subproblems, each of which may be of special interest to those analyzing one particular part of the government's tax-enforcement machinery or one specific aspect of policy choice. Which subproblem is relevant is not always made explicit in discussions of the normative economics of evasion. However, the primary goals cited above appear in different guises within each of these subproblems, and require careful specification of the associated constraints; for example, in order to give meaning to the policy goal "efficiency" we have to discuss efficiency *relative to* a set of feasible alternatives. So let us briefly set out the basic constraints for the optimization problem as a whole, and examine the ways in which some of these constraints may characterize interesting subproblems of policy design.

For simplicity, let us take the elementary model of the public sector introduced in chapter 4, where we suppose that a fixed sum $\overline{R}$ is required to be raised in tax. We further simplify by supposing that there are n identical individual taxpayers from whom this tax is to be raised.[3] Once again we assume that p—the probability of investigation, detection, and conviction —is uniform across taxpayers and across levels of reported income. If the tax authority enforces a probability p, then it incurs a cost $\varphi(p)$ per taxpayer. We also take n to be sufficiently large that, in view of the homogeneity assumption, p can be taken as the proportion of taxpayers investigated, so the expected return to evasion, $\overline{r}$, is also the known average loss to the government per dollar of tax evaded.

Given these simplifications, we may write the government's budget constraint as

$$nT - n\,\varphi(p) \geq \overline{R} \tag{7.5}$$

where $T := t[y - \overline{r}e]$ is the total expected amount of tax revenue raised per person. Within the context of the models we have developed, it seems reasonable to insist that 7.5 be satisfied under *all* circumstances. There are, however, two other constraints on the policy which *may* be applicable under *some* circumstances.

The first of these two additional constraints is this:

$$1 - p - ps \leq 0. \tag{7.6}$$

Obviously this says nothing new; it is simply a restatement of the restriction on tax-enforcement parameters that will be required if taxpayers are to be forced to choose honesty.

The other possibly relevant constraint concerns the available policy instruments. Ostensibly the government and its tax authority have at their disposal the full set of tax-enforcement parameters $\tau = (p, s, t)$ with which to control the private sectors (official and unofficial) of the economy. In practice, this can be too sweeping a supposition. The wonderful integration of public administration achieved by the Jackson family in Waugh's Republic of Ishmaelia (cited in the epigraph at the beginning of this chapter) is seldom achieved outside the pages of fiction. There is usually a "separation of powers," so that different arms of the government—for example, the revenue-raising and enforcement agencies—have to operate independently. If there is, then the constraints on the problem ought to take this into account—in which case one has to focus on a particular *subproblem* in which one or more of the components of τ are assumed to have been fixed.

For example, we might usefully isolate the *pure enforcement* subproblem, in which the tax rate t is predetermined and the tax authority's only option is the selection of the parameters p and s. Or consider the *tax legislation* subproblem: If the economy is lumbered with an incorrigibly rickety enforcement agency that would never achieve complete effectiveness in detection and conviction no matter what resources were made available, then it may be reasonable to take the probability of detection p

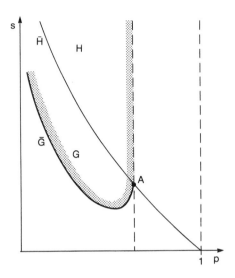

Figure 7.1
The feasible set: enforcement subproblem.

as fixed. This subproblem may thus be treated as one of fixing discriminatory tax rates, $[1 + s]t$ and t, on two specific groups in the community: the demonstrably guilty and the presumed innocent.[4]

These constraints—the fundamental restriction 7.5 and the additional constraints that define the various subproblems—can be conveniently represented in diagrammatic form as in figures 7.1 and 7.2.[5] The set G is the government's *feasible set*; it represents the values of the tax-enforcement parameters τ that satisfy equation 7.5. The curve labeled $\bar{G}$ represents the boundary of the government's feasible set.[6] The slope of $\bar{G}$ is given by

$$\frac{ds}{dp} = \frac{\varphi_p(p) - T_p}{T_s} \tag{7.7}$$

and

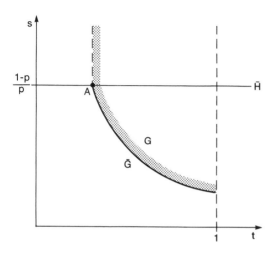

Figure 7.2
Enforcement subproblem: utilitarian optimum.

$$\frac{ds}{dt} = \frac{-T_t}{T_s} \tag{7.8}$$

in figures 7.1 and 7.2, respectively. The "enforced honesty" set H is the set of tax-enforcement parameters τ for which equation 7.6 is satisfied. The boundary of this set, $\bar{H}$,[7] intersects $\bar{G}$ at A. In figure 7.1 the set G cannot have any points to the right of A, because at that point the revenue constraint 7.5 has just been met by forcing every taxpayer to be honest, and so any further increase in p would just raise the enforcement cost $\varphi(p)$ without any increase in the collected tax T. All points above $\bar{G}$ and to the left of A must belong to G, and $\bar{H}$ must intersect the interior of G.[8] Also, because φ_p is strictly increasing, the slope of $\bar{G}$ is infinite in the neighborhood of A.

Either figure 7.1 or figure 7.2 by itself could be taken as a characterization of one of the particular subproblems that arise from the separation of powers that has just been described. To complete the specification of the overall optimization problem or of one of the subproblems, all we need now is a description of the government's social-welfare function. This will provide a system of contours in figures 7.1 and 7.2 from which one could immediately deduce the solution. However, this apparently simple requirement brings us immediately to the second of the two main reasons that policy discussion tends to be rather patchy.

This second reason is simply that the welfare-economic basis for such policy is rather unclear. In dealing with a relatively uncomplicated economic agent, such as a firm or a household, there is a presumption that there exists a clearly defined set of objectives which that agent pursues. However, in the case of a *society*, this presumption is no longer valid, for a number of reasons[9]—indeed, there may be some confusion between primary objectives and constraints.

Thus, it should not come as a surprise that there is no single universally agreed way to sketch a system of "preference contours" in figures 7.1 and 7.2. In fact, even the "preference direction" that such contours should have is far from obvious. Part of the problem is that governments may have in mind a number of quite different—and perhaps mutually contradictory —objectives.[10] What these objectives are, and how one objective is weighted against another, will determine the system of contours in figures 7.1 and 7.2, and will thus determine the optimal policy, if it exists.

For example, some might want to argue that honesty itself should be an overriding priority of the government. This view could be translated as "evasion is a bad thing and ought to be suppressed," in which case the optimization problem reduces to a search for the combination of instruments that will get one into the set H in figure 7.1. However, as was noted in the introduction to this chapter, it is not obvious that inducing such behavior should take priority over such considerations as economic efficiency and distributional equity. On the other hand, might not the enforcement of honesty be consistent with these other social objectives? To deal with this question we have to be more specific about the criteria on which social welfare is to be based.

Social Welfare: The Utilitarian Approach

One of the most well-worked pieces of equipment in the normative economist's tool kit is the utilitarian social-welfare function. It appears in a number of different forms, depending on the exact interpretation of utilitarianism, but there is a very simple and obvious representation in the context of the model set out in the two preceding sections. It is that the government uses an *ex ante* social-welfare function—in other words, a function whereby social welfare is some function of the expected utility of each household before the random variable **r** is realized. Since all households have been assumed to be identical, this amounts to using as an objective function the expected utility of a representative individual:

$$W = p u(c'') + [1 - p]u(c') \tag{7.9}$$

$$= \mathbf{E}u \tag{7.10}$$

where the utility function u is that used in the last two sections and where the expectations operator $\mathbf{E}$ again applies to the simple probability distribution 7.3.

Put this way, the utilitarian assumption seems almost boringly trivial. However, there is rather more to this criterion than the stark simplicity of (7.10) might suggest, since it actually incorporates two distinct assumptions:

B1 The cardinal utility function u, which is used by individuals to weight stochastic payoffs against certain payoffs, is also used by the government to evaluate the social value of monetary payoffs.

B2 The same probabilities $(p, 1 - p)$ are used by both the government and the individual taxpayers.

Assumption B1 means that *ex post* (social) aversion to income inequality is taken to be identical to *ex ante* (private) risk aversion. Some economists[11] have argued that this is indeed a reasonable condition to impose on social welfare, although the case is far from overwhelming.

Assumption B2 means not only that private individuals are as well informed as the government about the probability of being investigated and convicted, but also that, *ex post*, investigated and guilty taxpayers are accorded the same social weight (for given disposable income) as the innocent or the uninvestigated. This assumption seems questionable, since p is not the probability of some exogenous event (such as bad weather) but is rather a *policy variable*. By increasing p the government or the tax authority "makes" more apparently poor people; however, these apparently poor people are exactly those who are acting in a socially irresponsible fashion, so there may be a case for dropping B2 in favor of an assumption that puts a specific discount on the utility of those who are known to be antisocial.

Setting these worries aside for the moment, let us see if the utilitarian framework helps in answering the question whether enforcing honesty is desirable. Take first the pure enforcement problem, whereby p and s are the choice variables and t is fixed. The contours of the function look like those illustrated in figure 7.3, where the arrow indicates the direction of increasing social welfare. The slope of a contour of W in (p, s) space is given by

$$-\frac{W_p}{W_s} = \frac{u(c'') - u(c')}{p\, u_c(c'')et} \tag{7.11}$$

which is negative if e is positive. For small values of e, the right-hand side of equation 7.11 becomes $-[1 + s]/p$—the slope of $\bar{H}$, the boundary of the enforced-honesty set. We can see, in fact, that $\bar{H}$ is itself one of the contours of the social-welfare function W.

Now notice that the contour $\bar{H}$ intersects the interior of the government's feasible set G. Evidently there must be another

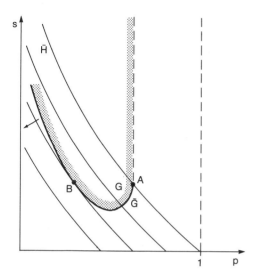

Figure 7.3
Enforcement subproblem: utilitarian optimum.

contour, below and to the left of $\bar{H}$, that also intersects the interior of G; this contour must represent higher social welfare. This simple observation has a strong implication. If social welfare is utilitarian and the tax rate t is taken to be fixed, then *eliminating evasion cannot be optimal.*[12] In fact the policy implication of utilitarianism in this case is easily seen. The highest feasible value of social welfare is attained at the point B, where the "social marginal rate of transformation" (equation 7.7) equals the "social marginal rate of substitution" (equation 7.11):

$$\frac{T_p - \varphi_p}{T_s} = \frac{u(c'') - u(c')}{p\, u_c(c'')et}. \tag{7.12}$$

However, if we change the type of constraints imposed on the optimization problem, then we arrive at a very different answer. Suppose we take the tax-legislation subproblem described above, in which s and t are treated as control variables but p is taken to be fixed. The slope of a W contour in (s, t) space is given by[13]

$$-\frac{W_t}{W_s} = -\frac{y[1 + s]}{et}. \tag{7.13}$$

The relevant diagram is figure 7.2: Equation 7.13 implies negatively sloped contours that become vertical as they intersect $\bar{H}$, and the direction of increasing welfare is southwest. In view of the shape of the contours, it is clear that the optimum must be at A, where $\bar{G}$ and $\bar{H}$ intersect. Thus, if the probability of detection is fixed, the optimal utilitarian policy is always to increase s and reduce t until evasion is eliminated: If people are risk-averse, then you might as well persuade them not to take the risk.

Does this result generalize? To answer this, let us amalgamate the two component subproblems—pure enforcement and tax legislation—and consider optimization with respect to *all* the parameters p, s, and t simultaneously. Now that it has this extra degree of freedom, should the government still try to eliminate evasion?

The answer is No. Worse than that, in this general case there is actually no optimal solution. To see why this occurs, examine figures 7.2–7.4. Imagine p fixed at some initial value, p_0. The optimal policy, conditional on p_0, is to set

$$s_0 = [1 - p_0]/p_0$$

and

$$t_0 = [\bar{R}/n + \varphi(p_0)]/y.$$

This is point A_0 in figure 7.4. But, from figure 7.3, this solution is not optimal; given t_0, it would be better to raise s and lower p so as to reach point B (where $p = p_1$). This then shifts the curves $\bar{G}$ and $\bar{H}$ in figure 7.4 so that the new policy, given p_1, is at A_1. Since φ is strictly increasing, this sequence can be repeated indefinitely; one continues cutting the tax rate and cut-

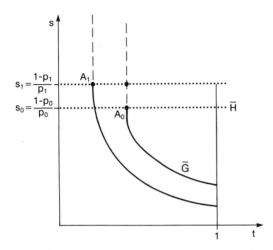

Figure 7.4
Absence of general solution.

ting back on the resources for law enforcement while augmenting the penalty so as to instill a wholesome horror of tax
evasion that is just sufficient to balance the government's budget. The idea is to threaten offenders with a very, very tiny
probability of very, very awful punishment.[14]

To summarize: The utilitarian welfare criterion, when applied
to the basic model of tax-evasion behavior (fixed incomes and
independent, well-informed, risk-averse, rational taxpayers[15])
yields results that are quite sensitive to the assumed constraints
on policy. Only with the tax-legislation subproblem will the
appearance of "the eradication of evasion" on the policy agenda
be consistent with the principles of utilitarianism.

Let us see what may be said if we broaden the concept of
social welfare.

Social Welfare: A General Approach

The policy suggested by the approach outlined above is, evidently, far from encouraging to those of the "abolish evasion"

school of thought who look to standard welfare economics to support their case. And in some respects it is patently absurd.

The absurdity lies in the slavish adherence to the von Neumann-Morgenstern model and its associated set of beliefs. The model is doing double duty here, as a device for (supposedly) explaining how people behave in the face of uncertainty and as a criterion of government action.

As far as people's behavior is concerned, there is considerable evidence to suggest that, in some important respects, people's preferences do not conform closely to those implied by assumption A4 of chapter 4.[16] Even if this objection could be set aside, the problem of how people *in practice* form their beliefs about the probability of uncertain events would remain. Whatever the government's official propaganda may say, a policy that relies on a minuscule p is not going to generate much admonitory court action on which the public can confirm their beliefs; it may literally be incredible.

From the standpoint of policy, to adopt utilitarianism begs some important questions. Should compliant citizens and dissenters have an equal voice in the social-welfare function? Should people's apparent preferences in the face of risk always be respected as a basis for public policy, even when their beliefs may be mistaken? In this section we shall look at some alternatives that attempt to take these issues into account. In particular, we shall introduce the possibility that the state may want to place a relative emphasis on the welfare of convicted tax evaders that is different from the implicit weight p in equation 7.9 and the possibility that the state may concern itself directly with the individual *ex post* realizations of consumption (c' and c'') rather than just relying upon people's *ex ante* evaluation of the prospect of that consumption. Accordingly, we shall abandon *ex ante* utilitarianism in favor of an *ex post* social-welfare function[17] with an explicit social valuation of offenders' welfare.

Obviously there is a wide variety of forms in which such a generalized social-welfare function could be represented. To keep the analysis simple, let us insist on two relatively innocuous assumptions:

B3 The social-welfare function is individualistic.

B4 The social-welfare function is symmetric and additively separable.

Assumption B3 means that social welfare could be written as some function of the values of (c', c'') for each person in the community.[18] Assumption B4 means that this function, in turn, must be expressible as the sum of a function of c' and a function of c'' for each person in the community, with the *same* pair of functions used for everyone. If we apply assumptions B3 and B4,[19] then, in a community of identical individuals, we may write social welfare as

$$\hat{W} = \hat{p}(p)\hat{u}(c'') + [1 - \hat{p}(p)]\hat{u}(c') \qquad (7.14)$$

$$= \hat{E}\hat{u} \qquad (7.15)$$

where $\hat{p}$ and $1 - \hat{p}$ are, respectively, the social weights given to "unsuccessful" and "successful" outcomes *for each person*, and hence are the weights given to the investigated (and guilty) and to the uninvestigated (and presumed innocent) *groups* in the community. The symbol $\hat{E}$ in equation 7.15 refers to the "expectation" taken with reference to *these assigned weights* and not to the probabilities $(p, 1 - p)$. The function $\hat{u}$ is not an individual utility function, but rather an *ex post* social evaluation function for the realized value of disposable income for each person; it is assumed to be increasing and concave.

Now to the contours of the function 7.14 as they would appear in our fundamental diagrams. The boundary of the honesty set, $\bar{H}$, is always one of the contours of $\hat{W}$ in figure 7.1 (but not in figure 7.2), since, if t is constant and e is zero, then 7.14 shows that social welfare is constant at some value $\overline{W}$ for all p

and s. However, because the specification of the function $\hat{W}$ in 7.14 is so general (all sorts of functional forms are valid candidates for $\hat{p}$ and $\hat{u}$), we cannot immediately say whether the value $\overline{W}$ actually represents a maximum or a minimum. It is not clear which is the direction of increasing social welfare in either figure 7.1 or figure 7.2, nor is it clear in which direction the contours slope once we move away from $\overline{H}$.

Despite this vagueness about the general appearance of the welfare contours on our diagrams, we can use this general specification to investigate two different aspects of social attitudes toward the distribution of income. To see this, write the slopes of the contours as

$$-\frac{\hat{W}_p}{\hat{W}_s} = \frac{\hat{p}_p[\hat{u}(c') - \hat{u}(c'')] - \hat{\mathbf{E}}(\hat{u}_c\mathbf{r})te_p}{\hat{\mathbf{E}}(\hat{u}_c\mathbf{r})te_s - \hat{p}\,\hat{u}_c(c'')te} \qquad (7.16)$$

and

$$-\frac{\hat{W}_t}{\hat{W}_s} = \frac{y\hat{\mathbf{E}}\hat{u}_c - \hat{\mathbf{E}}(\hat{u}_c\mathbf{r})[e + te_t]}{\hat{\mathbf{E}}(\hat{u}_c\mathbf{r})te_s - \hat{p}\,\hat{u}_c(c'')te} \qquad (7.17)$$

in figures 7.1 and 7.2, respectively.

In the first place we can examine the role of *aversion to ex post inequality*, a property associated with the concavity of the function $\hat{u}$. A strictly concave $\hat{u}$ implies that greater weight is to be given to people with low incomes; it satisfies the Pigou-Dalton transfer principle. Making $\hat{u}$ more concave[20] would be equivalent to imputing to society a system of values that is unambiguously more averse to inequality. In the case where $\hat{p}$ is independent of p, such an increase in concavity would increase the right-hand side of equation 7.16: The indifference curves in figure 7.3 would become flatter.[21] Thus, we might expect that, as we impute to society a greater aversion to *ex post* inequality, the optimal policy shifts in favor of using lower penalties but higher detection probabilities. Likewise, we see that, if the amount evaded is small, then as $\hat{u}$ is made more concave the right-hand side of equation 7.17 decreases. This suggests that if the social evaluation function $\hat{u}$ is more concave than the private utility function u then the solution to the tax-legislation subproblem in figure 7.2 will remain at A, but if $\hat{u}$ is less concave than u then the solution may shift to some other part of the feasible set.

The second feature of social attitudes we may examine is the *relative weight given to the welfare of known evaders*, $\hat{p}$. If this weight is arbitrarily increased, the right-hand side of equation 7.16 increases and that of equation 7.17 decreases. Thus, if more weight is given to the *ex post* welfare of malefactors, we expect the optimum in the pure-enforcement subproblem to be one where the surcharge s is lower but the probability of detection p is higher. Again if the weight $\hat{p}$ is made more sensitive to changes in p, then—in the neighborhood of the utilitarian solution where $\hat{E}(\hat{u}_r\mathbf{r}) = 0$—we find that the right-hand side of 7.16 will increase, so that the contours in (p, s) space become flatter.

These results suggest that the utilitarian rules discussed in the preceding section might be modified in the following ways: If, in the pure-enforcement subproblem, more weight is given to known evaders, or if *ex post* inequality aversion is greater than *ex ante* risk aversion, there should be greater reliance on detection probability than on surcharges. If, in the tax-legislation subproblem, *ex post* inequality aversion is less than *ex ante* risk aversion, rigid enforcement of honesty may no longer be optimal. However, these suggestions are tentative, since some of them have been established only locally (for social-welfare functions that are "close to" utilitarianism). As we shall see, this reasoning may not be valid in general.

It is difficult to obtain many more specific insights from a general formulation such as equation 7.14, and so we shall look at three special cases. None of these cases can of itself be claimed to represent the views that one might realistically expect a policymaker to hold. However, each of them contains an element (somewhat caricatured) of some value judgment that is commonly brought to bear on the subject of tax evasion.

In the first of these cases, let us assume that the social judgment is that *inequality is irrelevant*. The government then takes as its objective function some weighted average of the disposable income (consumption) of the two groups. The weights $(\hat{p}, 1 - \hat{p})$ might be the actual population proportion $(p, 1 - p)$, or they might be chosen to incorporate some fixed discount on the proportion of national income that is found to be generated in the black economy. The *ex post* welfare function is

$$\hat{W} = \hat{p}c'' + [1 - \hat{p}]c'. \tag{7.18}$$

Substituting in the values $c' = [1 - t]y + te$ and $c'' = [1 - t]y - ste$, we can easily derive the following:

$$\hat{W}_p = -\hat{p}_p[1 + s]te + [1 - \hat{p} - \hat{p}s]te_p \tag{7.19}$$

$$\hat{W}_s = -\hat{p}te + [1 - \hat{p} - \hat{p}s]te_s \tag{7.20}$$

$$\hat{W}_t = -y + [1 - \hat{p} - \hat{p}s][e + te_t]. \tag{7.21}$$

If $\hat{p} = p$ then equations 7.19–7.21 reduce to[22]

$$\hat{W}_i = -T_i, \quad i \in \{p, s, t\};$$

thus, the slopes of the contours of $\hat{W}$ in figures 7.1 and 7.2 are given by $-T_p/T_s$ and $-T_t/T_s$, respectively. It then follows that, if $\varphi_p > 0$, the slope of any $\hat{W}$ contour where it cuts $\overline{G}$ in figure 7.1 is steeper than the slope of $\overline{G}$ itself. From this and from the fact that $\overline{W}$ is now a minimum level of welfare (the direction of increasing welfare being leftward), we may deduce that the pure-enforcement subproblem has no solution; you can always increase social welfare by reducing the probability of detection a little and increasing the surcharge on evaded tax. This outcome runs into exactly the same objections as the outcome of the utilitarian model.

On top of this, we now find that the tax-legislation subproblem does not have a unique solution. To see this, observe that the direction of increasing welfare is again southwest (observe the signs of expressions 7.20 and 7.21), and that the boundary of G in (s, t) space is itself a contour of $\hat{W}$ if $\hat{p} = p$ (since 7.18 can then be rewritten $\hat{W} = y - T$). So any point on $\overline{G}$ represents a solution to the problem "Choose s and t to maximize $\hat{W}$ given p." This means, in effect, that it does not matter whether you raise the required revenue through determinate or stochastic taxes. The result also means that, even in the tax-legislation subproblem, the government is not bothered about whether taxpayers are honest or not. *Indifference to inequality implies indifference to honesty, as long as the government's bills are met.*

In our second specific example, *ex post inequality has the highest priority.* In this case the government shows overwhelming concern for the living standards of the worst-off individuals in the community.[23] Since our model assumes everyone to be identical in terms of their true income y, this criterion implies exclusive concern for the realized utility levels of the unfortunates who happen to get caught. The *ex post* welfare function is now

$$\hat{W} = c''. \tag{7.22}$$

Since c'' falls with e, we have $\hat{W} \leq \overline{W}$ in this case. Differentiating equation 7.22, we find

$$\hat{W}_p = -st e_p > 0 \tag{7.23}$$

$$\hat{W}_s = -et - s e_s t \tag{7.24}$$

$$\hat{W}_t = -y - s[e + t e_t] < 0. \tag{7.25}$$

Expression 7.24 is positive or negative as the elasticity of evasion with respect to the surcharge is less than or greater than -1; for e close to 0 it must be positive.

Consider the question of welfare maximization for the pure-enforcement subproblem in figure 7.1. In the neighborhood of the maximal welfare contour $\overline{H}$, the contours of the social-welfare function are negatively sloped, the direction of increasing welfare being northeast. For this subproblem there is evidently a simple optimum: Given t, one should increase p and/or s so that the taxpayer is forced into H. Thus, one achieves the maximum welfare level, $\overline{W}$. In like manner, it is easy to see that there is a unique optimum to the tax-legislation subproblem: The contours of $\hat{W}$ are positively sloped in the neighborhood of point A in figure 7.2, the direction of increasing welfare being northwest.

However, once again there is no general optimum. Consider any point on $\overline{H}$ to the left of A in figure 7.1, which represents a solution to the tax-legislation subproblem; this lies in the interior of the feasible set G, so that a small reduction in t could be achieved while still maintaining the budget constraint 7.5. Such a reduction would increase social welfare, and would reduce the size of G in figure 7.1 as $\overline{G}$ is shifted upward. Obviously, as long as $p > 0$ one can always do this (the tax burden on everyone can be cut, and total honesty will be enforced by the threat of a sufficiently high penalty s); however, p can never be reduced to zero, so nT remains strictly greater than $\overline{R}$.[24]

This special case illustrates the limitations of the "local" argument about the effect of changing the specification of the social-welfare function. For functions that are "close to" the utilitarian case, a small increase in the concavity of $\hat{u}$ or in the level of $\hat{p}$ seems to shift the choice of policy in favor of lenient penalties and more rigorous policing; but this conclusion is not true for changes in the social-welfare function that are so large as to reverse the sign of $\hat{W}_p$ and $\hat{W}_s$. In the case of any social-welfare function for which these partial derivatives are positive (the opposite sign to the utilitarian case), *elimination of evasion is desirable*. If this is so, then one might as well achieve this enforced honesty through enormous (but uninvoked) penalties rather than through costly policing; such a move would release resources that would permit a reduction of the general tax rate and a consequent rise in welfare.

Our third and final special case is that of a *bias toward honesty*: The social values are such that overwhelming weight is to be granted to the welfare of those citizens who are presumed to be honest. One obvious way of modeling this case is to take the counterpart of the case we have just discussed and assign a social weight of zero to any private benefit derived from the proceeds of evasion, which in our model means putting $\hat{p} = 0$ and selecting the parameters τ so as to maximize c'. However, this procedure is not as reasonable as it might appear. The implicit social value amounts to cynical adoption of the eleventh commandment ("Thou shalt not get caught"), since c' is actually the *total* income of the uninvestigated (and apparently good) members of the community, *including their successfully concealed "black" income*. To calculate c' you still need to estimate e—presumably from the sample of evaders whom you have caught, and whose welfare you promptly ignore. Moreover, if you do adopt c' as a social objective, then it gives rise to a policy that actively encourages evasion, subject to constraint 7.5 being met.[25]

A more promising approach is to abandon assumption B3 and to assume that social welfare is to be based only on that which can be observed. If so, then giving priority to the group that is presumed innocent implies

$$\bar{W} = [1 - t][y - e]. \tag{7.26}$$

This is a "see no evil" social-welfare function: Only legitimate, reported disposable income is counted as socially worthy.

Since $\bar{W}_p$ and $\bar{W}_s$ are evidently positive, the direction of increasing welfare in figure 7.1 must be northwest; thus, it is clear that in the pure-enforcement subproblem one really would want to force people into the honesty set. It is also clear that for e close to zero, $\bar{W}_t$ must be negative, so that in figure 7.2 the contours of $\bar{W}$ will be upward-sloping where they intersect $\bar{H}$.[26] It follows that in the tax-legislation subproblem you should adjust s and t so that the system is at point A, where evasion is

Table 7.1
Desirability of honesty under various welfare criteria.

Social-welfare function	Is honesty desirable?
Utilitarian (W)	No
Individualistic non-utilitarian ($\hat{W}$)	Maybe
"Observables only" non-individualistic ($\bar{W}$)	Yes

eliminated and the tax rate is minimized subject to the constraint 7.5. Since, once again, you can apparently go on cutting p and raising s so as to terrify people into honesty, there is no globally optimal policy, as in previous cases.

The conclusions obtained from our various types of social-welfare function are summarized in table 7.1. Notice that the last line of this table covers both the second and the third of the special cases we have just considered. Any social-welfare function that has "observables only" as arguments implies that it is always desirable to enforce honesty. However, even where it is clear that enforced honesty is desirable, it is still true that there is no optimum in situations where *all* the τ parameters can be varied. The result is robust in that it does not depend on the specification of a special form of the social-welfare function.

As was noted above, the difficulty really lies in relying on the underlying model of behavior, and in particular in relying on the assumption that the probability of detection that the authorities propose to enforce will actually be believed by the tax evaders at large. Casual evidence suggests that there is indeed quite a credibility gap.[27] If so, then this imposes on the selection of policy parameters another constraint that ought to be incorporated in figure 7.1. One might sketch an "incredibility strip" down the left side of the diagram—a zone to the left of some number $\underline{p}$ below which the probability of detection is no longer believed to be positive. If the authorities knew exactly what $\underline{p}$ was, then optimum policies would be clearly defined. But this is unlikely to be easy.

Social Justice and Evasion

Besides the purely technical matter of the possibly nonexistent optimum, there seems to be another reason why the analysis of the past two sections is a little disquieting: A policy of frightening people into obedience to the state just does not seem right. There are two basic reasons for disquiet.

The deterrent may fail. It is clear that some of the results are very sensitive to the conventional assumptions (A3 and A4 of chapter 4) that individual taxpayers are "rational," risk-averse, and accurately informed about the risks involved. The results may not hold up very well in a world of heterogeneous individuals, where both taxpayers and government agencies may make mistakes. Suppose that there are a few people who— through folly, miscalculation, or risk-neutrality—actually do evade taxes even though the expected returns are nil. Then the above type of massive-threat policy implies that there is a positive probability that the penalties really will be imposed on somebody.[28] The supposedly deterrent policy may have been *ex ante* optimal, but the result is a group of impoverished malefactors who just happen to have had the misfortune of being caught. This is not going to look very satisfactory from the standpoint of the sort of *ex post* values many people would want to apply.

The deterrent may succeed all too well. In fact it is not very hard to imagine countries with a system of social organization under which threats of appalling retribution for minor infringements are indeed credible and do indeed ensure the compliance of the citizenry. But such countries would not seem to be wonderfully attractive places in which to live.

If we take these two objections together, it is evident that the policy agenda cannot be considered complete until the penalties for tax evasion are placed in the context of the whole structure of law enforcement and punishment within the community. There seems to be a good case for asserting that penalties for one particular crime should not be wildly out of line with those for other crimes, and that these penalties should not outrage public opinion as to what is just. If the penalties do not fit into a graduated structure, then the effectiveness of punishment may be blunted for certain types of crimes—one might as well be hung for a sheep as for a lamb. Public opinion as to what is just can, of course, be pretty quirky, and should not be taken as binding upon legislators. Nevertheless, it should be worthwhile to note the results of several studies that have specifically set out to investigate people's opinions of the gravity of tax evasion and the penalties it might merit.

The results of these surveys run counter to the more loudly proclaimed views that one hears in the public bar. Roughly speaking, people appear to rank the crime of tax evasion somewhere between stealing a bicycle and stealing a car.[29] In Western capitalist economies it is not regarded as warranting particularly heavy punishment, if any at all,[30] and the picture is probably not very different in socialist countries.[31] In view of this, it seems rather unlikely that a policy of astonishingly severe punishment for fairly small amounts of evasion would command wide support, let alone that it could actually be made to work. There may well be some room for an increase in penalties, but legislators should recognize that it may not be possible to push them very far without violating the public's sense of what is fair and reasonable.

Finally, note that there is an interesting paradox here: If public opinion really was so dead set against tax evasion as a crime that it was prepared to countenance horrible penalties to deter it, then presumably moral pressure might prevent much of it from happening in the first place.

The Cost of Evasion

Some people might wonder whether all the argument about welfare functions and social justice is not missing the point. After all, the armchair economist's answer to the question "Why should the government encourage honesty?" is probably something like "Because of the crippling cost of dishonesty." To which one ought to respond "What is this cost, and in what way might it be crippling?"

In fact we have already taken into account two substantial components of the cost of evasion. Obviously there is the direct public resource cost φ of administering the tax-enforcement system. In addition, though, we should count the *private* cost incurred by those who are bearing the burden of risk: the poor old tax evaders. This may not immediately seem like a cost, but if tax evaders are risk-averse and if their utility is to be respected—as one presumably respects the utility of entrepreneurs, financiers, deep-sea divers, and other risk-takers—there is no avoiding the issue. The tax evader incurs risks in pursuit of his activity[32] just as the taxpayers in Ishmaelia incurred risks from General Jackson's marauding tax gatherers, and this should be included in any assessment of social welfare. This conclusion applies to a broad range of social-welfare criteria, not just to utilitarianism.

Forcing people to act honestly would clearly eliminate this private component of cost; as we now know, however, such a course is not optimal in many versions of the elementary policy model. It is easy to see how the argument would go through using the concept of the private cost of evasion in a utilitarian context. Suppose the authorities increase p from a very low starting point: Down goes evasion, up goes expected government revenue which could be returned to taxpayers by way of a rebate; hence down goes the cost of evasion net of this rebate, but up goes the enforcement cost $\varphi(p)$. Clearly you should raise

p just enough so that the marginal reduction in the one cost equals the marginal increase in the other.[33] This may not seem to be a palatable conclusion, but it is inevitable unless one adopts an explicitly "honesty-regarding" criterion—such as $\bar{W}$ in equation 7.26—as a measure of social welfare. However, once we relax the restrictive assumption of fixed taxable income y, there are clearly other components of the "cost" of evasion. If incomes are endogenously determined, and if various goods and services differ in their liability to tax or in the opportunities they afford for evading tax, then we also have to reckon with the impact of evasion on price distortions. We have to allow for both the distortions that may have already been induced by the tax system and the distortions that evasion may itself engender[34]—and it is by no means clear that, on balance, evasion of the tax actually "worsens" the distortions (for example, in terms of increasing the dead-weight loss of the tax system).

As a very simple example of the issues involved, take the incentive effects of taxation on factor supply, which were discussed in chapter 5. The imposition of the income tax clearly drives a wedge between the marginal rate of transformation and the marginal rate of substitution between time and other goods. In the absence of tax evasion, this results in an efficiency loss *relative to* the hypothetical situation in which the government raises the required revenue by lump-sum taxation. Allowing the possibility of evasion alters this wedge; in the extreme, anyone who was absolutely successful at concealing his black-economy activity would find that this distortion had apparently been eliminated. Although there will still be costs of the sort we have considered in the fixed-income case, it is conceivable that for some tax systems evasion may actually *reduce* the efficiency loss.

This illustrates the caution with which apparently practical arguments based on a superficial appeal to the cost of evasion must be used. There is, of course, a contrary view (taken by other armchair economists) in which it is the *suppression* of black-economy activity that imposes the crippling cost on the community—our fifth objection to the abrupt stamping out of evasion. This does not, of course, imply that the government can blissfully ignore evasion (after all, it still needs the money); rather, it implies that, in a productive economy, there is a fine balance to be determined between the assertion of fiscal authority and the incentive to enterprise, taken in the light of the technology of the economy and the structure of information. Policy for the control of evasion becomes, inevitably, bound up with the problem of tax design.

How one deals with these issues is examined more fully in chapter 8.

Summary: Nelson or Byng?

The economist eager to prescribe policies for tax enforcement might do well to ponder on the record of the British Admiralty in the age of sail. The far-flung interests of the Navy, the temperament of the commanders, and the limitations of the available technology gave rise to some obvious problems of information and the enforcement of authority. It was difficult to keep the admirals under control. Admiral John Byng did not do terribly well against the French and was, consequently, shot— *pour encourager les autres.*[35] Admiral Horatio Nelson—the focus of social scandal, the disobeyer of orders, and the turner of the blind eye—was made Commander-in-Chief, and a Viscount to boot. Which sort of treatment should be the model for guiding tax authorities in their similar problems of information and control?

Whether the matter at hand concerns officers of flag rank or humble taxpayers, there is a fundamental question of objectives to be addressed: How highly should one esteem compliance *per se*, as against the getting of immediate results? Compliance might be readily enforceable (although there is good reason for skepticism about superficially easy solutions), but everybody could nevertheless appear to be better off if the authorities were to be a little permissive.

Viewed through the eyes of the welfare economist, the validity of the adage "honesty is the best policy" depends on the type of optimization problem (or subproblem) that is relevant and on the type of social-welfare function that is to be used. Enforced honesty is to be seen as a goal that should be derived from more fundamental policy objectives rather than as an absolute desideratum; there might not even be such a thing as a "best" policy. As we have seen in the discussion of table 7.1, the important issues to be settled are these: Are welfare criteria to be based on the *full* income of all persons, or only upon observed incomes? What degree of *ex post* inequality aversion is appropriate? In addition, enforced honesty may be an appropriate prescription in cases where the model of isolated individuals is inappropriate—for example, where there is substantial interaction among taxpayers, so that evasion has an "epidemic" effect.

However, in practice, this type of analysis is bound to have limitations. Sophisticated theories of justice and welfare economics are probably an insufficient basis on which to draw up the policy agenda. In addition, we have to bring in two rather humdrum factors.

The first of these factors is the climate of opinion regarding the responsibility of citizens to the state, the legitimacy of authority, and the appropriateness of punishment. If there are strong views about the use of terror to enforce honesty, about the disproportionate severity of the punishment for evasion, or about shooting admirals, those views are bound to affect what can reasonably be proposed for the control of evasion. Swingeing penalties for that which is perceived as petty will be rejected as unjust. The public's revulsion at the prospect of a police state may be stronger than its appetite for the goods and services that the missing tax would have financed.

The second is the need to get things done. The Nelson touch may be required to guarantee the survival of some categories of "socially useful" economic activity—a fact of life that is widely recognized by pragmatic public officials everywhere. Italian civil servants customarily knock off early to get to their second jobs; the French cheerfully accept the blatant appearance in company accounts of *rémunérations occultes* covering illegal consultancy fees from the private sector to public employees; the Soviet government acquiesces in a significant loss of control of its planned economy through the "evasion" of the plan by those supposed to carry it out: the practice of *ochkovtiratel'stvo*—translated as "spectacle-wiping" or, more fetchingly, as "eyewash."[36]

This has been only an outline of the principles for public action (or inaction) on tax evasion. What form that action might take is the subject of the next chapter. However, it is clear from our simplified discussion that the action cannot be based on the mere supposition that people can be frightened into compliance. Nor should one accept the notion that all forms of evasion are automatically detrimental to economic welfare. That, too, is eyewash.

8   Policy Design

tax collector. A highwayman; occ. a footpad: late C. 18–early 19.
Eric Partridge, *A Dictionary of Slang and Unconventional English*

In purely economic terms, highway robbery has much to recommend it. Administratively efficient. Precious little waste. Probably few production distortions.[1] And, insofar as he managed to hold up the right stagecoaches, the highwayman's every theft would surely satisfy the Pigou-Dalton transfer principle. Could a modern-day tax administration, one wonders, perform so uniformly well?

This chapter deals with the subject of improving the performance of the tax administration—the collection and enforcement agencies. Comparing the Internal Revenue Service, the Inland Revenue, Her Majesty's Customs and Excise, and their distinguished counterparts elsewhere with the common highwayman is not entirely frivolous. The government obviously has to be sure of raising taxes in order to pay its way, but it is clear that people often feel that the tax authorities make a bad job of it. Even if they are broadly in favor of their government's expenditure policies, they may resent the form of the taxes, the apparently haphazard distribution of the tax burden, and what they perceive as the overmastering force which is used to enforce the payment of tax: They feel they are being robbed.[2] It might be tempting to dismiss all this as a failure of perception or, more cynically, as the inevitable reaction to the inevitable errors and injustices involved in the practical task of gathering taxes. Nevertheless, no matter how unjust we may personally feel the tax system to be, we would probably agree that the tax administration does not, and should not, expropriate funds from the populace with quite the capriciousness or the ruthlessness of a fiscal Dick Turpin.

If the government and its agents are not to act in a capricious or ruthless fashion, they will need to pursue a coherent set of goals in a manner that is perceived to be tolerably efficient and reasonably just. Presumably the economist can give some guidance on the best way of achieving such goals. This chapter is devoted to examining the form that such guidance might take. Chapter 7 introduced in a general way the aims and objectives that might be on a policymaker's agenda—the specific meanings that might be given to the vague feeling that "something ought to be done." We now want to look at the ways in which those objectives might be translated into practicable rules of action. We need to develop an explicit normative *model* of public policy.

Fundamental Constraints

Since we have already discussed the general principles underlying the normative economics of tax evasion in some detail, it is tempting to go straight on to describe policy rules for enforcing the tax system. Before we attempt to do that, however, we need to take another look at the constraints on the government and on its tax-collection and enforcement agencies. These constraints fall roughly into three categories: the facts of life, political expediency, and the problem of information.

Perhaps the most obvious fact of life facing any economic agent is that it has to remain solvent. In the case of a constitutional government,[3] this takes the form of a budget constraint:

Taxes, net of any leakages to the black economy and net of administration costs, must be at least as great as revenue. This may be reproduced from our previous analysis as follows[4]:

$$R \leq tY - \bar{r}\bar{E}t - \Phi \tag{8.1}$$

where R is net government revenue, t is the average tax rate, Y is the tax base (national income), $\bar{r}\bar{E}t$ is the expected aggregate loss through tax evasion, and Φ represents the total resource costs of enforcement.

As was noted in chapter 4, for some purposes it is appropriate to see this government revenue as an end in its own right, in which case one may simply replace constraint 8.1 with the condition $R = \bar{R}$, an exogenously given number. However, there are also important questions of public policy that concern the use of that revenue, net of any pure transfers. In this case we shall also need to reintroduce the production constraint for public goods:

$$z \leq R/\psi \tag{8.2}$$

where ψ is the constant marginal rate of transformation of private goods into public goods.

The brutally simple facts of life—insofar as they concern the financial and technical limitations on government policy—capture some of the most obvious elements of the enforcement problem facing those who make social decisions. They appeal to the instincts of those who adopt a conventional economic approach to such policy issues, and they are attractively similar to the constraints facing other decision-making entities such as households and firms. They are certainly easy to model.

However, there are two other types of constraints—no less important—which are less susceptible of the modeler's craft: the *legal and political* constraints imposed by the constitution, or by the level of competence of the administration that will have to carry out the policy; and the *informational* constraints imposed by the organization of production, the technology of communication, and the degree of sophistication of the taxpaying community. It is just not practicable to write down neat formal expressions that adequately capture the economic implications of different versions of each of these two sorts of constraints, and the relationships among them. As a second-best approach we might try asking the following questions: What weapons does the tax enforcer have in his armory? How much help can he get from the way in which the system of tax collection operates? What perceptions does the taxpaying public have concerning the policy he intends to enforce? How accurately can he, and they, determine what is actually going on? In the next four sections we shall examine a number of ways in which these questions have been answered. As a first glimpse of the role that these fundamental constraints play in the design of policy, let us analyze a very simple version of the full normative model of tax enforcement.

Some Elementary Rules

Economists traditionally have a penchant for simple marginal rules. Profit maximization by firms, consumer optimization, and social efficiency conditions all give rise to well-known marginalist maxims. The problem of tax enforcement can usefully be seen within this context too, since it is, after all, a branch of the theory of taxation in which there is a long history of policy analysis based upon elementary optimization models. As such, it too has marginal rules of its own to summarize some of the basic propositions about optimization by the government, or the tax authority, on behalf of the community.

The simplest of these rules might be expressed in this way: "The anti-evasion instruments should be set in such a way that the expected revenue raised by a marginal change in each instrument should exactly equal the marginal cost of changing that instrument."[5]

This certainly seems to appeal to common sense: If the marginal benefit of a particular instrument happens to exceed its marginal cost, then why not go ahead and use that instrument more intensively? However, it presupposes that the "benefit" to be achieved by a tighter control of tax evasion is to be understood purely in terms of public revenue—"tax farming." It also presupposes an agreed understanding of the notion of the cost of tightening up. Neither of these points should be accepted lightly, for reasons which may be familiar by now.

In fact, although this sort of marginal rule might be considered acceptable as a simple rule of thumb for tax gatherers, it neglects some important issues of economic policy. The government as a whole is presumably concerned with some notion of social welfare that is rather broader than just the amount of public revenue; it has to take into account what the revenue is to be used for, who benefits from an enforcement policy, and resource costs other than those required to police the tax system. As was noted in chapter 7, issues such as social justice and the efficiency of the production sector ought to be on the policy agenda; otherwise, simple-minded pursuit of a single objective can lead to absurdities.[6] Accordingly, the rules for the design of an enforcement policy need to be put on a firmer footing.

To do this we must first take account of the constraints that were reviewed in the preceding section. The government's budget constraint will be discussed in detail in each of our two examples. For the *informational constraint*, we shall assume throughout this section that the government or the tax administration has little or no prior information as to where the black-economy activity is to be found, so it faces a simple "quality control" problem whereby it attempts to persuade people to be honest through a system of random audits: It "samples" the taxpaying population (with the probability of inclusion in the sample being p) and imposes surcharges on evaded tax at a rate s. As we saw in chapter 7, this approach may make sense only if it is interpreted subject to an additional *political constraint* whereby some policy variables are assumed to be predetermined. To capture this additional constraint, let us imagine ourselves in the situation of a tax-enforcement authority that is instructed by the government to use its resources optimally in the pursuit of tax evaders. The value of s and t are taken to be fixed (they are not the responsibility of our department). How should p be determined?[7] To complete the definition of the problem, we must introduce two further components to the normative model: an *objective function* and a *system response*. We have met both of these components before.

How to specify the objective function was discussed in chapter 7; we shall adopt the pragmatic approach of trying a number of reasonable versions of these policy goals. As our standard case, we shall assume that the social-welfare function W is utilitarian, and that individual citizens are identical. From chapter 7 we may write down the objective function in this case as

$$W = \mathbf{E}u. \tag{8.3}$$

Now let us consider the system response, which was introduced in a series of models described in chapters 4–6. In general, the system response depends on the assumed relationships among the government, the tax authority, and the taxpayers, and on the way in which individuals decide how much income to earn and how much tax to evade. We shall adopt a standard procedure whereby the government or the tax authority is assumed to take the role of a "leader" and the individual agents in the economy act as "followers," in that they may be taken to be passive respondents to the policy of the tax administration. The individual taxpayer—though he be fit for treasons, stratagems, and spoils—is just too small relative to the community to organize a coordinated strategy of resistance to the fiscal authority. The government and its tax authority know of the collective response of the individual taxpayers and tax evaders in the private sector and incorporate this knowledge into their plans for the tax structure and the enforcement of taxation. For the purposes of this section, the response of the taxpayers will be based on the standard model of the tax evader as gambler that was developed in chapters 4 and 5.

As a first attempt let us make the simplifying assumptions that there is a fixed sum $\bar{R}$ to be raised through the tax system, a proportional tax at rate t, full employment of resources, and no government transfers, and that individuals may be regarded as essentially identical in their attributes a (including their taste for risk) and in their market opportunities. In view of the assumption of a homogeneous population, if there are n people in the community, then $\Phi(p)$, the cost of enforcement with detection probability p, can be written as $n\,\varphi(p)$, the tax base Y is ny, and $\bar{r}\bar{E}t$ becomes $n\bar{r}et$. As in previous chapters, y denotes individual income, e denotes the amount of income concealed, and $\bar{r}$ equals $1 - p - ps$, which is the expected rate of return to evasion.

As part of the system response we need to specify how the individual incomes are determined. To do this we shall adopt the model of endogenous income developed above, in which there is a legal sector (0) and an illegal sector (1) and the wages and hours worked in the two sectors are given by $\mathbf{w} = (w_0, w_1)$ and $\mathbf{h} = (h_0, h_1)$ respectively.[8] If we write $\mathbf{c}$ for consumption and ℓ for leisure, then from our previous work in chapters 4 and 5 we may write[9]

$$e = w_1 h_1 \tag{8.4}$$

$$y = w_0 h_0 + e \tag{8.5}$$

$$\mathbf{c} = [1 + t]y + \mathbf{r}te \tag{8.6}$$

$$\ell = 1 - h_0 - h_1 \tag{8.7}$$

where $\mathbf{r}$ is a random variable that takes the value $-s$ with probability p and the value 1 with probability $1 - p$. Each potentially dishonest taxpayer is assumed to maximize his expected utility $\mathbf{E}u(\mathbf{c}, \ell)$ by choosing $\mathbf{h}$, given the potential wage rates $\mathbf{w}$ and the tax-enforcement parameters $\tau = (p, s, t)$; because everyone has the same market opportunities (they all face the same $\mathbf{w}$), the same $\mathbf{h}$ will be chosen by all n people. The solution of this optimization problem is straightforward, and we may proceed right away to write down the appropriate *indirect* utility function, giving the maximum attainable value of individual expected utility for specified values of the parameters τ and $\mathbf{w}$; we may write this as $\mathbf{E}u = v(\tau, \mathbf{w})$.

Once the "production" assumptions (those concerning the determination of individual incomes y) are introduced to the fundamental constraint (8.1), it is clear that, since the n members of the community are identical, this constraint may be rewritten as

$$w_0 h_0 t + p w_1 h_1 t [1 + s] - \varphi(p) \geq \overline{R}/n. \tag{8.8}$$

As one final simplifying assumption, let us take the special case in which the gross wage for legal work is the same as that for illegal work: w_0. Using this and the government's budget constraint (8.6), we have the following Lagrangian:

$$v(\tau, \mathbf{w}) + \lambda[w_0 h_0 t + p w_0 h_1 t [1 + s] - \varphi(p) - \overline{R}/n] \tag{8.9}$$

where λ (the Lagrange multiplier for the constraint 8.8) has the interpretation of the marginal value (in utility terms) of public funds.

As we have seen, one way to make sense of this sort of model is to suppose that t and s are somehow predetermined and to investigate the choice of p. In order to see the effect of increasing the probability of detection on social welfare, differentiate expression 8.9 with respect to p so as to obtain

$$v_p dp + \lambda w_0 t[-d\ell - \overline{r} dh_1] + \lambda[w_0 h_1 t [1 + s] - \varphi_p] dp \tag{8.10}$$

where v_p is the partial derivative of $v(\tau, \mathbf{w})$ with respect to p, which is negative if people are actually involved in evasion, and where φ_p is the (positive) first derivative of φ.

Setting expression 8.10 equal to zero and using equation 8.4, we find the necessary condition for an optimum:

$$\varphi_p = [1 + s]te - \overline{r}t\frac{\partial e}{\partial p} - w_0 t\frac{\partial \ell}{\partial p} + \frac{v_p}{\lambda}. \tag{8.11}$$

Equation 8.11 gives the simple utilitarian rule for tax enforcement in an economy with identical taxpayers and uniform gross wages. The left-hand side of the equation is the marginal resource cost of increasing the detection probability. The first term on the right-hand side is the direct marginal yield from doing so; a simplistic application of the marginalist rule mentioned above would take only this term and φ_p into account. However, the direct marginal yield is modified by three other terms in the following order of appearance: the indirect yield from increasing p as taxpayers are induced to behave more honestly, the impact of the implicit change in the effective real wage on the labor supply and hence on total income, and the direct impact on individual utility. It is clear that the three indirect effects on the right-hand side of equation 8.11 contain both positive and negative terms, which suggests that the impact on social welfare of an increase in detection probability is generally not clear-cut.[10] This conclusion would still hold *even if marginal enforcement costs were zero.*

There are two main reasons for the apparent ambiguity. The first is that utilitarianism requires that the expected utility of everyone—the righteous and the unrighteous—has to be respected, and that raising p, whatever other social good it may accomplish, certainly reduces the expected utility of the unrighteous: the negative v_p term. The second is that raising the probability of detection may have an adverse effect upon production incentives: the $-w_0 t\partial \ell/\partial p$ term, which is equivalent to $t\partial y/\partial p$. It appears that the government may be able to increase social welfare from the status quo by being (a little) permissive toward dishonesty.

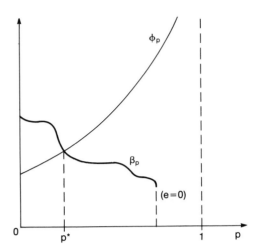

Figure 8.1
The optimum degree of enforcement.

We have already encountered arguments of this sort in chapter 7.[11] Now that we have a more general model of the economy, it is of interest to inquire how the details of the marginal rules on tax enforcement will be affected by changes in the parameters that characterize the model. Let us first take the simple identical-household model at face value and then move on to more interesting cases.

We may examine the effects of changing the parameters that characterize the behavior of the economy by using figure 8.1. Denote the right-hand side of equation 8.11 by β_p, the marginal social benefit from increasing detection probability; then the intersection of the φ_p curve and the β_p curve determines the optimal intensity of "quality control" p^* as shown. Take the second and third terms on the right-hand side of equation 8.11; if tastes change so that evasion becomes more responsive to deterrents (p or s), or so that the labor-supply wage elasticity falls, then the β_p curve will shift upward. The last term in equation 8.11 will be greater in absolute size the greater is individual risk aversion (since this increases $-v_p$) and the smaller is the shadow price of government revenue, $\bar{R}$.

The next step is to make the model of the system response a bit less restrictive. Let us do this step by introducing three important modifications to the model: heterogeneous taxpayers (distinguished by their personal attributes a), distinct market wages (w_0, w_1), and public goods z. We may assume that all tax revenue, net of enforcement costs, is spent on public goods, the amount of which is determined by the production constraint 8.2. These modifications will obviously make the mathematical expression of the model more complex, but they do not unduly complicate the economic intuition associated with the policy rules that can be derived.

In the modified model, a particular taxpayer will be characterized by the particular pair of wage rates $\mathbf{w} = (w_0, w_1)$ and the particular list of personal attributes a that apply to him. In line with the usage of previous chapters, let us call him a $(\mathbf{w}, a)$-type. If the level of public-good provision is z, then the (maximized) expected utility level of an individual of type $(\mathbf{w}, a)$ may be expressed as $v^a(\tau, \mathbf{w}, z)$ where τ again represents the tax-enforcement parameters. Suppose that the market opportunities $\mathbf{w}$ and the personal attributes a are distributed in the population according to some distribution function $F(\mathbf{w}, a)$. Then it is clear that the utilitarian social-welfare function may now be written as

$$W = \int v^a(\tau, \mathbf{w}, z) \, dF(\mathbf{w}, a). \tag{8.12}$$

Hence, under the twin constraints 8.1 and 8.2, the Lagrangian now becomes

$$\bar{v}(\tau, z) + \Lambda \left[\frac{tY - t\bar{\tau}\bar{E} - \Phi}{\psi} - z \right] \tag{8.13}$$

where $\bar{v}(\tau, z) := \int v^a(\tau, \mathbf{w}, z)dF(\mathbf{w}, a)$ (the average utility in the population given the tax-enforcement parameters τ and the public-good provision z) and where Λ is the Lagrange multiplier for the new combined government revenue-and-production constraint. Again we seek to analyze the welfare significance of an increase in the detection probability. We have to be more careful here because some of the characteristics in a person's list of attributes a will be observable, and it is reasonable to suppose that the tax authority may use different detection probabilities $p(a)$ for different a-types. A variation dp can be interpreted as an *across-the-board* increase in the detection probabilities $p(a)$. The *tailoring* of these probabilities will be considered in more detail below. Differentiating expression 8.13 and rearranging, we now find

$$\Phi_p = -\frac{\partial (t\bar{\tau}\bar{E})}{\partial p} + t\frac{\partial Y}{\partial p} + \frac{\psi}{\Lambda}\bar{v}_p. \tag{8.14}$$

If the level of public goods has been optimally determined, then the Lagrange multiplier will be given by

$$\Lambda = \bar{v}_z(\tau, z)\bigg/\left[1 + \frac{1}{\psi}\frac{\partial (t\bar{\tau}\bar{E})}{\partial z}\right]. \tag{8.15}$$

The denominator in equation 8.15 may differ from unity because of the impact of z on evasion behavior.

A brief examination of equation 8.14 reveals that the same type of considerations enter the optimal enforcement rule as in the simplified model with identical taxpayers: The left-hand side is again the marginal resource cost of enforcement; and the right-hand side is the marginal benefit β_p, which consists of the marginal yield of an increase in enforcement (including the induced greater honesty), the overall output effect, and the immediate impact on the average citizen's utility (evaluated in terms of the willingness to pay for public goods). Once again the same type of reasoning as was used for figure 8.1 can be brought to bear on the relationship between the optimal amount of enforcement and certain important characteristics of the economy in question. For example, it is easy to examine the role of the assumed responsiveness of total output to the rigor of tax enforcement (the term $\partial Y/\partial p$), or that of the risk aversion of the average citizen (captured in the term $\overline{v}_p$).

Finally, let us consider social-welfare functions other than the utilitarian criterion (equation 8.3 or 8.12). There are two departures from simple utilitarianism that ought to be considered.

The first of these is where social welfare is no longer taken as a simple sum of the expected utility levels of all the citizens, but is taken as some more complicated function of their expected utility. For example, one might consider

$$W' = \int \Omega(v^a(\tau, \mathbf{w}, z)) dF(\mathbf{w}, a) \tag{8.16}$$

where the first derivative of Ω, evaluated at $U = v^a(\tau, \mathbf{w}, z)$, gives the *marginal social evaluation* assigned to a person with expected utility level U.[12] This modification actually changes very little of the analysis. Observe that the right-hand side of equation 8.16 can be written as

$$\int \tilde{v}^a(\tau, \mathbf{w}, z) dF(\mathbf{w}, a)$$

where the function $\tilde{v}^a$ is defined as $\Omega(v^a)$. It is then clear that the analysis of this case follows immediately from that of our previous model with v^a replaced by $\tilde{v}^a$: If the function Ω were to be assumed strictly concave (representing strict *ex ante* inequality aversion by society), this would have the same effect on the policy rule as would the assumption that everyone had become more risk-averse. In other words, if the community becomes more sensitive to inequality (expressed in terms of *ex ante* utility), then, other things being equal, we should expect a lower intensity of investigation at the optimum.

The second modification goes deeper. It supposes that social welfare is to be evaluated *ex post* and does not necessarily respect people's *ex ante* perceptions of the risks involved in their choices. As a community we might feel an extraordinary compassion for poverty-stricken convicted criminals (even though it is "all their own fault"); we might pay exclusive attention to those who are presumed innocent; or we might give equal weight to income of all sorts, whether illegal or legal.[13] More generally, the community imposes its own evaluation of the random consumption prospect facing each tax evader thus: $\hat{u}^a(\mathbf{c}, \ell)$. We find that the social-welfare function is now modified so as to read

$$\hat{W} = \int \mathbf{E}\hat{u}^a(\mathbf{c}, \ell) dF(\mathbf{w}, a) \tag{8.17}$$

where $\mathbf{c}$ and ℓ are determined by individual utility maximization given the parameters $\mathbf{w}$ and τ and the constraints 8.4–8.7. Now, except in very special cases, social welfare *cannot* be written as a function of maximized *ex ante* expected utility levels $v^a(\tau, \mathbf{w}, z)$.

Replacing the actual (maximized) utilities $v^a(\tau, \mathbf{w}, z)$ with the imputations $\hat{u}^a$ introduces an important modification to the fundamental policy rules. The standard marginal condition 8.14 has an additional term in the marginal-benefit computation, so that we now find

$$\Phi_p = \beta_p + \int \mathbf{E}\left(\hat{u}_c^a \mathbf{r} t \frac{\partial e}{\partial p} + \hat{u}_\ell^a \frac{\partial \ell}{\partial p} \right) dF(\mathbf{w}, a) \tag{8.18}$$

where β_p is the expression on the right-hand side of equation 8.14. The additional term in equation 8.18—the whole integral expression—can be considered as the "paternalism factor": If $\hat{u}^a$ were to be identical to actual preferences u^a,[14] then this term would vanish and the rule 8.14 would be restored. If $\hat{u}^a$ is a strictly concave transformation of u^a, so that society is prepared to place greater weight on unfavorable outcomes for its citizens than do the citizens themselves, then marginal benefit is clearly shifted downward relative to the utilitarian case.[15] The opposite will hold if $\hat{u}^a$ is less concave than u^a.

These lessons on elementary policy rules can be drawn together as follows:

• If the investigation process is of the "quality control" variety, then the optimal value of the probability of detection is found by equating the marginal resource cost of investigation to the marginal benefit from enforcement.

• The marginal benefit from enforcement includes the expected yield given the current amount of evasion and also the yield from the induced increase in honesty.

• In a productive economy, the marginal benefit from enforcement should also incorporate the indirect effects on the size of national income that would be entailed by a change in the degree of enforcement via its effect on the size of the black economy.

• If the policy is based on welfare and the social-welfare function is utilitarian, then the imputation of marginal benefit from enforcement should allow for the adverse direct impact on individual expected utility.

• Nonutilitarian social-welfare criteria may involve augmenting the marginal benefit from enforcement by an amount that reflects the extent to which the state assumes that people will misjudge their own interests when they make decisions about tax evasion.

However, there is the nagging feeling that the government (or its tax authority) can surely do better than this. Perhaps it can. In the next two sections we shall examine two directions in which an improvement in tax enforcement could be sought.

Designing Taxes and Penalties

That the design of tax-enforcement policy is closely linked to the design of the tax system is almost self-evident. As we have observed, both the structure of the system of taxation and the opportunities for individuals to dodge it arise from similar information problems that confront governments and administrators. There may be some justice in the claim that ill-thought-out tax systems are themselves a cause of evasion. If so, then modifying the system that you are trying to police may be more efficacious than reinforcing the police.

Some elementary administrative steps might improve compliance by making evasion more difficult—a simple switch from voluntary reporting to withholding system, or perhaps a shift from direct to indirect taxation.[16] Beyond these considerations, some major issues of economic principle bear upon the structure of taxes and penalties. We shall examine three of these: how evasion will affect policy choices on tax progressivity, how the penalty system should be designed, and how evasion behavior is affected by the legal opportunities for tax avoidance.

Let us take the first issue first. The *progressivity* of the tax system is itself a matter of governmental choice. How that choice is made will be affected by the government's objectives (how much weight it places on distributional equity, for example) and by the system response (e.g., what losses in output might be induced through the labor supply's responses to tax changes). How will these choices be further affected by the presence of the underground economy? To address this question, we may use the framework that was developed in the previous section. Let us examine the implications of the "tax-legislation" subproblem in the case of an economy with heterogeneous taxpayers, a variable factor supply, and utilitarian social objectives. Using the government's budget constraint and production constraint (8.1 and 8.2) and the social-welfare criterion (8.12), it is clear that once again we have the problem of maximizing the Lagrangian (8.13). In this case the maximization is with respect to the parameters s and t. Assuming that there is an interior maximum to such a problem, then, instead of equation 8.14, we would now find

$$0 = -t\frac{\partial(\overline{r}\overline{E})}{\partial s} + t\frac{\partial Y}{\partial s} + \frac{\psi}{\Lambda}\overline{v}_s \tag{8.19}$$
$$[+] \qquad\quad [?] \qquad [-]$$

and

$$0 = [Y - \overline{r}\overline{E}] - t\frac{\partial(\overline{r}\overline{E})}{\partial t} + t\frac{\partial Y}{\partial t} + \frac{\psi}{\Lambda}\overline{v}_t. \tag{8.20}$$
$$[+] \qquad\qquad [?] \qquad\quad [?] \qquad [-]$$

(The signs of the terms are indicated in brackets immediately underneath.)

Three points are worth noting immediately about equations 8.19 and 8.20. First, the zero on the left-hand side of each of these equations is a reflection of the fact that there are no *direct* resource costs to an increase in either s or t. (Contrast this with the Φ_p term in equation 8.14.) Second, if $\psi = 1$, then equation 8.20 can be used to represent an increase in the progressivity of the tax. (In this case, the good z is delivered as a purely rival commodity, distributed to the community in the form of a lump-sum grant which is a perfect substitute for private consumption. In equation 8.20, the marginal tax rate t is being increased and the resultant increase in public funds R, given by the constraint 8.1, is used to increase disposable incomes across the board.) Third, in a productive economy the utilitarian approach to evasion policy does *not* imply that evasion should be eliminated were there to be no other constraints on the rates at which penalties may be set—it is not always socially beneficial to reduce tax evasion wherever this can be done without resource cost. This conclusion is due in part to the structure of the second-best problem: If taxes are distortionary and if evasion provides a way of overcoming such distortions, then the social value of reducing evasion becomes ambiguous.

To see the implications of all this for the tax rate, let us examine equation 8.20 in more detail. Take the case outlined above where the z is in fact just an income transfer provided to all the population. Then $\bar{v}_z$ is the (average) marginal utility of a lump-sum subsidy, and we may write

$$v_t^a = -yv_z^a. \tag{8.21}$$

Hence

$$\bar{v}_t = -\text{cov}(y, v_z^a) - Y\bar{v}_z \tag{8.22}$$

where cov denotes covariance over all $(\mathbf{w}, a)$-types and where y is determined by equations 8.4 and 8.5.

Substituting equations 8.21 and 8.22 into equation 8.20, we derive

$$t = \frac{1}{\theta}\left[\frac{\text{cov}(y, v_z^a)}{\Lambda} + \bar{r}\bar{E} + Y\frac{\partial(\bar{r}\bar{E})}{\partial z}\right] \tag{8.23}$$

where $\theta := \partial[Y - \bar{r}\bar{E}]/\partial t$. The expression θ gives the impact upon aggregate reported personal incomes—allowing for all incentive effects—of an increase in the marginal tax rate; we may take this as negative. The first term inside the brackets gives the conventional expression for the optimal income tax problem, which may also be taken as negative.[17] The second and third terms indicate the modification to the optimal tax rate due to the leakages into the underground economy.

Although equation 8.23 shows the relationship among the various factors that determine the optimal tax rate, it cannot be taken as an explicit formula; the variable t enters expressions on the right-hand side as well as appearing on the left. However, it does make one point clear: The notion that the presence of the underground sector should automatically force the authorities to adopt a less progressive tax structure is manifestly untrue.

Let us now use this type of model to address the second issue: the structure of *penalties*.[18] Is a similar type of result available? To answer this, let us suppose that one has the opportunity of imposing a fixed penalty S either in conjunction with or instead of the surcharge on evaded tax, s. For simplicity, let us take the case where the aggregate income Y and the probability of detection p are constant. If we use the government budget constraint 8.1 and consider variations in S and s such that government net revenue R remains unchanged at $\bar{R}$, then it is clear that

$$p\, dS = -ptE\, ds + \bar{\tau}t\, dE \tag{8.24}$$

must be satisfied. Now let us differentiate the social-welfare function 8.12 with respect to S and s, incorporating the constraint 8.24. We find, after some simplification,

$$\left.\frac{\partial \bar{v}(\tau, \mathbf{w}, z)}{\partial s}\right|_{R=\bar{R}} = t\,\text{cov}(v_S^a, e) + \bar{v}_S \frac{\bar{\tau}t}{p} \left.\frac{dE}{ds}\right|_{R=\bar{R}} \tag{8.25}$$

where $v_S^a = [v_s^a(\tau, \mathbf{w}, z)]/et$. The term $\bar{v}_S$ is zero or negative, and the "cov" term denotes the covariance (across the various types of taxpayers) between the impact on the taxpayer's utility of a marginal increase in the fixed penalty S and the taxpayer's optimal amount of evasion e.

To examine the implication of equation 8.25, consider the case of total reliance on the fixed penalty S. In this case $s = 0$, and it is evident that the covariance term must be positive.[19] Thus, if aggregate evasion E falls with the increased progressivity of the penalty structure, the right-hand side of equation 8.25 will be positive. Welfare must increase if s is increased from zero and S is decreased accordingly. There is thus a case for punishing people by an amount related to the evaded tax rather than merely imposing a fixed penalty.

The structure of formal penalties for evasion (s and S) is clearly a matter for the legislature rather than the tax authority. Nevertheless, there may be a role for the authority to play in the design of penalties when we consider the mechanisms of social interaction discussed in chapter 6. Recall the importance, in terms of a possible "watershed" effect, of perceptions formed by potential tax evaders concerning the behavior of others: If evasion is kept largely under control, then few people will know of others who are evading; people will, therefore, be somewhat disinclined to evade by the external effect of everyone else's behavior (see the equilibrium at 0 in figure 6.1). But if you let matters get out of hand, it becomes very much harder to dissuade any one individual from evading—and people learn rapidly from their peers[20] ("everyone else does it, so why shouldn't I?"—the equilibrium at K in figure 6.1). The authority might try to exploit this social-stigma mechanism by, for example, publicly pillorying the culpable wealthy.[21] Could it attempt more than that? Since it will probably have little freedom to adjust the formal penalties for evasion (the fines and surcharges are presumably set by the legislature), exploiting the taxpayers' self-esteem and fear of disgrace may be a useful additional weapon.[22] Appeals to morality and public-spiritedness—and their counterpart, the heaping of shame upon transgressors—could be effective alternatives to the stiffening of legal sanctions. However, this lever should be used cautiously. If used in a community already blighted by cynicism, revivalist calls for fiscal probity may just have the perverse effect of spreading disaffection.[23]

Finally, let us examine the third issue: how evasion policy will be affected by *avoidance*, the legal alternative to evasion. The structure of the tax system may offer some easy methods of reducing a tax bill other than by cheating.[24] If so, we would expect some people to take advantage of this. Let us look at a heavily oversimplified story of this choice that yields some useful insights into people's evasion behavior and into its implications for policy.

We assume that the tax laws do not quite match the ideal of the economic advisers or the intentions of the legislators: Sharp-eyed accountants have spotted that there are legal opportunities for taxpayers to engage in "tax sheltering." Suppose that it costs a fixed amount $\bar{\Gamma}$ (in money or in inconvenience) to transform one's income into a form that is suitable for sheltering and to search for a suitable shelter,[25] and suppose that this cost is common knowledge. Then anyone who takes the sheltering option is virtually making a public announcement about the size of his true income (it must obviously be at least as large as $\bar{\Gamma}$). This announcement may make it inadvisable to try *evading* taxes at the same time; by choosing to shelter income, the individual draws attention to himself and therefore becomes a prime target for investigation. We might reasonably conclude that the relevant model of evasion in the presence of legal tax shelters is one where there is a polarization between the evaders and the shelterers.[26]

It would be interesting to know how the tax-enforcement parameters τ affect the choice between sheltering and evasion, and which type of taxpayers in the community will choose one or the other method of reducing their tax liability. To do this, let us take income y as exogenous and compare $u^a(y - \bar{\Gamma})$, the benefit that the individual would get from the sheltering scheme, against $v^a(\tau, y)$, the maximum utility attained by a (y, a)-type individual if the tax-enforcement parameters are set at τ. To do this, define the function

$$g(y; \tau, a) := u^a(y - \bar{\Gamma}) - v^a(\tau, y). \tag{8.26}$$

Under the polarization assumption, people choose sheltering rather than evasion if and only if $g(y; \tau, a)$ is positive.

If t is increased, then utility v^a falls; if s or p is increased, and if $e(\tau, y, a) > 0$, then again v^a falls. In each case, the function g is shifted upward; thus, as we might expect, increasing the tax rate or tightening up on enforcement tends to shift people away from evasion and into sheltering.

Now let us turn to a comparison of choices made by different groups of individuals. Take first a group whose members differ in their personal attributes, a, but have the same income, y. Some of these persons evade tax; others shelter income. Consider the subgroup of those with attributes $\tilde{a}$ who are indifferent between evasion and sheltering. Anyone with income y who is more risk-averse than a member of this $\tilde{a}$ subgroup will choose the (risk-free) sheltering option; conversely, those with relatively low risk aversion will choose the (risky) evasion option.

Now consider instead a group of the population with identical a but with differing incomes. It is clear that $g(y; \tau, a) < 0$ for people with very low incomes, because they cannot afford the fixed costs of sheltering; but it remains to be seen whether the rich all choose to shelter rather than evade. Differentiating equation 8.26 with respect to y, we find

$$g_y(y; \tau, a) = u_c^a(\overline{c}) - v_y^a(\tau, y)$$

$$= u_c^a(\overline{c}) - \mathbf{E}u_c^a(\mathbf{c})[1 - t] \qquad (8.27)$$

where $\overline{c} := y - \overline{\Gamma}$. If we use assumptions A1–A4 of chapter 4, then as long as $[1 + s]t$ (the penalty tax rate on concealed income) exceeds 100 percent it can be shown that equation 8.27 is positive.[27] Under such conditions, we would find some critical income level $\tilde{y}$ such that all those with $y < \tilde{y}$ evade tax whereas all those with $y > \tilde{y}$ shelter income.

Obviously the complexity of tax law, with its loopholes, idiosyncrasies, and anomalies, cannot be forced into a model that is as simple as the one we have just examined. However, the principal point to be drawn from the model is surely one that applies more generally: If the authorities tighten up on the enforcement of the tax law, then some taxpayers will switch from evasion to avoidance (rather than to honest behavior); and, on the whole, it will be the risk-averse and the rich who find that they can afford the financial advice and the adjustments to their personal circumstances that are required in order to make the switch.

Information and Audit Design

Throughout this book we have been concerned with the topics of information and uncertainty. (Without uncertainty in some form, there would be no possibility of people cheating the government.) However, we now need to look more closely at the economic role of information in the design of audit policy. We do this by assuming that the tax rate and the penalty for tax evasion (the surcharge *s*) are exogenously given and examining the strategic potential afforded by the uncertainty inherent in the relationships between the taxpayer and the tax authority.

The five rules given above can, in one sense, be regarded as astonishingly primitive. The tax authority appears to behave as if it were playing the parlor game "lucky dip." Common sense suggests that there must be a better way of catching cheats.[28] To see what this better way might be, let us move away from the view of enforcement as a simple "quality control" exercise and consider it as part of an exercise in the interpretation of messages.

Perhaps the first question to ask is: Where do the messages come from? There are two primary sources: from information currently supplied by the private sector and from history.

Take the matter of history first. There are many signals about a taxpayer's behavior that can be picked up by the tax authority and put to good use—for example, evidence of sudden changes in reporting. As a very simple example of what can be done with limited information, consider the following. Return to the basic model of evasion that we adopted in chapters 4 and 7 and assume that the tax authority cannot afford to eliminate tax evasion by raising the detection probability until the expected rate of return, $\bar{r}$, is zero. Nevertheless, the authority may be able to reduce evasion below that which would arise were it just to carry on sampling the population with uniform probability *p* and imposing the surcharge *s*. Suppose that both the tax authority and the taxpayers know that the process of investigation will be repeated over many time periods. Then, in addition to the current rate of return, the taxpayers also have to take into account the consequences of their current actions on their *future* reputation. The tax authority can categorize taxpayers according to their past records, and can apply a different intensity of investigation to different categories—those with bad records get audited more frequently. Public awareness of this approach may induce a certain amount of compliance. Once they have been convicted of tax evasion, people improve their behavior because they know that they will be more closely scrutinized in the future.[29]

There is, of course, no road-to-Damascus conversion of the erstwhile cheats to a life of blameless behavior. People will still fiddle their taxes if they can afford to do so; on the whole, they cheat until they are caught and then report honestly until the record of their crime has been expunged. However, for any given expenditure on enforcement, the amount of evasion, *on average*, is less than would have arisen under a simple system with uniform probability of detection and no powers of recall. The use of the tax authority's memory to augment the deterrent effect of stigma is evidently a much sharper tool than purely random auditing.

If it were possible to hone the cutting edge of this tool or to enhance the tax authority's memory, even more might be achievable. For example, if tax law and accounting practice were to enable the tax authority to look *back* into a newly discovered evader's past taxpaying record—perhaps over many years—this would have a substantially greater effect on compliance than a system that starts each financial year with a clean sheet.[30]

Let us now ignore history and examine the scope for the use of currently available information. The obvious source of this information is the report that the taxpayer makes to the tax authority. What is the nature of the "report"? It certainly need not be a W-1 or some other official form, but it is more than just general information about potential wrongdoers. Even ghosts provide information, if you know where to look. However, the kind of tracking one must do to deal with ghosts is fundamentally different from the one-to-one communication of specific details that characterizes the situation for nonghosts. The act of reporting establishes a *relationship* between the author of the report (the taxpayer) and its recipient (the tax authority).

This relationship introduces a new possibility: the tailoring of audit schemes to convey a message that will be clearly understood by the recipient and will influence his behavior. For this approach to work, there are two major prerequisites: The message must get through, and the recipient must act on it in a predictable fashion. In other words, individuals must be well-informed and rational. These assumptions are important because the tax authority is, in turn, assumed to build the taxpayer's expected responses to the scheme into the design of the investigation rules.

Now consider the material upon which the tax authority's message can be based. As we saw in chapter 3, there are two sets of characteristics that are relevant to tax policy. Set a consists of personal attributes, which are fully known only to the taxpayer; set b consists of behavior, which is potentially observable by the tax authority and everyone else. We assume that informational constraints preclude an imputation $\hat{u}^a(\mathbf{c}, \ell)$ that is conditioned on the individual's attributes a; rather, the investigator needs a model of the process $a \to b$ in order to refine his policy.

To see how this type of refinement might work, take a particularly simple example. Suppose that in a particular economy there are only two levels of taxable income and only two types of personal attributes a. Everyone has at least income y_0, and there are some people who have $y_0 + \Delta y$ (where Δy is a fixed, positive number). The proportio of the population who have low incomes (who receive a per capita income of y_0) is α_0. All this is publicly known. Furthermore, there is a proportion of the population, α_1, who have both a high income ($y_0 + \Delta y$) and personal attributes such that they would not be prepared to risk tax evasion. The remaining proportion, α_2 (which equals

$1 - \alpha_0 - \alpha_1$), consists of "chancers"—people with high income and with a values such that they would be prepared to evade taxes under some circumstances. This too is assumed to be known. Under these restrictive assumptions, no low-income person will ever evade. (Because everyone knows that every person in the economy has at least y_0, no one will believe a tax return that reports any lesser amount.) But what of the high-income people? The situation that confronts each one of them and the tax authority is a simple modification of table 6.1, reproduced here as table 8.1 (the ys have merely been replaced with Δys). It *might* be worth their while to evade taxes, depending on what form the relationship between the tax authority and taxpayer takes. We consider two possibilities.

First we take the position that has been adopted all along thus far: The tax authority acts as a "leader"—it lays down, and sticks by, the rule of investigation—and each taxpayer as a "follower."[31] A glance at table 8.1 reveals that in this case the authority can score a hole in one. Suppose it announces that *all* tax returns reporting low incomes will be audited. Then no high-income person will dare to evade *any* income; if he were to report y_0 he would be audited and exposed (upper left cell), and if he were to report anything other than the two known income levels (y_0 and $y_0 + \Delta y$) no one would believe it for a moment. As long as $\alpha_0 \varphi$ (the total cost of auditing the low-income people) does not exceed $\alpha_2 t \Delta y$ (the gain in tax yield from the high-income people), this "bang-bang" policy—with $p = 1$ for

Table 8.1
Payoffs to high income receivers and the tax authority.

		Tax authority	
		"Investigate"	"Not investigate"
	"Cheat"	$([1 - t - st]\Delta y, [1 + s]t\Delta y - \varphi)$	$(\Delta y, 0)$
Taxpayer			
	"Not cheat"	$([1 - t]\Delta y, t\Delta y - \varphi)$	$([1 - t]\Delta y, t\Delta y)$

low reported income and $p = 0$ for high reported income—is feasible and has enforced honest behavior by everyone. The authority has coerced the high-income taxpayers into accepting the situation in the lower right cell of table 8.1, and it does not even have to use a heavy surcharge s to achieve this result.

There could be a catch, though. This policy suggests that one might find a tax authority repeatedly and exclusively targeting a segment of the community in which it appears to lose money on every single audit (each audit costs φ, and it yields nothing since all the y_0 people report y_0). If the authority has an iron resolve or sufficient bureaucratic inertia, this apparently odd state of affairs may be accepted by everyone. But if the populace guesses that the authority's resolve is about as strong as a wet paper bag and that there is substantial room for discretionary action on the part of tax officials, then the authority's message that it will stick to this policy just will not be believed.

In the light of this, consider an alternative relationship that might exist between taxpayer and tax inspector.[32] Suppose that each party pursues a policy of narrow self-interest, conditioned by a set of beliefs about what the "other side" is doing. The tax authority knows, for example, that the α_0 segment of the population has to report y_0, that the α_1 segment feels bound to report (truthfully) $y_0 + \Delta y$, and that each person in the α_2 segment could go either way; we take it that the authority *assumes* that a proportion $\underline{\pi}$ of this last segment will cheat (report y_0) and that a proportion $1 - \underline{\pi}$ will act honestly (report $y_0 + \Delta y$). The taxpayer, for his part, knows that the tax authority will never audit a high tax return, but that it may audit a low one; we take it that the taxpayer *assumes* that the authority actually audits a proportion $\underline{p}$ of such low-income reports.

Suppose that the authority perceives its interest as maximizing revenue, net of audit costs.[33] If it actually chooses to audit a proportion p of the low income reports, then, given its assumption about taxpayers' behavior, it perceives the probability of catching an evader to be θp where $\theta := \alpha_2 \underline{\pi}/[\alpha_0 + \alpha_2 \underline{\pi}]$—the presence of the genuine low-income people (α_0) "dilutes" the effectiveness of the investigation policy. The expected net revenue from the policy is thus

$$[\alpha_1 + [1 - \underline{\pi}]\alpha_2]t\Delta y + \theta p[1 + s]t\Delta y - \varphi p. \qquad (8.28)$$

Let us define the number

$$\pi^* := \frac{\varphi \alpha_0}{\alpha_2[[1 + s]t\Delta y - \varphi]}.$$

Expression 8.28 can then be written as

$$\text{constant} + \frac{\varphi \alpha_0}{\alpha_0 + \alpha_2 \underline{\pi}}[\underline{\pi}/\pi^* - 1]p.$$

It is then clear if $\underline{\pi} > \pi^*$ the expected net revenue increases everywhere with p, in which case the authority would investigate *all* low income reports ($p = 1$); if the authority believes that $\underline{\pi} < \pi^*$, the expected revenue decreases with p, and it will choose $p = 0$.

Now look at the taxpayers' position. Clearly we do not have to worry about the α_0 and α_1 segments, whose behavior is fixed. But what of the α_2 segment, consisting of high-income "chancers"? From table 8.1 we see that they will get expected utility

$$\underline{p}u^a([1 - t]y_0 + [1 - t - st]\Delta y) + [1 - \underline{p}]u^a([1 - t]y_0 + \Delta y) \qquad (8.29)$$

if they cheat and

$$u^a([1 - t][y_0 + \Delta y]) \qquad (8.30)$$

if they do not.

Evidently the relative size of expressions 8.29 and 8.30 depends on the assumed investigation proportion $\underline{p}$, and there is some particular value p^* (which will depend on s, t, and the function u^a) that equates these two expressions. If the chancers believe that $\underline{p} < p^*$ then all will cheat ($\pi = 1$); if $\underline{p} > p^*$ then none will cheat ($\pi = 0$).

Of course this model is most interesting at the point where the two sets of beliefs and actions are consistent—in fact, it is arguably the only point at which the model is interesting. If π^* and p^* each lie between 0 and 1, then this situation of mutually consistent beliefs occurs where $\underline{\pi} = \pi^*$ and $p = \underline{p} = p^*$.

The net result is as follows. None of the tax returns reporting high incomes will be audited. Some of the low income reports—a proportion p^*—will be audited. None of the genuinely low-income people cheat, but some of the high-income people—a proportion π^* of the "chancers"—will cheat. Contrast this with the "bang-bang solution" outlined above, where none of the high-income people are audited and none of them cheat. The equilibrium proportion p^* evidently decreases with s and decreases with taxpayers' risk aversion. The equilibrium proportion π^*—the amount of evasion that is "tolerated" in this solution to the problem—increases with φ and decreases with s.

The same type of approach can be applied to more complex and interesting cases although the derivation of an explicit investigation rule (the tailoring of probability of audit p to observed behavior b) would inevitably be more complex. To some extent the complexity can be mitigated by partitioning the taxpaying population into relevant subclasses (according to occupation, age, region, ...) and targeting each of these with an appropriate intensity; however, the rule is likely to be quite sensitive to specific details about the underlying distribution of incomes and personal attributes, F. Nonetheless, even though the "leader-follower" and "mutually consistent beliefs" paradigms may be crude ways of representing the interaction between taxpayer and tax authority, the intelligent use of information that comes free with the tax returns has obvious potential in improving the aim of investigative effort.

A few cautionary remarks follow.

• By modifying the probability of investigation in the light of the individual taxpayers' reports, the tax authority may achieve an improvement of the policy rules in only *one* direction: that of raising more revenue for a given resource cost. If one takes into account other objectives of social welfare, then "tailoring" can have unfortunate side effects. Consider, for example, the objective of distributional equity: Tax systems and enforcement schemes that hit the poor more heavily than the rich are going to appear inequitable *ex post*. However, this is precisely what a discretionary audit system does,[34] either in the community as a whole or within each separate category of taxpayers that is targeted by the tax authority.

• One should not underestimate the crucial role of information and accurate perceptions. If either side in the game consistently gets this wrong, then—even though it may have been exquisitely tailored— the audit scheme may not fit the stringent requirements of the informational equilibrium on which the design is based.

• If there are ghosts about, all the above schemes run into problems. Tightening up on taxpayers who submit false reports can make opting out of the legitimate economy altogether (as described in chapter 5) seem an attractive prospect to some of them. Pursued to the extreme, a clever audit scheme that should have yielded information and tax revenue can in practice backfire. Ghosts do not report.[35]

Mistakes

It would be idle to pretend that the administration of the fiscal system is, or could be, flawless. Mistakes will happen, and the potential for these mistakes should influence the design of policy.[36] There are basically two sorts of mistakes to be taken into account: those made by the tax authority and those made by the taxpayer. Each has a similar impact on the optimization problem.

Recall the points made in chapter 7 about the penalty imposed upon tax evaders, namely the surcharge s. A hike in s will usually increase compliance—since it is apparently costless to raise s, you might as well raise it so far that the expected return to evasion $\bar{r}$ falls to zero; then you could further increase welfare by cutting p and raising s (so as to keep $\bar{r}$ at zero) and using the resources saved to augment private incomes.

However, as we now know, this apparently logical chain has potentially frightful consequences: It results in the occasional use of huge penalties as a spur to honest behavior. Such an outcome may appeal to the barroom policymaker who views million-dollar fines or the shooting of convicted tax evaders as legitimate weapons, but it is open to criticism on several grounds. Apart from the importance of setting the penalties for tax evasion within the context of those for other crimes and the straightforward moral objections to awful punishment, there is an argument based on the problem of imperfect information. It can be characterized as follows: The sort of dire policy prescription outlined above would not be so bad if the tax authorities could be trusted to get it right; but bitter experience suggests they cannot be trusted; and since they cannot, awful penalties should not be used. The wrong person may be hanged. Let us examine the practical difficulties.

For a start, it may be very difficult to establish conclusive proof that an offense has been committed. All along we have adopted a convenient fiction of supposing there to be a well-defined lump of income that may just happen to have been concealed under a cover of dishonest practice; at a given moment, the cover is whipped off and the truth is plain for all to see. Complicated cases are obviously not like that. Even when an audit uncovers an apparent irregularity in reporting, it may be difficult for those taxpayers whose circumstances are unconventional but who have acted within the law to establish their fiscal innocence. That being so, an enforcement system that makes mistakes and yet relies on the deterrent effect of heavy penalties may impose severe welfare losses *ex post*.[37]

Second, if *both* sides can make mistakes, the main thrust of this argument is strengthened. The criterion for punishment becomes less easy to define, and the distinction between honest and dishonest behavior becomes less clear cut. The information available after an audit may offer only a partial picture of what has "really" been happening. Although the taxpayer (or his adviser) will often have a clearer idea about his true tax position than the tax authority, and although an audit will usually redress this imbalance, the audit may not be decisive in clarifying whether there had been an *intention* to cheat the government. Because of this an effective enforcement system may still have to penalize honest mistakes.[38]

Third, the tax code may well be beset by ambiguities, in which case the concept of the "true tax position" is far from clear.[39] If this is so, how does it affect the policy options for the administration?

The immediate answer seems to be that we would have to modify the optimization rules set out earlier in this chapter to allow for this further component of risk. This modification raises no great new issues of principle, although the imputation of a plausible probability distribution representing the risk may present considerable practical difficulty. However, there is a more fundamental point: The additional aspects of uncertainty may actually change the nature of the economic problem in certain important respects. In particular, the structures of certain social institutions may take on special significance. Two instances of this are particularly important: the tax code and the possibility of taxpayer appeals.

Let us first consider the tax code. Clarity of expression of the law, and a lack of ambiguity in the implication of the law for the taxpayer, will play an important part in determining the range of acceptable enforcement policies. If it is unclear which people have broken the law and how grievously they have broken it,

draconian measures of enforcement will be seen as unaccept-
ably inequitable—the public may not be prepared to have a
well-meaning simpleton's wife and children turned out into the
street just because he worked out his capital gains incorrectly.

This possibility of innocent confusion has some obvious
implications for the authorities. Legislators should examine
closely the way their intentions are expressed in the letter of
the law. Those who design the institutional mechanisms of
taxation systems should take human fallibility into account;
there may be a strong case for automaticity in tax collection.[40]

A less obvious implication is that innocent confusion may
also influence the way in which legislators select the proposed
tax base and plan the structure of tax rates. Unsophisticated
taxes—which might be a little short on the refinements that the
champions of social justice would like to see—may be preferable to nicely graduated schedules that are difficult to imple-
ment and costly to enforce. They may be preferable not only
on the grounds of crude savings in tax-collection costs but also
with regard to the *effective* justness of the tax—the perceived
fairness or unfairness of the tax once the workings of the
systems of assessment and enforcement have been taken into
account.

Now let us turn to the possibility of legal process. If the tax
authority is not capable of assessing incomes correctly or distinguishing between different categories of taxpayers, constitutional provision of appeal procedures becomes crucial. If it is
relatively inexpensive for a taxpayer to appeal a decision by the
tax authority, then the significance (in terms of economic welfare) of mistakes made by the tax authority is relatively minor.
The court becomes a method for mitigating the *ex post* injustices
that would otherwise arise.

Suppose, then, that the tax authority well knows that it
makes mistakes when it classifies people for tax purposes.
Should it be terribly worried about this? Perhaps not. In fact,
there is a way in which mistakes could apparently work to the

community's advantage. Official carelessness could even play the part of a policy instrument.[41] Suppose that when the tax authority audits people's incomes it randomly over- or underestimates them and uses these erroneous estimates as a basis for demanding tax payments and a surcharge. Those who are dishonest run the risk of being forced to pay the tax and the surcharge on both their concealed income *and* any overestimate of their income. This may induce them to reduce the amount that they choose to evade, to the consequent benefit of others. This benefit may be sufficient to offset the losses of taxpayers for whom the authority's assessment of their tax liability is too high, and who are thus unjustly surcharged. If a wrong assessment can be appealed, these individual losses can actually be made good through the courts. The situation would be even more favorable to the honest taxpayer if the law were to require that the cost of successful appeals be borne by the tax authority.

However, if the tax authority bears the cost of appeals, then the court can, apparently, also become a convenient device for eliciting information about a taxpayer's position. Consider the following "tax authority as mad axeman" scenario. If the inspectors go beserk and start producing ludicrously inflated assessments, this will abruptly change the expected returns to evasion. All taxpayers will report honestly, because then the worst that can happen to them is that they will have to pay for the time of a real tax inspector doing his job seriously, and if the above law on appeals is in force then they do not even have to pay that. By using this device the tax authority has managed to reintroduce the "solution" (outlined in chapter 7) in which the threat of absurdly high assessments is used as a perfect substitute for a very high surcharge s. If the cost of an appeal does not exceed the resource cost (to the tax authority) of accurately auditing a tax return, then there should be an overall gain in welfare. The approach is cynical, but potentially effective.

Hence, even if the parameters s and t are beyond the control of the tax authority, there may in practice be policy parameters other than p that it could deploy in enforcing the tax system. Or so it appears. In fact it is clear that although a mild application of the "mad axeman" strategy may produce desirable results,[42] rigorous use of the device is unattractive because it relies heavily on the rational and well-informed use of the legal machinery by all citizens. Tough methods of enforcement—even if indirect and irregular—may still mean that some of the innocent get hurt.

Quis Custodiet Ipsos Custodes?

There is one final factor to mention. It concerns a feature of the tax system that, if neglected, could undermine the most carefully designed policy. Up till now we have assumed that the government has at its disposal an invisible army of enforcement agents who loyally investigate the incomes of those liable to tax. However, tax inspectors and auditors are real people like you and me. They are also, presumably, subject to the same sorts of temptations. What if the government's agents are themselves cheating the government?

Again we need to examine the nature of the *economic* issue that is involved. It is not just a problem of grit in the machinery of tax collection; that problem has already been allowed for in the above discussion of the relationship between taxpayer and tax authority. The "invisible army" might be inefficient—ill-informed and prone to mistakes, perhaps; bumbling even—but not crooked. Crookedness, in this case, implies that agents of the tax authority are susceptible to subversion by others in the economy. To see how this subversion might occur, consider briefly the means by which the mechanism of assessment and enforcement operates.

In some cases the system of tax assessment relies to an extent on the services of professional private accountants, who supply general information about a firm's financial soundness and can also provide specific information to the tax authority about their clients' liability to tax.[43] It should not be taken for granted that the auditors are on the side of the tax authorities. They have to be won over. The authorities could do this by offering economic inducements that make it worth the accountants' while to keep their professional house in order. Such inducements might take the form of statutory protection of the profession's monopoly. This gives rise to a two-stage system of policing in which the tax authorities check up on a sample of the company auditors and threaten those who break the code of the profession by conniving with their clients to evade taxes with the prospect of being struck off.[44] The judgment required on the part of the authorities is as follows: If they are overgenerous with the protection, then there will be social losses from the excess monopoly rents accrued by the accountancy profession; but if the protection is insufficient, the authorities run the risk of causing widespread disaffection among the body that is supposed to act as their "deputies" (with a potentially catastrophic loss of tax discipline and revenue).

Of course, the economic problem may actually be simpler than that. Even if there were no outside professional body whose loyalty was in question, the employees of the tax authority might be open to offers of bribes.[45] The concealment of corrupt officials within the authority can vitiate an otherwise effective enforcement policy. Prospective tax evaders may be able to "buy themselves a cop"; in that case, conventional sanctions against the evaders may not have the desired effect in the long run—if the penalty for evasion is increased, then all that may happen is that the equilibrium price of a tame "policeman" rises while everyone carries on as before. If the venality of tax officials is a significant feature of a country's bureaucracy, then combating corruption in the public sector may be a more effective way of controlling tax evasion in the private sector.[46]

Summary

In abstract terms, the design of tax-enforcement policy can be treated as just one more branch of some well-known public-finance theory. Nonetheless, it contains problems that are particularly interesting. What make them so is the set of choices to which it gives rise.

Evidently there is a fundamental choice to be made between threats and thoroughness. Should the policymaker rely on high tax surcharges, or on efficient detection? As we saw in chapter 7, *ex post* inequality aversion will influence the choice of policy instruments if evasion is to be not eliminated but merely attenuated to a degree sufficient to ensure that the government's budget constraint is met. The more acute is society's concern for *ex post* inequality, the more it will rely on rigor of enforcement (p) rather than on severity of sentence (s).[47]

Another series of difficult choices concern the type of information and the type of institutional structure that are relevant to a particular community. The precise details of the tax law will determine what can be done to control evasion without permitting leakage through legal escape routes, and without imposing severe injustices in the course of enforcement. And although it obviously makes sense for enforcers to put readily available information to good use, it is not immediately obvious how this should be done; the answer will depend on the structure of the taxpaying population, on the social norms, and on the relationships between individual taxpayers and the state. The issues are likely to be complex.

However, because the issues are complex they should not be brushed aside as time-consuming niceties that practical administrators can ill afford. As in other branches of public finance, it is important that the rules of tax enforcement be based on economic reason rather than on hunch or blind prejudice; otherwise the tax inspectors may find that they have been holding up the wrong stagecoach after all.

9   Conclusion

An economy breathes through its tax loopholes.
Barry Bracewell-Milnes

Tax Evasion as a Serious Subject

Cheating the government is occasionally regarded as something of a sport or a curiosity. It should be treated as neither. It is, rather, an intrinsically interesting economic problem with profound implications for the fiscal relationship between government and citizen. Those who are not persuaded of this might reflect on two basic questions.

Is evasion inevitable? In all but the most trivial types of economy the answer must be "Yes, almost certainly." It is true that one can easily imagine particular communities whose members —motivated by religious zeal, altruism, or civic pride[1]—willingly supply the resources required for collective consumption, redistribution, or whatever without the need for government compulsion. However, in the everyday world of selfish humankind, which is the usual subject matter of economics, such situations are exceptional. There will normally be a fundamental conflict between private gain and public duty that makes "dodging the column" appear an attractive option to many citizens. Honesty is not the natural fruit of self-interest.

Do economists have any useful contribution to make to an understanding of the problem? The problem of tax evasion might be thought to be a purely administrative issue. However, the possibility of cheating in the relationship between individuals and the government significantly affects the working of the economic system. In fact the economist can contribute to an understanding of the subject in three principal areas: description, analysis, and prescription.

The Evidence

Describing the problem in quantitative terms is not easy. A quick skim through the many empirical studies of tax evasion and the underground economy prompts two questions that ought to be asked more frequently: What is the evidence *of*, and what is it *for*?

   This is a topic about which there is much passion but for which reliable numbers are at a premium. Because of the inevitable problems of getting data, and the inaccuracy of such data as can be obtained, there is a tendency to spend more time writing about how to measure evasion activity than about the actual estimates. Such estimates as are available often provide evidence of the inadequacy of the techniques rather than of the size of the black economy. The problem is usually exacerbated by official ignorance, and perhaps in some cases by the officials' proneness to corruption.

   In the absence of the evidence that we would like to have, what should the presumption be? It is as unrealistic to assume that the underground economy does not exist as to suppose that the entire fiscal system is about to implode under the pressure of tax cheating. The very large estimates of the underground economy usually depend on techniques of estimation that are not wonderfully robust, or they apply to particular cases from which it would be unwise to generalize. On the other hand, even the modest estimates are not trivial in their implications for the tax authorities— 2 percent of several trillion dollars is still quite a lot.

However, simply putting a percentage on the underground sector does not of itself provide much guidance as to the importance of tax evasion as an economic issue. Sheer size is not the point. Cheating the government does not take place in a political and social vacuum. The practice is evidently alive and flourishing in most countries—developing and developed, Eastern and Western—and it is *within the context* of a particular economic system that one should try to analyze what is going on and what, if anything, should be done about it. Detailed evidence—whether from official audits, private enquiry, or indirect inference—can be useful as a guide to policy, but only in conjunction with an appropriate analytical framework.

The Role of Economic Theory

The phenomenon of tax cheating poses some particularly interesting analytical questions. In tackling such questions one has to address major issues that lie at the heart of public economics; in fact, the phenomenon casts doubt on some of the conventional wisdom.

Take one example of this: the issue of personal taxation and its supposed incentive effects. Considerable research effort has been devoted to theoretical and empirical analysis of one particular area of personal and household choice: decisions about whether to participate in the labor market, and how much time to supply to that market. Clearly such research is of tremendous importance; clearly, too, precise estimates of the labor supply are likely to be sensitive to the assumptions made about the availability of alternative, unobserved opportunities in the labor market. In some circumstances, opting in or out of a part of the shadow economy may be a margin of choice that is as significant for the public as the margin between work and leisure. Such a phenomenon would have serious positive and normative implications—the apparent labor-supply responses reflected in conventional elasticity estimates are likely to be biased, and the inferences drawn concerning the impact of taxation on social welfare could be quite misleading.

Economic theory can enlighten us to some extent as to what is going on at this margin of choice. However, it is not immediately evident what should be the appropriate analytical apparatus for this purpose. The standard economic models of crime and the control of crime—models in which individuals are motivated by the expected returns to wrongdoing and deterred by the risks of punishment—provide a promising basis on which to work, but they are incomplete in two important respects: First, in economic terms, evasion is not an ordinary crime. Embedded in the problem of financing government by means of taxation is a potential distortion of information that is fundamental to the problem of evasion; hence an adequate model of evasion should take explicit account of the role of the public sector. Second, as chapters 4–6 have argued, no single tale of the malefactor's motivation is entirely adequate. The issue of evasion is not a mere textbook exercise like the purchase of lottery tickets. This is not to play down the role of prospective personal gain; although people do evade taxes for reasons other than money (such as social protest or sheer bloody-mindedness), it would be unreasonable to suggest that these alternatives are the *principal* driving force of evasion. However, one needs to give careful attention to the way in which individuals' motivations are incorporated into a model of the collective response to the system of taxation and tax enforcement.

The analytical framework developed in this book can help in answering some basic questions concerning the underground economy. How does its growth come about? Chapter 4 offers a simplified story: If the government enlarges the public sector through taxation, then it is likely that the underground economy will grow too, a long as this switch of resources away from the private sector is broadly perceived to increase social welfare; beyond that point, further tax hikes will have the opposite effect. Why is tax evasion often associated with a distinct, segregated sector of the economy? Why might there be a self-perpetuating "culture" of evasion activity? Chapters 5 and 6 suggest simple economic mechanisms that will induce the behavior that leads to such phenomena. Understanding such mechanisms is an important first step in drawing up a policy for dealing with the problem.

Policy

But is a *policy* toward tax evasion really necessary? If it is actually true that an economy breathes through its tax loopholes, then might not any such policy—trying to close off loopholes and hunt down those who manage to wriggle through any remaining cracks—prove counterproductive? Put bluntly: Should the government raise a white flag in its battle against the black economy?

To answer this basic question properly, you first need to pose even more basic questions about the economic role of "honesty": Is it a social good in its own right, or a secondary objective that is logically entailed by other more basic goals, or what? In the absence of a clear view on this issue, an economic adviser would be in the invidious position of giving policy guidelines without knowing who is supposed to be doing what and to whom.

Standard welfare economics does not suggest that there is a terribly strong case for the suppression of tax evasion. Evasion is regarded as a public ill only insofar as the private risks of detection and punishment impose welfare losses upon the sufferers (the evaders). If people are not particularly risk-averse, then, according to the conventional argument, official zeal for enforcement need only be sufficient to ensure that the government can pay its bills. If the case against tax cheating is weak, does this mean that there is a case for *encouraging* evasion?

Maybe. However, the case would rest on a very special set of conditions—for example, that the marginal gains in productive efficiency in the underground sector be greater than the cost of the risk borne by the tax evaders.[2] Moreover, this type of economic argument, which concentrates on the small change of marginal decisions to engage in wrongdoing, may actually neglect a more substantial but less easily quantifiable issue: The public sector can work only through cooperation or coercion. If the spirit of cooperation is not present in sufficient measure, then, in the "common-sense" view, nothing should be allowed that will undermine the effectiveness of those who have the authority to coerce; that way lies Chaos.[3]

This point is analogous to the popular wisdom on "the battle against inflation." Economic theory offers several formal arguments about the welfare losses from steady-state inflation, but none of these is overwhelmingly convincing. Perhaps what people are really worried about is *uncertainty* (as distinct from quantifiable *risk*)—the possibility that a lax attitude toward inflation may lead to a loss of confidence and to the collapse of the state's authority. Similarly with evasion. As we have seen, there may be a welfare-based argument for reducing the amount of cheating, but the argument looks decidedly flaccid. The problem is that cheating *might* become an epidemic, thus destroying the fiscal basis for the support of the state.[4] Tight control is required to avoid the spread of mutiny below decks.

Of course, even if you accept that control is necessary, there remain the questions of how far you want to go and how you should go about it.

The first of these two questions involves a balance between law enforcement and personal freedom. Some people will argue that big punishments are morally objectionable, period—that even if they were to be effective as a deterrent, so that they never had to be invoked in practice, they would still be unacceptable in a civilized society. Such arguments clearly set bounds on what may be prescribed and, therefore, on what is achievable. On this basis, outright eradication is unlikely to be practicable within the sort of society that one observes around the world, and with the sort of citizens who live around the corner.

The second question—how enforcement policy should be designed—raises more complex issues. Although this is obviously not a cookbook for tax enforcers, we are interested in the principles upon which investigation rules are based. It is probably a good idea that enforcement policy should be informed by economic analysis rather than just relying on hunch or tradition. However, the appropriate economic principles will depend intimately upon the objectives of the government and the type of institutional setup within which one has to work.

The fundamental distortion of information evidently presents fiscal planners with an awkward problem of control. What will make a person tell the truth? Self-interest usually does not work, but what if this self-interest were to be modified by a governmental stick and carrot? Administrative cost—not to mention qualms about a police state—will restrict the frequency with which the stick can be brought to bear. But the force of the stick can be redoubled by social pressures if the tax authority is skilled at public relations, and the stick can be wielded more skillfully through the subtle use of information. Effective use of information could be enhanced by cooperation among fiscal agencies; for example an integrated taxation-*cum*-income-support system could provide valuable opportunities for effective monitoring. Nevertheless, it would require starry-eyed optimism to suppose that even this will guarantee honest behavior, in the face of the human scope for misinterpretation and the human capacity for making mistakes.

A Final Word

Away from the headline-grabbing stories of the underground economy, there is an important story to be told and an important branch of economic behavior to be analyzed. The subject matter of this book is not just an intellectual curiosity, but touches on people's everyday experiences. Consider the following:

The hit movie of 1984 was a Soviet-made comedy called *The Blonde Around the Corner*, which was based on the lives of people on the fringes of the black economy. It was an affectionate portrait of the life of easy money and lavish parties. Although it ended in approved Soviet style, with the loose-living blonde married to a devout young research worker who wanted to settle in Siberia, build the future, and raise a family, the reason for the film's success was that it portrayed a life that so many Russians could recognize. (Walker 1986)

For the immediate future, at least, cheating the government is here to stay.

Notes

Chapter 1

1. See the interview in *Izvestia*, June 2, 1986, page 3. In this case the black-economy activity consists in the illegal use of state-owned equipment.

2. A tax scam sometimes used in the U.K.—see *The Independent*, October 24, 1987, p. 2.

3. Another tax scam—see *Washington Post*, August 17, 1986, p. D5.

4. For surveys of the recent literature, see Cowell 1985c; Jackson and Milliron 1986, Pommerehne 1985, Pyle 1987, and Witte and Woodbury 1983. Other works giving a general introduction to the topic are Bawly 1982, Feige 1987, Heertje et al. 1982, Simon and Witte 1982, Skinner and Slemrod 1985, Smith 1981a and 1981b, Smith 1986, Smithies 1984, Tanzi 1983, and Weigel et al. 1987.

5. For a good introduction, see Anderson 1976, Cameron 1988, Heineke 1978, McKenzie and Tullock 1978, and Pyle 1983.

6. Rice 1956.

7. There are exceptions, such as vigilante groups and lynch mobs, but these are relevant to rather special circumstances.

8. See Graetz and Wilde 1985.

9. For example, in the Soviet Union, although there may be draconian summary penalties for overdue payments of tax (Newcity 1986, p. 194), tax evasion as such is not actually against the law; there is no article in the criminal code that punishes it, except in times of war

(Maggs 1979). There is an important economic counterpart, however: "crimes against the central planner."

Chapter 2

1. The distinction made in French between *l'évasion fiscale* and *la fraude fiscale* runs into this kind of problem, but it is not quite identical to the distinction made by Anglophones between "avoidance" and "evasion."

2. The complementary argument, that certain types of officially designated evasion are really not all that bad, has also been made; see Bracewell-Milnes 1979.

3. Seldon (1979) introduced the term "tax avoision." Cross and Shaw (1981, 1982) use the more emotive "tax aversion."

4. See Boidman 1983 and International Bar Association 1982 for a general discussion. The differences between the British and American tax systems, and their opportunities for evasion and avoidance, are discussed further in Feldman and Kay 1981; the similarities between the two countries in actual rulings on cases is noted in Millett 1986.

5. Geeroms and Wilmots (1985) investigated attitudes toward tax avoidance and tax evasion on the basis of the official Belgian definitions and found that avoidance and evasion are close substitutes. See also Lewis 1979.

6. For example, note the distinction made in English law as recently clarified by the Judicial Committee of the Privy Council. In the majority judgment on the appeal in the case of *Inland Revenue v Challenge Corporation Ltd.* ([1986] STC 548) it was stated that there is a discernible difference between (i) a transaction that is a sham, (ii) a transaction that effects the evasion of tax, (iii) a transaction that mitigates tax, and (iv) a transaction that avoids tax. In case i the transaction creates a false impression in the eyes of the tax authority. In case ii the tax commissioner is not informed about circumstances relevant to an assessment of tax. Income tax is mitigated—case iii—if the taxpayer reduces his income or incurs an expenditure that reduces his tax liability, as for example when making payments under covenant or when making an irrevocable settlement. Income tax is avoided—case iv—if the taxpayer suffers no loss of income, and incurs no expenditure, but nevertheless enjoys a reduction in liability to tax as if he had.

7. These may not be confined to financial penalties; see chapter 6.

8. Such costs should be distinguished from compliance costs. See Sandford 1980 for a detailed discussion of the relationship among compliance costs, evasion, and avoidance; see Slemrod and Sorum 1984 for an estimate of compliance costs in the U.S.

9. A dramatic example of such a response is the threat of retroactive penalties, as in the famous Rossminster case in the U.K. (Smithies 1984, p. 145).

10. Compare the distinction made between "legality" and "control" when defining the "second economy" in the USSR (Feldbrugge 1984).

11. A nice distinction along these lines is made by Kay (1980, p. 136): "Evasion is concerned with concealing or misrepresenting the nature of a transaction; when avoidance takes place the facts of the transaction are admitted but they have been arranged in such a way that the resulting tax treatment differs from that intended by the relevant legislation. The incidence of evasion is therefore a function of the mechanisms by which tax is assessed and collected, and the extent to which they can be controlled or monitored; the incidence of avoidance is a function of the tax base and depends on the extent to which evasion is successful in expressing the underlying economic concepts." Nevertheless, as Kay acknowledges, there still remains an area of overlap between the two concepts as defined in this way.

The problem of avoidance and of the definition of income is discussed further in Feldman and Kay 1981, using the Simons (1938) approach.

12. Some illicit activities, such as Social Security fraud, are legally distinct from, but economically similar to, evasion. Compare the very broad interpretation of "black economy" used by Smithies (1984).

13. In the Soviet Union, production after hours in the illegal sector is said to be "na levo"—"on the left."

14. "Black economy" and "underground economy" are used as synonyms in this book. The former is probably the more usual term in the U.K.; the latter is the more common usage in the U.S.

15. See the surveys of the empirical literature in Carter 1984, Feige 1984, Marrelli 1987, and Smith 1986.

16. Women's work in the home is usually classified as "unproductive." This official convention has not always applied, however: see Lewis

1984 for a discussion of how the official U.K. census classification changed during the nineteenth century.

17. I say "at least three" because some students of the subject would want to distinguish yet other boundaries, and hence other subcategories. For example, there is a difficulty with the classification of many criminal activities inside or outside boundary I: Should prostitution and the narcotics industry be included in definitions of the "informal economy"? For an introduction to the subject see Henry 1978, Gershuny and Pahl in Henry 1981, and Wiles 1987. For an excellent overview of the issues see Blades 1985.

18. For the U.S., see the Tax Compliance Measurement Program reported in U.S. Dept. of Treasury Internal Revenue Service 1979 and in Long 1980. This is dealt with in more detail in chapter 4. In some cases official records have been fruitfully combined with academic research facilities to provide an estimate of tax noncompliance—see Alm and Bahl 1985 and Bahl and Murray 1986 for the case of Jamaica.

19. See Brown et al. 1984 and method 4 below.

20. This type of study tends to miss the "ghosts" (discussed below).

21. See Dilnot and Morris 1981 and Smith 1986. The method is discussed in detail in chapter 5 below.

22. See Macafee 1980 and Ross 1978.

23. Gutmann followed a technique pioneered by Cagan (1958). For detailed comments on Gutmann's technique see Bowsher 1980, Garcia 1978, and Laurent 1979.

24. Even the more sophisticated attempts at estimating a demand-for-currency equation by which to deduce the size of the economy seem to be subject to this type of problem, and produce some very strange results—see Klovland 1980 and chapter 4 of Tanzi 1982b. For an excellent critical analysis see Barthelemy 1988.

25. See Frey et al. 1982 and Frey and Weck 1983a,b. The approach is based on that of Kofler and Menges (1976).

26. See the criticisms in Helberger and Knepel 1988.

27. The problems of underdeveloped countries are discussed further in Chopra 1982, Herschel 1978, and Jain 1972, 1974, 1986. Inter-country comparisons are made in Alden and Saha 1978, Frey and Pommerehne 1982 and 1984, Frey and Weck 1983a,b, and O'Higgins

1985. The scope and the size of the "second" economy in socialist countries are discussed in Brezinski 1985, Galasi 1985, Grossman 1977, and O'Hearn 1980.

28. Table 2.2 can usefully be contrasted with Gutmann's (1977) estimate of $176 billion as the total underreported income.

29. O'Higgins (1989) suggests that 5 percent is probably a reasonable figure for the U.K. The Institute for Fiscal Studies suggests a figure nearer 2 percent, although their estimate for the self-employed sector is much higher (Dilnot and Morris 1981; Smith 1986). The U.S. Department of the Treasury (1979) suggested 6–8 percent for the U.S. (probably an underestimate); Hansson (1980) reports an estimate of 8–15 percent by the Riksskatteverk for Sweden. The much higher estimates of Gutmann and Feige have been challenged by Denison (1982) on the basis of employment/population ratios.

30. See Dubin et al. 1987. The hypothesis that the black economy is growing alarmingly in developed market economies is also put in doubt by such detailed survey evidence as is available (see chapter 5 below). On the basis of two surveys in Norway in the early 1980s, Isachsen and Strøm (1985) found that there was no evidence of increased participation in "black" labor-market activity—a conclusion which is borne out by Wolff's (1985) study of domestic servants in the U.S.

Chapter 3

1. Probably the earliest analytical treatment of the economics of tax evasion and enforcement is Schleicher 1971.

2. The standard reference, Atkinson and Stiglitz 1980, has one footnote on the subject.

3. See Dornbusch and Fischer 1984, pp. 526–528.

4. There are other objections as well. For example, even if it were possible to charge for publicly supplied goods, the pricing scheme might be distributionally inequitable. For a further discussion of these problems and of public goods in general, see chapters 6, 8, and 12 of Cowell 1986b.

5. This is the "Prisoner's Dilemma" game form. There is a close similarity between this behavior and that of individual firms within an oligopolistic market structure.

6. This is the "Chicken" game form. Anyone who has lived in a group household will be familiar with this as the problem of who fills the refrigerator.

7. The logic underlying such rules is discussed in Brennan and Buchanan 1985. For discussions of how cooperation can be rationally established in various types of Prisoner's Dilemma and Chicken games, see Hardin 1971, Kreps et al. 1982, and Lipman 1986; see also Guttman 1987. For extensive general discussions of the game-theoretic approach, see Sugden 1986 and Taylor 1987. For some negative evidence on the practical importance of defection in small communities, see Schneider and Pommerehne 1981; for some persuasive argumentation on the "preference revelation" problem, see Johansen 1977. For evidence on the apparent disparity between public and private attitudes, see Zweifel and Pommerehne 1985.

8. Under these circumstances the case depicted in table 3.1 is likely to be more relevant than that of table 3.2.

9. The "government" in this two-person economy is a disembodied but not omniscient spirit. For examples of this type of approach to the tax-evasion problem, see Gaertner 1987, Gottlieb 1985, Laurin 1983, and Maital 1982.

10. As in the case of the American couple who divorced and married each other three times in order to reduce their tax bill (*Washington Post*, July 7, 1986, p. D3).

11. The distinction here may be quite subtle. As an example, consider the problem of paying for public broadcast TV. Until quite recently, the available technology made it impractical to monitor people's consumption of public broadcast output so as to impose a charge based on quantity consumed (as with excise taxes). What could be done was to tax the presence in a building of an installed TV set (the situation in the U.K.). A decision for *potential use* of a TV set was thus considered to be observable behavior for the purposes of levying charges (taxes); the *amount of use* was not.

12. The classic example of this was the bricking-up of windows in order to escape liability for window taxes. However, the principal source of this diversion of resources is to be found in the problem of "household production" (see Sandmo 1986).

13. For a general discussion of the economics of avoidance see Stiglitz 1985. As was noted in chapter 2, the important distinction here is

between that which is ruled unlawful in practice and that which is not. The form that avoidance takes varies greatly according to the nature of the tax system and the method of enforcement: In the U.K. (until very recently) you bought a forest; in the U.S. you set up your own church.

14. These are known technically as "crimes against the central planner" (Lampert 1985, Orland 1987, Pomorski 1979).

15. See the "income distribution game" outlined in Kurz 1977.

16. The failure to file tax returns need not imply an intention to misrepresent information or defraud the authorities. Take the sad plight of Bundy Bynum, a United Methodist minister who did not file a single tax return in 25 years (*Washington Post*, April 20, 1985, p. G11). In the light of psychiatric evidence, the IRS took a sympathetic view of the case, allowing "fear of filing" as a legitimate phobia.

17. For a general introduction to this type of problem see Arrow 1985, Cowell 1986b, and Rees 1985. For an application of this in the context of public administration see Cullis and Jones 1987. The implications for a tax-enforcement agency are discussed in chapter 8 below.

18. Although, as we have just seen, the exact comparison between personal expenditure and income taxes in terms of evasion opportunities will depend in each case on whether an automatic or a self-declaration system of tax assessment is in force.

19. There is evidence that people who might be supposed to be quite well informed are often unaware of basic information, such as their own marginal tax rate (Brown 1968, Lewis 1978). The complexity of tax guides presumably exacerbates the problem of misperception (James et al. 1981).

20. Compare the irritation felt by some about the treatment of alcoholic drink in the U.K.: An excise duty based on the alcohol content is levied on each bottle or can. A VAT is then assessed on the whole, *including* the excise duty. This "tax on tax" approach appears to be perceived as particularly unjust, irrespective of the actual levels of taxation involved.

21. Although the nonpayment of tax in such cases is usually regarded by the law as "evasion," this form of open protest is rather different from the type of behavior that we examine in most of this book. The people involved—such as pacifists—are unlikely to be bought off by

financial incentives, and are usually undeterred by the severe penalties they receive in the courts. Consider the case reported in the *Times* (London) of April 13, 1985: A pacifist refused to pay £109.05 to the Inland Revenue. He received a 21-day prison sentence, and the IR obtained a court order to enter his home and seize his property.

22. On tax revolts see Brennan and Buchanan 1980.

23. Sometimes the distinction between tax evasion and outright protest can become blurred. Take, for example, the sad case of the tax-evading farmer in the Guangxi region of China, reported in *The Guardian* for May 19, 1988: He was sentenced to death for driving his tractor over a tax inspector.

24. For example, there is the special type of model, discussed by Weiss (1976) and Stiglitz (1982), in which random taxation appears to be desirable. Other examples are discussed in chapter 7.

25. On this see Adam and Ginsburgh 1985, Ginsburgh et al. 1985, Lai and Chang 1988, Pandit 1977, Peacock and Shaw 1982, Ricketts 1984, and Thomas 1985.

26. This is the issue of the Laffer Curve; see Feige 1987, Feige and McGee 1982, 1983, and McGee and Feige 1982 for an aggregate approach. Greenberg et al. (1981) provide evidence from microdata on the Gary negative income tax experiment which suggests that underreporting in such experiments may be substantial, and that as a consequence the estimates of the labor supply may be biased upward.

27. Schmähl (1985) discusses the relationship between the Social Security system and the black economy.

28. This is similar to the concept of the "Bad Man" sometimes used in discussion of the fundamentals of law; see Holmes 1897.

Chapter 4

1. This approach is standard in the literature. See Allingham and Sandmo 1972.

2. The analysis can easily be adapted to a tax base other than income. It can also be fairly easily extended to the problem of welfare fraud (Yaniv 1986). In this case we may have the situation where the budget line in figure 4.2 is extended down and to the right of B, so that the consumption of a successful fraudster exceeds his gross income. By

extending the line AB in this way we can also model the case where it is possible for the tax evader to report a loss ($e > y$).

3. Incorporating these features into the utility function is not difficult for so simple a choice problem, but makes little difference to the analysis of this chapter. Possibly the most important consequence of relaxing this assumption is that some individuals may choose not to evade at all even though they have positive marginal utility of consumption and are faced with a strictly positive rate of return to evasion (see equation 4.3a and note 6). Although the von Neumann-Morgenstern assumption is not particularly restrictive in the present context, more care is required when one examines normative aspects of tax evasion.

4. To see this, note that, for any consumption prospect c, the marginal rate of substitution of consumption-if-caught (c'') for consumption-if-escape (c') is

$$[1 - p]u_c(c')/[pu_c(c'')];$$

setting $c' = c''$ gives the result.

5. Of course, if one were to introduce a specific disutility to the act of evasion (as we will in chapter 6), or if there were certain fixed transaction costs to evasion, then a condition corresponding to 4.3a would still be relevant. If $[1 + s]t > 1$ and $p > 0$, an equilibrium of type 4.3b is ruled out (Yitzhaki 1974).

6. See Arrow 1965, 1970; Pratt 1964.

7. See Allingham and Sandmo 1972; Cowell 1985c, p. 171.

8. This type of constraint is commonly used in full models of the black economy; see Sandmo 1981.

9. It is easy to extend this to the case where the probability of detection is conditioned on the observable components of personal attributes a. The probability of detection must then be written $p(a)$, and the expression Φ is evaluated over the entire range of a.

10. See Cowell and Gordon 1988. The level of provision of the publicly supplied good is not necessarily optimal, but is just determined by the tax-enforcement parameters τ, the technology, and the evasion behavior. The appropriate level of provision is discussed further in chapter 8.

11. See Ahsan 1974, Cowell 1975, Mossin 1968, Stiglitz 1969.

12. It is straightforward to show these results using the first-order condition 4.3c and differentiating. We find

$$te_p(\tau, y, a) = [su_c^a(c'') + u_c^a(c')]/\mathbf{E}(u_{cc}^a \mathbf{r}^2)$$

and

$$te_s(\tau, y, a) = [pu_c^a(c'') - psteu_{cc}^a(c'')]/\mathbf{E}(u_{cc}^a \mathbf{r}^2).$$

Both of these expressions are clearly negative.

13. This result is due to Yitzhaki (1974). Because individual incomes are assumed to be exogenous, tax evasion increases both in absolute terms and as a proportion of taxable income. However, if the penalty is not proportionate to the evaded tax, the simplicity of the result disappears (Cowell 1985c, p. 171).

14. This type of model has been discussed by Ali (1976) and by Koskela (1983a); its structure is similar to that dealt with in the literature on risk-taking (Ahsan 1974, Cowell 1975). Koskela also shows that, if one makes the additional assumption of decreasing absolute risk aversion (see below), then this result holds for the case where the tax parameters are adjusted such that the expected revenue raised by the government from a particular taxpayer stays constant. For taxpayers who are not at the appropriate "break-even" point, one can predict the outcome by combining the result on the "pure progression" change with the result on the change in lump-sum income.

15. See Christiansen 1980. Because the structure of the random prospect is particularly simple in the case of the basic tax-evasion model (there are only two possible outcomes), a mean-preserving spread has an unambiguous effect on the risk-taking (Rothschild and Stiglitz 1970, 1971).

16. Differentiating constraint 4.6, it is easy to see that the feedback effect on E of a change in p or s via the amount of z will be smaller than the corresponding effect arising from a change in t.

17. Here u_{ci}^a is the appropriate second derivative for a (y, a)-type person, and the (c, z) arguments have been suppressed.

18. See Yitzhaki 1974, Christiansen 1980, and Cowell and Gordon 1988. These references use a result from chapter 2 of Arrow 1970.

19. If the appropriate model is the one *without* public goods (constraint 4.5 above), or if $u_{cz} = 0$ as in Gottlieb 1985, then this term

must be zero. Hence, as was noted above, an increase in the tax rate results in a *reduction* in evasion. On the importance of public expenditure in the evasion decision, see Becker et al. 1988 and Weck-Hannemann and Pommerehne 1988.

20. See Cowell and Gordon 1988.

21. The case of non-Ziff public goods is discussed further in Cowell and Gordon 1988.

22. Fishburn (1981) discusses the effect of price inflation in this type of model by examining the exogenous deflation of real income with the tax system fixed in nominal terms.

23. Yet this has been done; see Isachsen, Samuelson, and Strøm 1985 and Mork 1975. This work will be discussed further in chapter 5.

24. Although the data are based on an analysis of individual tax returns, they are made available to researchers only in a form that aggregates the observations by region to the level of the three-digit Zip code.

25. See Clotfelter 1983, Poterba 1987, Tauchen and Witte 1985, Witte and Tauchen 1987, Witte and Woodbury 1985.

26. Clotfelter's approach can be criticized on methodological grounds, since he does not model the "rationing" of evasion, and there may be multicollinearity among some of the regressors—see Baldry 1984b and Cox 1984.

27. See Crane and Nourzad 1985, 1987.

28. The world has, unfortunately, been deprived of some important case-study evidence on the behavior of the tax evader as gambler. The *Washington Post* of September 14, 1985 reports that one John A. Shorter, a prominent Washington defense attorney indicted on tax-evasion charges, maintained in court that he was not guilty because he was a "compulsive gambler." He regularly took all his fees in cash, he kept no bank account, and he was "compelled by his mental disorder to spend nearly all his money on gambling," according to an expert whom he wanted to produce as witness in court. The judge disallowed the testimony.

29. The basic model has been elaborated in a number of directions. McCaleb (1976) adapts it to deal with the case of differential taxation on capital and labor income. Büchner (1987a) modifies the cardinal

utility function so that it has *two* arguments: c and $y - c'$. (The latter acts as a proxy for subjective pain felt by the evader, irrespective of whether he is discovered.) Other authors have introduced a progressive tax system and a progressive system of penalties; this makes the model less tractable than the linear one discussed above, but it retains many of the standard results on the effects of changing the marginal penalty for evasion or the probability of detection—see Fishburn 1981, Srinivasan 1973, and Sproule et al. 1980. Nayak (1978) investigates the opposite case of regressive taxes and suggests that similar results are obtainable; but in this case the budget set may be nonconvex, which can lead to problems of nonuniqueness of the solution and difficulties in interpreting the comparative statics. Persson and Wissen (1984) show the implications for the observed income distribution with respect to the true income distribution.

Chapter 5

1. See Atkinson and Stiglitz 1980, p. 29. If $B > 0$, and the marginal tax rate t is constant, then the average tax rate, $t - B/y$, rises as income rises. The tax system can be made more progressive by increasing t and B simultaneously. The tax-transfer system modeled here can be interpreted as a crude approximation to the effects of a Social Security system (Schmähl 1985).

2. For examples of this type of model in the context of the black economy see Cowell 1985b, Garber et al. 1982, Houston 1987, Marchon 1979, Neck et al. 1989, Sproule 1985, and Yaniv 1988. For an elementary treatment see Block and Heineke 1973. The model is based on the analysis of labor under uncertainty as in Cowell 1981a and Tressler and Menezes 1980.

3. Once again the second-order conditions will be satisfied by the concavity of u^a and the convexity of the budget set.

4. If "$<$" holds in 5.4, then $h_0 = 0$; if "$<$" holds in 5.5, then $h_1 = 0$.

5. This sort of perversity has been noted by Baldry (1979) and by Pencavel (1979). The specific example will be discussed further in the next section.

6. See Atkinson and Stiglitz 1980, pp. 119, 37.

7. This "two-stage" model is discussed in Cowell 1981a and Cowell 1985b. The utility function u^a may be written

$$u^a(c, \ell) = \alpha(\beta(\ell)c + \gamma(\ell))$$

where α, β, and γ are increasing functions. See also the similar model of savings under uncertainty discussed by Drèze and Modigliani (1972). This functional form is different from the additively separable form used in Andersen 1977, which does not yield readily interpretable results.

8. It is assumed that the individual is currently participating in both sectors and that A5 holds. The reason for the result is that the given wage (w_0) fixes the amount of leisure demanded (ℓ), and hence fixes the total time to be divided between the two sectors. The problem then reduces to that discussed in Stiglitz 1969.

9. The result also goes through for cases where $w_0 < w_1$—see Cowell 1981a, 1985b. See Fluet 1987 for a discussion of the case $w_0 > w_1$.

10. Observe that the expression $e(\tau, w_0[1 - \ell], a)$ in equation 5.8 is essentially identical to $e(\tau, y, a)$ in chapter 4 for a person with given market opportunities $\mathbf{w}$ and separable decisions. However, note that assumption A5 is now extended so as to apply to *both* arguments of the utility function—see Fluet 1987.

11. This follows from the fact that a change in the marginal tax rate works in exactly the opposite direction to a proportionate increase in $\mathbf{w}$, the returns in both sectors.

12. An example of this is the Pay As You Earn tax system in the U.K. In the U.S. a similar distinction may be made: Wage and salary income is reported directly to the IRS (on form W-2, for example). Garber et al. (1982) incorporate this explicitly into their model of evasion.

13. It may be at one's regular place of work, however. In many countries it is quite common for "black economy" car repairs to be carried out on the firm's premises during days off. There is also, of course, the possibility that the *employer* may cheat the tax authority by understating the wages or salaries paid to workers (Yaniv 1988).

14. As can be seen, the acceptance set $A(\mathbf{w}, a)$ has the property that, if any $\tau = (p, s, t, B)$ is a member of the set, then so also is (p', s', t, B) where $p' \geq p$ and $s' \geq s$.

15. See Cowell 1985b, Isachsen and Strøm 1980, and Isachsen, Samuelsen, and Strøm 1985. The economic problem is similar to that

treated in Block and Heineke 1973, 1975, Block and Lind 1975a, 1975b, Cowell 1981b, and Heineke 1978.

16. The term is used in this sense by the Inland Revenue

17. The result depends on the assumption that leisure is a normal good (Cowell 1981a, 1981b). As in chapter 4, D denotes the appropriate second-order term; in this case it is

$$- \mathbf{E}(u_{cc}^a w_1^2 [1 - t + t\mathbf{r}]^2 - 2w_1 u_{c\ell}^a [1 - t + t\mathbf{r}] + u_{\ell\ell}^a),$$

which is strictly positive.

18. See Cowell 1985b.

19. Observe that the numerator in equation 5.17 has the same sign as the differential of $L(c'', \ell)$ with respect to w_1.

20. This is achieved by increasing s and reducing p simultaneously so that $\bar{r}$ stays unchanged.

21. This applies only *within* one or other of the two regimes described in equation 5.9. It is quite conceivable that an increase in B may cause τ to cross the boundary of $A(\mathbf{w}, a)$ and thus induce a switch from $h_0 = \bar{h}_0$ to $h_0 = 0$ and a corresponding positive jump in h_1.

22. This conclusion has to be modified slightly. The way we have modeled the penalty structure, raising the marginal tax rate would also increase the penalty for evasion st, and so there would be an additional effect on work in the illegal sector (equation 5.17).

23. See Dilnot and Morris 1981 and Smith 1986.

24. The criteria used by Dilnot and Morris (1981) to flag such excess-expenditure households were essentially pragmatic and attempted to make allowances for items of nonrecurrent expenditure, such as the buying of consumer durables during the period covered by the interview.

25. This feature also appears in the U.S. TCMP data—see Clotfelter 1983 and table 2.2 above.

26. See Smith 1986, pp. 144–153. Smith and his collaborators fitted equations of the form

$$\log c = \mathbf{az} + b_1 x + [b_2 + b_3 x] \log y$$

where c is the expenditure on a particular group of commodities, $\mathbf{z}$ is a vector of household characteristics, x is a dummy variable (equal to 1 if the household is self-employed, 0 otherwise), and y is household income. This equation was estimated for eight different commodity and occupational groupings; the coefficient b_1 was positive and significant (at the 5 percent level) in four of these.

27. Both surveys were carried out by Markeds-og Mediainstituttet, a private polling organisation. The interviewer, on concluding the session, would ask the respondent to accept a questionnaire on the hidden economy. The response rate was quite high. Of 1,198 persons contacted in the September 1980 survey, 73 percent complied by completing the questionnaire; of 1,041 persons contacted in the April 1983 survey, 69 percent complied. See Isachsen, Klovland, and Strøm 1982 and Isachsen, Samuelsen, and Strøm 1985.

28. See Isachsen, Samuelsen, and Strøm 1985. The dependent variables were labor in the black economy, labor in the legitimate economy, and tax underreported. The authors attempt to deal with obvious "corner solution" problems, where certain individuals do not participate in evasion *at all* on the grounds of morals or lack of opportunity.

29. Contrast this with the findings of a previous study reported in Mork 1975. Using the Norwegian Occupational Life History Study (in which respondents were asked about their income in 1970) and the publicly available tax declarations, Mork found that the ratio [Income reported to the authorities]/[Income reported in the interview] fell as one moved upward through the income classes. In fact, these two results—less *activity* in the black economy but more *concealed income* as you move up the income classes—are mutually consistent and are actually predicted by the models we developed above.

30. See Watson's (1985) model of labor-market equilibrium.

31. As far as evasion of *income tax* is concerned, of course, there is no reason to suppose that dentists or lawyers are any more or less honest than other self-employed individuals.

32. This type of effect has also been examined by Fortin and Hung (1987), Hansson (1985), and Kesselman (1989). Although I have assumed segregation, it is evident that this analysis would go through in modified form were this segregation to be not quite perfect.

33. The production-possibility frontier will have this shape if there is a second factor (capital, say) used in production.

34. This assumption means that we do not have to worry about distinguishing between the ex-tax price ratio P_0/P_1 and the tax-inclusive price ratio. If the expansion were financed by changing the rate of a sales tax or a value-added tax, then we would obviously have to take into account the distortionary effect of the tax change.

35. In some countries it is *possible* that the expansion of government activity principally calls upon the services of the illegal sector. Let us hope these are special cases.

36. For models that deal with the market power of those buying factor services, see Cowell 1984, de Gijsel 1983, and Fortin and Hung 1987.

37. See Büchner 1987b and Marelli 1984a, 1984b. As is well known, the tax rate too will be irrelevant if taxes are based solely on gross profit.

38. This will be possible if the ex-tax relative price advantage $P_1/P_0 - 1$ is less than the *ad valorem* rate of indirect tax, and if the customers (because of differing degress of risk aversion, taste for reputation, and the like) form two distinct groups. For a model of this sort see Gordon 1988 and Cowell and Gordon 1989.

39. Note Ashenfelter and Smith's (1979) remark concerning the impact of minimum-wage laws: "The structure of wages ... cannot be fully understood without reference to the interaction between legal and economic behavior."

Chapter 6

1. See Witte and Woodbury 1985.

2. The above-mentioned Scandinavian studies provide an interesting exception. However, where it has been possible to check self-reported behavior against actual behavior, it appears that self-reports (and therefore questionnaire evidence on actual evasion) are decidedly unreliable; see Elffers et al. 1987 and Hessing et al. 1988.

3. See Aitken and Bonneville 1980, Dean et al. 1980, Dornstein 1976, Frank and Dekeyser-Meulders 1977, Geeroms and Wilmots 1985, Groenland and van Veldhoven 1982, Keenan and Dean 1980, Laurin 1983, Lewis 1978, 1979, 1982, Mason and Calvin 1978, 1984, Porcano 1988, Schmölders 1980, Song and Yarbrough 1978, Spicer and Lundstedt 1976, Vogel 1974, Wallschutzky 1984, and Wärneryd

and Walerud 1982. The approach is based on the pioneering work of Schmölders (1959) on fiscal psychology. See Wallschutzky 1984 for a summary discussion of the propositions about the economic psychology of taxation that have been confirmed by such attitude surveys.

4. In some studies the subjects in the simulation are actually offered an *unfair* gamble—i.e., one were $\bar{r} < 0$. That people are willing to take such gambles is interesting, but not terribly informative. The acceptance of such gambles is not unusual (racetrack betting is a well-known case in point), but it makes extrapolation from the laboratory (where a few dollars may be at stake) to real life (where a livelihood may be at stake) somewhat precarious.

5. Webley and Halstead (1986) and Webley et al. (1985) cast some doubt on the finding of Friedland et al. (1978) that large fines may be more effective as a deterrent than a high probability of audit.

6. For example, the probability of audit stipulated in the experiment may not satisfactorily represent the likely action of a tax authority nor the taxpayer's perceptions of any such possible action. Also, when people are asked in experiments to assume that *they themselves* are the evader, they respond differently (as to the factors causing evasion, for example) from the way would they respond if it were a third party doing the evasion (Hite 1987, Thuman 1988). Moreover, people may modify their behavior in certain ways simply because they know it is an experiment—the "Hawthorne effect."

7. See Spicer 1975.

8. Also, people's attitude to risk appears to depend on their perceptions of the nature of the tax payment—whether it is perceived as reduced income or as a loss. See Chang et al. 1987.

9. Benjamini and Maital (1985) suggested that higher tax rates led to more evasion.

10. Spicer and Becker (1980) found that evasion was high for those who perceived substantial inequities in the tax system; compare the results of Thibaut et al. (1974) on obedience to rules. Webley et al. (1986) found the opposite of what Spicer and Becker found. Kaplan and Reckers (1985) found that beliefs about the fairness of the tax system were less important than beliefs about the morality of tax cheating (see also Kaplan et al. 1986). On the basis of survey evidence, Mason and Calvin (1984) argue that the effect of perceived inequity in evasion is probably not simple and direct. Becker, Büchner,

and Sleeking (1986) found that the perception of tax burden *and* the share in publicly supplied goods were important (see also Mackscheidt 1984).

11. See Hessing and Elfers 1985. Such interview responses could just be an *ex post* rationalization of greed.

12. D is the appropriate second-order term for the problem, as in equation 4.8.

13. The result is established in a way similar to the result on public goods discussed in chapter 4. To see this, observe that under the stated conditions μ the marginal rate of substitution of c for ι must be independent of c, and so the numerator on the right-hand side of equation 6.1 can be written as $\mu\mathbf{E}(u_{cc}^a\mathbf{r})$—which, in view of assumption A5, must have the sign of μ. Hence e_ι is positive if and only if μ is positive.

14. Consider the Australian attitudes reported in Wallschutzky 1984. The formal argument here is not restricted to a model with this specific way of representing inequity. The main result would still hold if $\mathbf{Ec}$ were to be replaced by $[1 - \alpha]c' + \alpha c''$ where α is some weight such that $\alpha < 1/[1 + s]$.

15. Once again one can write down appropriate corner conditions for equation 6.3.

16. And sometimes it is downright deceptive—witness the Congregational Church of Human Morality, which was investigated by the IRS as a tax scam (*Los Angeles Times*, August 29, 1986).

17. The concept goes back a long way in the writings of some German moral theologians and philosophers concerning taxation— for example, von Nell-Breuning (1930, p. 259) and Noldin (1907, 1909) distinguish between the impact on conscience of direct and indirect taxes. As far as the modern-day literature on evasion is concerned, "stigma" was introduced in an elementary form by Allingham and Sandmo (1972), although they did not discuss the dynamic model we deal with here. Stigma is often introduced into discussions of the "take-up" of Social Security or welfare benefits. It is claimed that many people who are entitled to such benefits fail to claim them because of the social stigma of doing so. However, there is some ambiguity as to what that stigma represents. It is not always made clear whether the stigma is actually just a type of transaction cost (the hassle of combat with the welfare bureaucracy) or whether it is a more complex type of

interaction, such as that outlined here. See Cowell 1986a and Klein 1975. On the general issue of social conscience in economics, see also Robinson 1964, chapter 1; for a discussion of its role as a general deterrent to crime, see Grasmick and Green 1980.

18. See Benjamini and Maital 1985, Maital 1982, Schlicht 1985, and (especially) Gordon 1989.

19. This is just one of several formulations that might represent social norms. Instead of E one might have the proportion of people evading tax, for example.

20. Learning by experience, from one's neighbors and from one's surroundings is certainly important in the behavior of gamblers—see Lea et al. 1987, p. 271ff.

21. The number of evaders personally known to a taxpayer is often cited as an important factor predisposing people to evasion (Schmölders 1970, Spicer and Lundstedt 1976, Vogel 1974).

22. Compare Benjamini and Maital 1985. The assumption implies that, whether or not one is evading, one's utility *at any given level of personal consumption* is increased by the evasion of others: On reading in the morning paper that another Harry Claiborne, Aldo Gucci, or Sun Myung Moon has been bilking the IRS of millions, one smiles indulgently. In fact, we could relax this assumption and still retain the characteristics of the model described below. For example, we might reasonably have $V_E^a(y, E) > 0$ and $V_E^a(0, E) < 0$—as the black economy grows, we are rather pleased about it if we happen to be evaders, but we are highly scandalized otherwise. Whatever the exact specification, the important point is that the $V^a(y, E)$ schedule should cut $V^a(0, E)$ from below.

23. For a further discussion of the economic interpretation of such reference groups, see Cowell 1986a.

24. For more sophisticated models of evasion epidemics, see Seidl 1974.

25. This assumption keeps the analysis reasonably simple while losing little that is essential to the present section.

26. Observe that e_0 will be given by $[1 - q(n)]e^*$ where e^* is the equilibrium value of each person's evasion.

27. There is no enforcement of the tax, so $p = 0$, and the $\mathbf{E}$ operator may be dropped.

28. Compare equation 4.9.

29. See Srinivasan 1973, Nayak 1978, and Sproule et al. 1980.

30. See Hoeflich 1983. The particular model used here is based on Corchon 1984.

31. After the manner of the Stackelberg model of oligopoly. There is a further problem, too: that of making sure that the agents nominally responsible to the government are really on the government's side.

32. See Graetz et al. 1984, Reinganum and Wilde 1984, 1985, and chapter 8 below.

Chapter 7

1. Recall from chapter 4 that if $\bar{r} > 0$ and if potential taxpayers correctly perceive this to be the case, then they will *always* evade.

2. On this point see Kolm 1973, Fishburn 1979, Kemp and Ng 1979, Koskela 1983b, Polinsky and Shavell 1979, and Singh 1973. Goode (1981) has some interesting comments on the practicality of this type of approach.

3. The uses of these funds $\bar{R}$—providing public goods, modifying the productive potential of the economy, income transfers—could play a significant part in the achievement of the government's fundamental objectives; however, for brevity these are omitted from the simplified model.

4. The separation of powers may impose even more restrictions on the parameter set. For example, the law that specifies the punishment for evasion—the surcharge s—may be taken to be given as well as t, so that the only degree of freedom is the investigation strategy (represented in our model as the simple probability p). We will examine this type of model in chapter 8.

5. The set is drawn on the assumption that $T_{ij} < 0$ for all i and j selected from $\{p, s, t\}$, and also on the assumptions $\varphi_p > 0$ and $\varphi_{pp} > 0$.

6. For example, $\bar{G}$ in figure 7.1 is the set of (p, s) values that would satisfy condition 7.5 with equality assuming that condition 7.2b holds (where e is strictly positive). Obviously values of $p > 1$ are irrelevant, and so $\bar{G}$ is truncated at the point where it intersects the line $p = 1$.

7. This boundary is, of course, given by the (p, s) values that satisfy equation 7.4.

8. If one considers a point on $\bar{H}$ to the left of A, this is, by definition, a situation where zero evasion is enforced at lower cost, so that realized government revenue is higher than $\bar{R}$.

9. See chapter 13 of Cowell 1986b.

10. Collard (1984) and Wertz (1979) discuss the policy implications of various types of "reduced-form" government objective functions.

11. See Harsanyi 1955.

12. See Baldry 1984a. The policy rule implied by equation 7.12 will be discussed in chapter 8.

13. The right-hand side of equation 7.13 follows from differentation of $Eu([1 - t]y + rte)$ and the use of equation 7.2c. Even though the function u is concave, the contours in figure 7.2 need be neither concave nor convex.

14. It is this problem that underlies the debate about Becker's "optimal fine" result. See Becker 1968, Carr-Hill and Stern 1977, Stern 1978, and Stigler 1970.

   If the marginal cost of enforcement were to be zero, this policy would be modified as follows: If t is exogenously fixed (the pure enforcement subproblem), the rule 7.12 still holds but with the left-hand side zero; and if $t > \bar{R}/ny$, then there is still no reason to eliminate evasion, so that one has a solution such as B, with $e > 0$. The solution to the tax-legislation problem (where p is fixed) is obviously no different from the standard model with $\varphi_p > 0$. However, in the general problem (all τ parameters variable) one reduces t until it equals $\bar{R}/ny$ and sets $s > [1 - p]/p$ with p fixed at any positive value—see Cowell 1989.

15. Heterogeneity of taxpayers can be introduced into the model fairly easily.

16. See, for example, the survey by Sugden (1986).

17. For further discussions of *ex ante* and *ex post* welfare criteria, see Cowell 1986b and Hammond 1981.

18. Recall that this means (consumption-if-not-caught, consumption-if-caught).

19. Notice that the utilitarian framework we adopted in the preceding section implies the use of assumptions B3 and B4.

20. To see what this means, examine the analogous point in the case of increased *risk aversion* illustrated in figure 4.3. For the interpretation of inequality aversion in terms of concavity, see chapter 13 of Cowell 1986b.

21. As $\hat{u}$ is made more concave, the ratio $\hat{u}_c(c'')/\hat{u}_c(c')$ decreases. On dividing the numerator and the denominator of equation 7.16 by $\hat{u}_c(c')$ and putting $\hat{p}_p = 0$, we see that the increased concavity of $\hat{u}$ has the stated result.

22. Since each of these expressions is negative, $\overline{W}$ represents a level of *minimum* social welfare in this case.

23. This is a crude representation of the principle of social justice discussed by Rawls (1971).

24. It might appear that the outcome is the same as that of the utilitarian case: an arbitrarily high surcharge, a very low probability of detection, and a low standard tax rate. There is an important difference, however. Under utilitarianism the instruments are adjusted so that evasion is merely reduced to an "acceptable" level, so *ex post* there will always be some people who actually suffer penalties. But in the present special case this is not so; the instruments are adjusted in such a way as to force everyone to be honest. There is nobody to be caught.

25. To see this point, notice that the contours of the social-welfare function in (p, s) space are identical to those of equation 7.26 but are ranked in the opposite direction, and that the contours of the social-welfare function in (s, t) space slope in the opposite direction to those of equation 7.26.

26. Although on the parts of figure 7.2 that lie far outside H it would be possible to have $\tilde{W}_t$ positive.

27. The probability of an audit by the IRS is perhaps around 2 percent, but casual evidence suggests that many people perceive it to be much lower. See the remarks of a New York waitress noted in Graetz and Wilde 1985. For an analysis of the problem of credibility of punishment, see Friedland 1982.

28. See Shavell 1987, in which the optimal policy will involve imposing the maximum available penalty. The problem is how this maximum is

to be determined. Notice that there is no *logical* upper limit (such as bankruptcy) to s: the actual fine paid is ste, so that for any finite s you could always find a small e such that $c'' > 0$. Of course, if the huge surcharge really were effective, no one would actually have to pay it anyway. Also, if the fines were really high, it might be the case that juries would refuse to convict; thus, p is effectively zero.

29. See Song and Yarbrough 1978, Vogel 1974. See also Grasmick and Scott 1982 on the intensity of guilt feelings for different types of theft.

30. See Aitken and Bonneville (1980), Groenland and van Veldhoven 1983, Lewis 1979.

31. See the contrast in views on "fiddling" in the USSR reported in Connor 1986.

32. This component of cost is measured by the amount that he would be prepared to pay in order to eliminate those risks. This amount, minus the revenue loss to the government caused by the evasion, can be seen as the "excess burden" of evasion (Yitzhaki 1987). In fact, the evader may also incur real resource costs in order to the reduce the risk of being caught and hence the burden of uncertainty. These concealment costs should be treated in the same way as the component of risk cost that we have just discussed. See the models of Mayshar (1986) and Usher (1982, 1987). The relationship between this cost-of-concealment approach and the basic model of chapter 4 is explained in Cowell 1988.

33. That is, the marginal excess burden of the tax equals the slope of the enforcement-cost function φ (Slemrod and Yitzhaki 1987). This is similar to the result we obtained in equation 7.12, where p was traded off against s.

34. Usher (1987) identifies four types of efficiency loss from theft. Three of these (loss of labor of the thief, loss of labor of the victim in self-protection, and destruction of the product) can be seen as related to the concept of private cost that we have just discussed; the fourth is the deadweight loss caused by the underproduction of goods that are particularly prone to theft. Alm (1985) analyzes economic distortions caused by the black economy in a Harberger-type general-equilibrium model.

35. The phrase is Voltaire's. The official reason for the Honourable John Byng's execution was "for not having done his utmost."

36. This is the common name given to crimes against the central planner mentioned in chapter 3 above (Feldbrugge 1979, Pomorski 1979). The different degrees of *de facto* tolerance by the Soviet government are discussed further in Ioffe 1985 and in Katsenelinboigen 1977. The supposed ideal of "optimal control" through procuratorial supervision, and the selective and strategic control that is achieved in practice, are discussed in Smith 1979.

Chapter 8

1. The suspected presence of highwaymen on one's route will induce a certain amount of wasteful self-protection, but this might not be very large compared with the private armies of accountants mustered in response to ill-drafted tax laws and arbitrary fiscal boundaries. See Usher 1987 and note 34 of chapter 7 (above).

2. See the passionate passages on pages 187–206 of Coffield 1970 and the article under the headline "Overtaxed agency: IRS is under pressure to raise its collections—without getting tough or abusive" in the *Wall Street Journal* of December 24, 1987.

3. Obviously a despot could obtain whatever resources he wanted by simply levying them off anyone he chose. But such despots are not economically interesting.

4. See equations 4.5, 4.6, 7.5. There are other sources of finance, such as direct charges for publicly supplied goods and services and net receipts from borrowing; these were discussed in chapter 3. However, introducing these to the budget constraint 8.1 would make the analysis much more complicated while yielding few additional insights.

5. This is the appropriate rule if the tax authority takes as its objective the maximization of expected revenue given the system of tax rates, allowances, and exemptions laid down by the legislature (Collard 1984, Reinganum and Wilde 1986).

6. For example, it can appear appropriate to use indefinitely large fines and minimal detection probabilities in order to enforce honest behavior.

7. This is a yet more restrictive case of the *pure enforcement* subproblem. We may take it that the tax authority has already used any discretion it might have had over the surcharge to raise it to the maximum allowed by law, the level $\bar{s}$.

8. Compare the approach used in Sandmo 1981.

9. The exogenous income model can be read off as a special case in the analysis that follows.

10. Note that $\bar{r}t\partial e/\partial p$ is negative, $\partial\ell/\partial p$ is of ambiguous sign, and v_p/λ is negative. The reasoning behind the first two of these is to be found in chapters 4 and 5. The reason for the last is that if a person is evading taxes, utility-if-caught is always strictly less than utility-if-not-caught; an increase in p shifts the weight from the latter to the former in the overall computation of expected utility (see assumption A4 above). Alternatively, the direct effect on v of an increase in p can be seen in terms of the additional private costs of concealment that would be incurred in order to offset the increase in risk.

11. On the first point, see chapter 7 above and Baldry 1984a. The second point is closely allied to the argument in chapter 7 on the "cost" of evasion. Observe the importance of the implicit assumption in our model that production techniques in sector 0 and sector 1 are identical, so that the gross-of-tax market rewards are identical. If it were somehow to be the case that production in sector 1 were less efficient than production in sector 0 (perhaps because of all the tiresome problems of concealment), so that the marginal costs of production were higher for evaders than for nonevaders, then social welfare could be improved by eliminating evasion. See Schweizer's (1984) model of the evasion of excise taxes.

On the conclusion about the desirability of permissiveness, see the points about random taxation in note 24 of chapter 3 (above) and Cowell 1985a.

12. Under utilitarianism the marginal social evaluation would be the same at all levels of utility. We could make equation 8.16 richer by assuming that the weight of each $(\mathbf{w}, a)$ type of person in the social-welfare function was not derived from their representation in the community (given by the gradient of the distribution function $F(\mathbf{w}, a)$), but from some other imposed weighting scheme; the argument would still go through as in the text.

13. These two extreme cases were represented as $\hat{W}$ in equations 7.18 and 7.22.

14. More generally, this result holds if $\hat{u}^a$ is an affine transform of u^a.

15. The argument can also be applied to the other type of departure from nonlinearity discussed in chapter 7: that where the community

imputes weights ($\hat{p}, 1 - \hat{p}$) rather than the true probabilities ($p, 1 - p$). If $\hat{p} > p$, then the marginal benefit schedule will be shifted upward.

16. Such moves may prove beneficial for reasons other than just reducing the opportunities for evasion. The room for making mistakes may be reduced. Also, taxpayers' perceptions about the nature of the tax may change. Loftus (1985) aruges that switching to a withholding system will mean that taxpayers no longer view income tax as a "potential loss" and, as a consequence, are less likely to accept the risks involved in tax evasion.

17. Those with high incomes have a low marginal utility of lump-sum income (Sandmo 1981).

18. The subject is relatively neglected in the literature. One of the few papers on tax evasion in which the equity implications of alternative penalty structures are considered is Bulckaen 1984. Polinsky and Shavell (1984) show that fines should be higher for better-off taxpayers.

19. With a flat-rate penalty, v_S^a becomes $-pu_c^a([1 - t]y - S, z)$. Clearly this *increases* with y; so too does evasion e.

20. See, e.g., Lea et al. 1987.

21. See Lewis 1982, chapter 10.

22. "People just don't feel gulity enough when they don't fill out their tax returns properly," according to a member of an American Bar Association commission (*Wall Street Journal*, December 24, 1987). That view concurs with the importance of guilt feelings reported from a number of recent studies of taxpayers attitudes (Furnham 1983, Thuman et al. 1984, Yankelovich et al. 1984). Scott and Grasmick (1981) showed the importance of the *perception* of penalties in the deterrence of evasion. Grasmick and Scott (1982) confirmed the results of Schwartz and Orleans (1967) on the potency of "conscience appeal" or "guilt feelings" as a social sanction.

23. See the fascinating results reported in Tittle and Rowe 1973. Under certain circumstances, this sort of drum-banging seems merely to convince people that everyone else is evading, so they might as well do so too.

24. For example, it used to be argued that the British Estate Duty was essentially a "voluntary tax."

25. "Sheltering" must be costly in some sense; otherwise everyone would make use of it and the government would collect no revenue. The sum $\overline{\Gamma}$ will include the costs of financial advice, the costs of rearranging one's income sources (e.g., between income from work and income from financial assets), and other costs such as that of living overseas as a tax exile. There may, additionally, be a positive marginal cost of sheltering each dollar, but we shall neglect that here. For a full treatment see Cowell 1988; see also Alm 1988.

26. See Cowell 1988.

27. Using equations 4.3c and 8.27, we find that this condition would require the expression

$$[1 - t][1 - p][1 + 1/s]u_c^a(c')/u_c^a(\overline{c})$$

to be less than 1. Since $\overline{c} < c'$,

$$u_c^a(c')/u_c^a(\overline{c}) < 1;$$

thus it is clear that equation 8.27 will be positive if s is "large enough." A sufficient condition for the condition to hold would be $[1 + s]t > 1$, which is also a sufficient condition for $e(\tau, y, a) < y$ (Yitzhaki 1974). If s is too small and people have decreasing absolute risk aversion, then $e(\tau, y, a) = y$ for large y, and g becomes negative for very large incomes.

28. For an introductory discussion of the issues involved, see Murphy 1959.

29. Greenberg (1984) provides a simple example where the authority has a one-period memory and the taxpayers are put into three categories. Those in category 1 have probability of investigation $p_1 = \frac{1}{2}\underline{p}$ where $\underline{p} := 1/[1 + s]$. Those in category 2 have a smaller probability: p_2. Members of category 3 are *always* investigated. In each period, taxpayers are shifted between groups: Those in category 1 who are caught cheating are moved to category 2; those in category 2 who are investigated are returned to category 1 if found truthful but are put into category 3 if found cheating; category 3 is a black hole for habitual cheats—once in it, the taxpayer stays there. If the taxpayers know about this rule, then it can be shown that, in equilibrium, a proportion α of the taxpayers will be found in category 1 (where everyone cheats) and a proportion $1 - \alpha$ in the larger category 2 (where no one cheats), such that α is less than the arbitrarily small

minimum tolerable amount of evasion and $\alpha p_1 = [1 - \alpha]p_2$. There will be *no one* in category 3. See also Landsberger and Meilijson 1982.

30. Even quite simple modifications of the tax authority's options can produce remarkable improvements. For example, Rickard et al. (1982) show that allowing retroactive penalties is much more effective at deterring evasion in a multiperiod model.

31. For examples of this type of "Principal and Agent" or "Master and Servant" model see Border and Sobel 1987 and Reinganum and Wilde 1985. The approach of Reinganum and Wilde is based on that of Townsend (1979). In such models, the mutual understanding between taxpayer and tax authority makes it possible to use the rules as a self-selection mechanism.

32. See Reinganum and Wilde 1986. Graetz et al. 1986, and Cremer et al. 1988. Cremer et al. imbed their analysis within a simple model of optimal taxation.

33. This is analogous to the budget-maximizing behavior of a bureaucratic agency (Niskanen 1971, pp. 38–42). See also the simple revenue-generating model of Balachandran and Schaefer (1980).

34. See Scotchmer 1987b, 1988.

35. See Cowell and Gordon 1989.

36. Some of the issues involved here can be seen as caricatures of arguments concerning capital punishment.

37. Establishing whether or not punishable evasion has occurred can pose some curious problems. Under the title "Big Bang Theory" the journal *Taxation* noted: "The Internal Revenue Service ... has published a study considering the tax collection problems that will arise in the event of a nuclear war. It concludes that tax-payers inconvenienced by the hostilities will have to be excused interest and penalties should they file their returns late."

38. In the U.K. the maximum penalty for negligent underpayment disclosure is the amount of underpayment plus £50; the maximum penalty for fraudulent underpayment is *twice* the amount of underpayment plus £50 (Bingham 1980).

39. See Scotchmer and Slemrod 1987, 1989.

40. It may also influence the choice of the tax base (Stern 1982).

41. Scotchmer and Slemrod 1989, Scotchmer 1989. For discussions of a celebrated case in the U.K. see Gillard 1987 and Tutt 1985.

42. In the U.K., if information is missing or if tax returns appear to be incomplete the Inland Revenue will issue tax demands based on absurdly high estimates of parts of your income. You then counter with documentation of your actual tax position. The matter is then often dropped.

43. See Scotchmer 1988.

44. This is the essence of the paper by Nitzan and Tzur (1987). They consider an extended game in which the players are the government, firms that are liable for taxes but would like to dodge them, and a body of private-sector auditors. Each auditor is caught between the government (which will penalize him for misconduct) and his clients (who may dispense with his services if he is insufficiently accommodating to their schemes to cheat the government).

45. See Virmani 1987.

46. See Chu 1987. It is interesting to note that in India during 1983–84 only 38 convictions for tax evasion were obtained out of 1,541 prosecutions; 223 convictions were obtained out of 244 prosecutions in the U.K. during the same period (Jain 1985). Jain reveals that this contrast is typical over recent decades, and argues that it is consistent with the general view that prosecutions are often conducted on frivolous grounds. Other explanations, of course, are also possible.

47. However, if it is a good idea to eliminate evasion completely, then, irrespective of the degree of inequality aversion, the same method of enforcement is suggested by the simple economic model: a low (but positive) probability of detection and a surcharge high enough to make the expected return to evasion zero.

Chapter 9

1. There is, for example the case of the funding by the ancient Israelites for Jehovah's tabernacle: Moses had to order them to *stop* making voluntary contributions because they had provided too much (Exodus 36: 6).

2. Some might nevertheless argue that there is a case for encouraging *avoidance* even if avoidance opportunities appear to be randomly

distributed among various categories of taxpayers. See note 24 to chapter 3.

3. See Karzon's (1983) argument on taxpayer demoralization, which echoes the article by Oldman (1965). Oldman argued that suppressing tax evasion is important to keep compliers happy in their compliance.

4. Compare Bayar and Frank's (1987) concern for the erosion of the tax base.

Bibliography

Aaron, H. J. (1981) *The Value-Added Tax: Lessons from Europe*. Brookings Institution, Washington.

Acharya, S. N. (1985) Aspects of The Black Economy in India: Report of a Study by the National Institute of Public Finance and Policy. Ministry of Finance, Government of India, New Delhi.

Adam, M. C., and Ginsburgh, V. (1985) "The effects of irregular markets on macroeconomic policy." *European Economic Review* 29: 15–33.

Ahsan, S. M. (1974) "Progression and risk-taking." *Oxford Economic Papers* 26: 318–328.

Aitken, S., and Bonneville, E. (1980) A General Taxpayer Opinion Survey. CSR Inc., Washington, D.C.

Alden, J., and Saha, S. (1978) "Analysis of second jobholding in the EEC." *Regional Studies* 12: 639–650.

Alessandrini, S., and Dallago, B. (1987) *Consequences and Perspectives in Different Economic Systems*. Gower, Aldershot.

Alexander, C., and Feinstein, J. S. (1987) A Microeconometric Analysis of Income Tax Evasion. Mimeo, Massachusetts Institute of Technology.

Ali, A. A. G. (1976) "Landowners' behavior under self-assessment: theoretical treatment." *Journal of Development Economics* 3: 171–179.

Allingham, M., and Sandmo, A. (1972) "Income tax evasion: A theoretical analysis." *Journal of Public Economics* 1: 323–338.

Alm, J. (1985) "The welfare cost of the underground economy." *Economic Inquiry* (April): 243–263.

Alm, J. (1988) "Compliance costs and the tax avoidance-tax evasion decision." *Public Finance Quarterly* 16: 31–66.

Alm, J., and Bahl, R. (1985) An Evaluation of the Structure of the Jamaican Personal Income Tax. Jamaica Tax Study Examination Project, Metropolitan Studies Program, Staff Paper 15.

Andersen, P. (1977) "Tax evasion and labor supply." *Scandinavian Journal of Economics* 79: 375–383.

Anderson, R. W. (1976) *The Economics of Crime.* Macmillan, London.

Arrow, K. J. (1965) *Some Aspects of the Theory of Risk-Bearing.* Yrjö Jahnssonin Säätio, Helsinki.

Arrow, K. J. (1970) *Essays in the Theory of Risk-Bearing.* North-Holland, Amsterdam.

Arrow, K. J. (1985) "The economies of agency." In Pratt, J. W., and Zeckhauser, R. (eds.), *Agency, The Structure of Business.* Harvard Business School Press.

Ashenfelter, O., and Smith, R. S. (1979) "Compliance with the minimum wage laws." *Journal of Political Economy* 87: 333–359.

Atkinson, A. B., and Stiglitz, J. E. (1980) *Lectures on Public Economics.* McGraw-Hill, New York.

Bahl, R., and Murray, M. N. (1986) Income Tax Evasion in Jamaica. Jamacia Tax Study Examination Project, Metropolitan Studies Program, Syracuse University, Staff Paper 31.

Balachandran, K. R., and Schaefer, M. E. (1980) "Optimal diversification among classes for auditing income tax returns." *Public Finance* 35: 250–258.

Baldry, J. C. (1979) "Tax evasion and labour supply." *Economics Letters* 3: 53–56.

Baldry, J. C. (1984a) "The enforcement of income tax laws: Efficiency implications." *Economic Record* 60: 156–159.

Baldry, J. C. (1984b) Income Tax Rates and Tax Evasion: Some Comments on Empirical Estimation of Tax Evasion Functions. Mimeo, University of New England.

Baldry, J. C. (1986) "Tax evasion is not a gamble: a report on two experiments." *Economic Letters* 22: 333–335.

Baldry, J. C. (1987) "Income tax evasion and the tax schedule: Some experimental results." *Public Finance* 42: 357–383.

Barry, D. B., Feldbrugge, G. J. M., Ginsburgs, G., and Maggs, P. B. (eds.) (1979) *Soviet Law After Stalin: Law in Eastern Europe*. Sijthoff and Noordhoff, Germantown, Maryland.

Barthelemy, P. (1988) "The macroeconomic estimates of the hidden economy: A critical analysis." *Review of Income and Wealth* 34: 183–209.

Barthelemy, P. (1989) "The underground economy in France." In Feige 1989.

Bawly, D. (1982) *The Subterranean Economy*. McGraw-Hill, New York.

Bayar, A., and Frank, M. (1987) "The erosion of the different tax bases." *Public Finance* 42: 341–350.

Becker, G. S. (1968) "Crime and punishment—An economic approach." *Journal of Political Economy* 76: 169–217.

Becker, W., Büchner, H.-J., and Sleeking, S. (1987) "The impact of public expenditures on tax evasion: An experimental approach." *Journal of Public Economics* 34: 243–252.

Benjamini, Y., and Maital, S. (1985) "Optimal tax evasion and optimal tax evasion policy: Behavioral aspects." In Gaertner and Wenig 1985.

Bingham, T. (1980) Tax Evasion: The Law and the Practice. Alexander Harden Financial Services, London.

Blades, D. W. (1985) "Crime: What should be included in the national accounts and what differences would it make?" In Gaertner and Wenig 1985.

Block, M. K., and Heineke, J. M. (1973) "The allocation of effort under uncertainty: The case of risk-averse behavior." *Journal of Political Economy* 81: 376–385.

Block, M. K., and Heineke, J. M. (1975) "Labor theoretic analysis of criminal choice." *American Economic Review* 65: 314–325.

Block, M. K., and Lind, R. C. (1975a) "Crime and punishment reconsidered." *Journal of Legal Studies* 4: 241–247.

Block, M. K., and Lind, R. C. (1975b) "Economic analysis of crimes punishable by imprisonment." *Journal of Legal Studies* 4: 479–492.

Board of Inland Revenue (1981) One Hundred and Twenty Third Report. Cmnd 8160, HMSO, London.

Boidman, N. (1983) "Tax evasion—The present state of non-compliance." *Bulletin for International Fiscal Economics* 37: 451–479.

Border, K., and Sobel, J. (1987) "A theory of auditing and plunder." *Review of Economic Studies* 54: 525–540.

Bowsher, N. N. (1980) "The demand for currency: Is the underground economy undermining monetary economy?" *Federal Reserve Bank of St. Louis Review* 62: 11–17.

Bracewell-Milnes, B. (1979) *Tax Avoidance and Evasion: The Individual and Society*. Panopticum Press, London.

Brennan, G., and Buchanan, J. (1980) *The Power To Tax*. Cambridge University Press.

Brennan, G., and Buchanan, J. (1985) *The Reason of Rules*. Cambridge University Press.

Brezinski, H. (1985) "The second economy in the Soviet Union and its implications for economic policy." In Gaertner and Wenig 1985.

Broesterhuizen, G. A. A. M. (1985) "The unobserved economy and the national accounts in the Netherlands: A sensitivity analysis." In Gaertner and Wenig 1985; reprinted in Feige 1989.

Brown, C. V. (1968) "Misperceptions about income tax and incentives." *Scottish Journal of Political Economy* 15: 1–21.

Brown, C. V., Levin, E. J., Rosa, P. J., and Ulph, D. T. (1984) "Tax evasion and avoidance on earned income: Some survey evidence." *Fiscal Studies* 5(3): 1–22.

Büchner, H.-J. (1987a) Steuerhinterziehung und subjektiv empfundene Steuerlast. Rheinische Friedrich-Wilhelms-Universität Bonn, Discussion Paper A-83.

Büchner, H.-J. (1987b) Der Einfluss der Steuerhinterziehung auf direkte und indirekte Steuern. Rheinische Friedrich-Wilhelms-Universität Bonn, Discussion Paper A-100.

Bulckaen, F. (1984) "Equità dei sistemi di controllo della evasione delle imposte personali sul reddito." *Rivista di Diritto Finanziario e Scienza delle Finanze* 63: 399–426.

Cagan, P. (1958) "The demand for currency relative to total money supply." *Journal of Political Economy* 66: 303–329.

Cameron, S. (1988) "The economics of crime deterrence: A survey of the theory and evidence." *Kyklos* 41: 301–323.

Carr-Hill, R., and Stern, N. H. (1977) "Theory and estimation in models of crime and its social control and their relations to concepts of social output." In Feldstein, M. S., and Inman, R. P. (eds.), *The Economics of Public Services*. Macmillan, London.

Carter, M. (1984) "Issues in the hidden economy." *Economic Record* 60: 209–211.

Chang, O. H., Nichols. D. R., and Schultz, J. J. (1987) "Taxpayer attitudes toward tax audit risk." *Journal of Economic Psychology* 8: 299–309.

Chopra, O. P. (1982) "Unaccounted income—Some estimates." *Economic and Political Weekly* 17: 739–744.

Christiansen, V. (1980) "Two comments on tax evasion." *Journal of Public Economics* 13: 389–401.

Chu, C. (1987) Tax Evasion with Venal Tax Officials. Mimeo, Institute of Economics, Academia Sinica.

Clotfelter, C. T. (1983) "Tax evasion and tax rates." *Review of Economics and Statistics* 65: 363–373.

Coffield, J. (1970) *A Popular History of Taxation*. Longmans, London.

Collard, D. (1984) Some Tax Investigation Rules. Mimeo, University of Bath.

Connor, W. D. (1986) "Social policy under Gorbachev." *Problems of Communism* 35 (July–August): 31–46.

Contini, B. (1981) "The second economy of Italy." *Journal of Contemporary Studies* 4: reprinted in Tanzi 1982b.

Corchon, L. (1984) A Note on Tax Evasion and the Theory of Games. Mimeo, Madrid.

Cowell, F. A. (1975) "Some notes on progression and risk-taking." *Economica* 42: 313–318.

Cowell, F. A. (1981a) "Taxation and labour supply with risky activities." *Economica* 48: 365–379.

Cowell, F. A. (1981b) "Income maintenance schemes under wage-rate uncertainty." *American Economic Review* 71: 692–702.

Cowell, F. A. (1984) The Firm and Illegal Employment: An Economic Analysis. Mimeo, London School of Economics.

Cowell, F. A. (1985a) "Public policy and tax evasion: some problems." In Gaertner and Wenig 1985.

Cowell, F. A. (1985b) "Tax evasion with labour income." *Journal of Public Economics* 26: 19–34.

Cowell, F. A. (1985c) "The economic analysis of tax evasion: A survey." *Bulletin of Economic Research* 37: 163–193.

Cowell, F. A. (1986a) Welfare Benefits and the Economics of Takeup. TIDI Discussion Paper 89, London School of Economics.

Cowell, F. A. (1986b) *Microeconomic Principles*. Philip Allan, Oxford.

Cowell, F. A. (1988) Tax Sheltering and the Cost of Evasion. TIDI Discussion Paper 119, London School of Economics.

Cowell, F. A. (1989) "Honesty is sometimes the best policy." *European Economic Review* 33: 605–617.

Cowell, F. A., and Gordon, J. (1988) "Unwillingness to pay: Tax evasion and public good provision." *Journal of Public Economics* 36: 305–321.

Cowell, F. A., and Gordon, J. (1989) On Becoming a Ghost. TIDI Discussion Paper 127, London School of Economics.

Cox, D. (1984) "Raising revenue in the underground economy." *National Tax Journal* 37: 283–288.

Crane, S. E., and Nourzad, F. (1985) "The time value of money and income tax evasion under risk-averse behaviour: Theoretical analysis and empirical evidence." *Public Finance* 40: 381–394.

Crane, S. E., and Nourzad, F. (1986) "Inflation and tax evasion: An empirical analysis." *Review of Economics and Statistics* 68: 217–223.

Crane, S. E., and Nourzad, F. (1987) "On the treatment of income tax rates in empirical analysis of tax evasion." *Kyklos* 40: 338–348.

Cremer, H., Marchand, M., and Pestieau, P. (1988) Evading, auditing and taxing: The equity-compliance tradeoff. Cornell University, Department of Economics. Working Paper 401.

Cross, R. B., and Shaw, G. K. (1981) "The evasion–avoidance choice —A suggested approach." *National Tax Journal* 34: 489–491.

Cross, R., and Shaw, G. K. (1982) "On the economics of tax aversion." *Public Finance* 37: 36–47.

Cullis, J. G., and Jones, P. R. (1987) *Microeconomics and The Public Economy*. Basil Blackwell, Oxford.

Dean, P. N., Keenan, A., and Kerney, F. (1980) "Taxpayers' attitudes to income tax evasion: An empirical study." *British Tax Review*: 28–44.

de Gijsel, P. (1985) "A microeconomic analysis of black labour demand and supply." In Gaertner and Wenig 1985.

De Grazia, R. (1980) "Clandestine employment: A problem of our times." *International Labour Review* 119: 544–583.

Denison, E. G. (1982) "Is US growth understated because of the underground economy? Employment ratios suggest not." *Review of Income and Wealth* 28: 1–16.

Dilnot, A., and Morris, C. N. (1981) "What do we know about the black economy?" *Fiscal Studies* 2: 58–73; reprinted in Tanzi 1982b.

Dornbusch, R., and Fischer, S. (1984) *Macroeconomics*, third edition. McGraw-Hill, New York.

Dornstein, M. (1976) "Compliance with legal and bureaucratic rules: The case of self-employed tax payers in Israel." *Human Relations* 29: 1019–1034.

Drèze, J. H., and Modigliani, F. (1972) "Consumption decisions under uncertainty." *Journal of Economic Theory* 5: 308–335.

Dubin, J. A., Graetz, M. J., and Wilde, L. L. (1987) "Are we a nation of tax cheaters? New econometric evidence on tax compliance." *American Economic Review, Papers and Proceedings* 77: 240–245.

Dubin, J. A., and Wilde, L. L. (1988) "An empirical analysis of federal income tax auditing and compliance." *National Tax Journal* 41: 61–74.

Elffers, E., Weigel, R. H., and Hessing, D. J. (1987) "The consequences of different strategies for measuring tax evasion behaviour." *Journal of Economic Psychology* 8: 311–337.

Erekson, O. H. and Sullivan, D. H. (1988) "A cross-section analysis of IRS auditing." *National Tax Journal* 41: 175–189.

Feige, E. L. (1979) "How big is the irregular economy?" *Challenge* 22(5): 5–13.

Feige, E. L. (1981) "The UK's unobserved economy: a preliminary assessment." *Economic Affairs* 1: 205–212.

Feige, E. L. (1987) "The anatomy of the underground economy." In Alessandrini and Dallago 1987.

Feige, E. L. ed. (1989) *The Underground Economies*. Cambridge University Press.

Feige, E. L., and McGee, R. T. (1982) "Supply-side economics and the unobserved economy: The Dutch Laffer curve." *Ökonomisch-statistische Berichten*.

Feige, E. L., and McGee, R. T. (1983) "Sweden's Laffer curve: Taxation and the unobserved economy." *Scandinavian Journal of Economics* 84(4): 499–519.

Feldbrugge, F. J. M. (1979) "Does Soviet law make sense?" In Barry et al. 1979.

Feldbrugge, F. J. M. (1984) "Government and shadow economy in the Soviet Union." *Soviet Studies* 36: 528–543.

Feldman, J., and Kay, J. A. (1981) "Tax avoidance." In Burrows, P., and Veljanovski, C. G. (eds.), *The Economic Approach to Law*. Butterworths, London.

Fishburn, G. (1979) "On how to keep tax-payers honest (or almost so)." *Economic Record* 55: 267–270.

Fishburn, G. (1981) "Tax evasion and inflation." *Australian Economic Papers* 20: 324–332.

Fluet, C. (1987) "Fraude fiscale et offre de travail au noir." *L'Actualité Économique. Revue d'analyse économique* 63: 226–242.

Fortin, B., and Hung, N. M. (1987) "Poverty trap and the hidden labor market." *Economics Letters* 25: 183.

Frank, M. (1972) "La sous-estimation et la fraude fiscale en Belgique: ampleur et remedes." *Cahiers Économiques de Bruxelles* 53: 5–46.

Frank, M. (1976) "Fraude des revenus soumis a l'impôt des personnes physiques et perte d'impôt qui en résulte pour le Tresor—étude méthodologique." *Public Finance* 31: 1–30.

Frank, M. (1977) *La Fraude Fiscale en Belgique*. Editions de l'Université de Bruxelles.

Frank, M. (1987) "La fraude et la sous-estimation fiscales et leur impact sur la distribution des revenus." In Ginsburgh and Pestieau 1987.

Frank, M., and Dekeyser-Meulders, D. (1977) "A tax discrepancy coefficient resulting from tax evasion or tax expenditure." *Journal of Public Economics* 8: 67–78.

Franz, A. (1985) "Estimates of the hidden economy in Austria on the basis of official statistics." *Review of Income and Wealth* 31: 325–333.

Frey, B. S., and Pommerehne, W. W. (1982) "Measuring the hidden economy: Though this be madness, there is method in it." In Tanzi, V. (ed.), *The Underground Economy in the United States and Abroad*. D. C. Heath, Lexington, Mass.

Frey, B. S., and Pommerehne, W. W. (1984) "The hidden economy: State and prospects for measurement." *Review of Income and Wealth* 30: 1–23.

Frey, B. S., and Weck, H. (1983a) "What produces a hidden economy? An international cross-section analysis." *Southern Economic Journal* 49: 822–832.

Frey, B. S., and Weck, H. (1983b) "Estimating the shadow economy: A naive approach." *Oxford Economic Papers* 35: 23–44.

Frey, B. S., Weck, H., and Pommerehne, W. (1982) "Has the shadow-economy grown in Germany? An exploratory study." *Weltwirtschaftliches Archiv* 118: 499–524.

Friedland, N. (1982) "A note on tax evasion as a function of the quality of information about the magnitude and credibility of threatened fines." *Journal of Applied Social Psychology* 12: 54–59.

Friedland, N., Maital, S., and Rutenberg, A. (1978) "A simulation study of tax evasion." *Journal of Public Economics* 8: 107–116.

Furnham, A. (1983) "The Protestant work ethic, human values and attitudes towards taxation." *Journal of Economic Psychology* 3: 113–128.

Gaertner, W. (1987) "Untergrundwirtschaft, Steuerhinterziehung und Moral." In Hesse, H. (ed.), *Wirtschaftswissenschaft und Ethik*. Dunbar and Humblot, Berlin.

Gaertner, W., and Wenig, A. (eds.) (1985) *The Economics of the Shadow Economy*. Springer-Verlag, Berlin.

Galasi, P. (1985) "Peculiarities and limits of the second economy in socialism." In Gaertner and Wenig 1985.

Garber, S., Klepper, S., and Rubenson, D. (1982) Tax Rates and Tax Evasion: Bringing the Theory Closer to the Evidence. Mimeo, Carnegie-Mellon University.

Garcia, G. (1978) "The currency ratio and the subterranean economy." *Financial Analysts Journal* 34 (November--December): 64–69.

Geeroms, H., and Mont, J. (1987) "Evaluation de l'importance de l'économie souterraine en Belgique: Application de la méthode monétaire." In Ginsburgh and Pestieau 1987.

Geeroms, H., and Wilmots, H. (1985) "An empirical model of tax evasion and tax avoidance." *Public Finance* 40: 190–209.

Gillard, M. (1987) *In The Name of Charity: The Rossminster Affair.* Chatto and Windus, London.

Ginsburgh, V., Michel, P., Padoa Schioppa, F., and Pestieau, P. (1985) "Macroeconomic policy in the presence of an irregular sector." In Gaertner and Wenig 1985.

Ginsburgh, V., Perelman, S., and Pestieau, P. (1987) "Le travail au noir." In Ginsburgh and Pestieau 1987.

Ginsburgh, V., and Pestieau, P. (1987) *L'Économie Informelle.* Editions LABOR, Brussels.

Goode, R. (1981) "Some economic aspects of tax administration." *International Monetary Fund Staff Papers* 28: 249–274.

Gordon, J. (1988) Evading Taxes by Selling for Cash. TIDI Discussion Paper 118, London School of Economics.

Gordon, J. (1989) "Individual morality and reputation costs as deterrents to tax evasion." *European Economic Review* 33: 797–805.

Gottlieb, D. (1985) "Tax evasion and the prisoner's dilemma." *Mathematical Social Sciences* 10: 81–89.

Graetz, M. J., and Wilde, L. L. (1985) "The economics of tax evasion: Fact and fantasy." *National Tax Journal* 38: 355–363.

Graetz, M. J., Reinganum, J. F., and Wilde, L. L. (1984) An Equilibrium Model of Tax Compliance with a Bayesian Auditor and Some 'Honest' Taxpayers. California Institute of Technology Social Science Working Paper 506.

Graetz, M. J., Reinganum, J. F., and Wilde, L. L. (1986) "The tax compliance game: Towards an interactive theory of law enforcement." *Journal of Law, Economics, and Organization* 2: 1–32.

Grasmick, H. G., and Green, D. (1980) "Legal punishment, social disapproval and internalization as inhibitions of illegal behavior." *Journal of Criminal Law and Criminology* 71: 325–335.

Grasmick, H. G., and Scott, W. J. (1982) "Tax evasion and mechanism of control: A comparison with grand and petty theft." *Journal of Economic Psychology* 2: 213–230.

Greenberg, D., Moffit, R., and Friedmann, J. (1981) "Underreporting and experimental effects on work effort: Evidence from the Gary income maintenance experiment." *Review of Economics and Statistics* 63: 581–589.

Greenberg, J. (1984) "Avoiding tax avoidance: A (repeated) game-theoretic approach." *Journal of Economic Theory* 32: 1–13.

Groenland, E. A. G., and van Veldhoven, G. M. (1982) "Tax evasion behaviour—A psychological framework." *Journal of Economic Psychology* 3: 129–144.

Grossman, G. (1977) "The second economy of the USSR." *Problems of Communism* 26 (September–October): 25–40.

Groves, H. M. (1958) "Empirical studies of income tax compliance." *National Tax Journal* 11: 291–301.

Gutmann, P. M. (1977) "The subterranean economy." *Financial Analysts Journal* 33 (January–February): 24–27.

Guttman, J. M. (1987) "A non-Cournot model of voluntary collective action." *Economica* 54: 1–20.

Hammond, P. (1981) "*Ex-ante* and *ex-post* welfare optimality under uncertainty." *Economica* 48: 235–250.

Hansson, I. (1980) "Sveriges svarta sektor." *Ekonomisk Debatt* 8: 595–602.

Hansson, I. (1982a) The Unobserved Economy in Sweden. Paper presented to conference on The Unobserved Economy, Wassenaar, Netherlands.

Hansson, I. (1982b) "The underground economy in a high tax country: The case of Sweden." In Tanzi 1982b.

Hansson, I. (1985) "Tax evasion and government policy." In Gaertner and Wenig 1985.

Hansson, I. (1987) "Optimal income taxation and the untaxed sector." In Alessandrini and Dallago 1987.

Hardin, R. (1971) "Collective action as an agreeable n-Prisoner's dilemma." *Behavioural Science* 16: 472–481.

Harsanyi, J. C. (1955) "Cardinal welfare, individualistic ethics and interpersonal comparisons of utility." *Journal of Political Economy* 73: 309–321.

Heertje, A., Allen, M., and Cohen, H. (1982) *The Black Economy*. Pan Books, London.

Heineke, J. M. (1978) *Economic Models of Criminal Behavior*. North-Holland, Amsterdam.

Helberger, C., and Knepel, H. (1988) "How big is the shadow economy?" *European Economic Review* 32: 965–976.

Henry, S. (1978) *The Hidden Economy*. Martin Robertson, Oxford.

Henry, S. (ed.) (1981) *Can I Have It in Cash?* Astragal Books, London.

Herschel, F. J. (1978) "Tax evasion and its measurement in developing countries." *Public Finance* 33: 232–268.

Hessing, D. J., and Elffers, H. (1985) "Economic man or social man?: A social orientation model for individual behaviour in social dilemmas." In Brandstaetter, H., and Kirchler E. (eds.), *Economic Psychology*. Linz, Trauner.

Hessing, D. J., Elffers, H., and Weigel, R. M. (1988) "Exploring the limits of self-reports and reasoned action: An investigation of the psychology of tax evasion behavior." *Journal of Personality and Social Psychology* 54: 405–413.

Hite, P. A. (1987) "An application of attribution theory in taxpayer noncompliance research." *Public Finance* 42: 105–118.

Hoeflich, M. M. (1983) "Of reason, gamesmanship, and taxes: A jurisprudential and games theoretical approach to the problem of voluntary compliance." *American Journal of Tax Policy* 2: 9–88.

Holmes, J. (1987) "The path of the law." *Harvard Law Review* 10: 458–478.

Houston, J. (1987) Participation in the Underground Economy. Federal Reserve Bank of Philadelphia, Research Department, Working Paper 87-10.

International Bar Association (1982) *Tax Avoidance, Tax Evasion.* Sweet and Maxwell, London.

Ioffe, O. S. (1985) *Soviet Law and Soviet Reality.* Martinus Nijhoff, Dordrecht.

Isachsen, A. J., and Strøm, S. (1980) "The hidden economy: the labour market and tax evasion." *Scandinavian Journal of Economics* 82: 304–311.

Isachsen, A. J., and Strøm, S. (1985) "The size and growth of the hidden economy in Norway." *Review of Income and Wealth* 31: 21–38.

Isachsen, A. J., Klovland, J. T., and Strøm, S. (1982) "The hidden economy in Norway." In Tanzi 1982b.

Isachsen, A. J., Samuelsen, S. O., and Strøm, S. (1985) "The behaviour of tax evaders." In Gaertner and Wenig 1985.

Jackson, B. R., and Milliron, V. C. (1986) "Tax compliance research: Findings, problems and prospects." *Journal of Accounting Literature* 5: 125–165.

Jain, A. K. (1972) "The problem of tax evasion in India." *Bulletin for International Fiscal Documentation* 26: 276–299.

Jain, A. K. (1974) "Tax avoidance through Hindu undivided family in India." *Public Finance* 29: 121–130.

Jain, A. K. (1986) Tax Avoidance and Tax Evasion—The Indian Case. Mimeo, London School of Economics.

James, S. R., Lewis, A., and Wallschutzky, I. (1981) "Fiscal fog: A comparison of the comprehensibility of tax literature in Australia and the U.K." *Australian Tax Review* 10: 26–35.

Johansen, L. (1977) "The theory of public goods: Misplaced emphasis?" *Journal of Public Economics* 7: 147–152.

Kaplan, S. E., and Reckers, P. M. J. (1985) "A study of tax evasion judgements." *National Tax Journal* 38: 97–102.

Kaplan, S. E., Reckers, P. M. J., and Reynolds, K. D. (1986) "An application of attribution and equity theories to tax evasion behavior." *Journal of Economic Psychology* 7: 461–476.

Karzon, A. U. (1983) "International tax evasion: Spawned in the United States and nurtured by secrecy havens." *Vanderbilt Journal of Transnational Law* 16: 757–832.

Katsenelinboigen, A. (1977) "Coloured markets in the Soviet Union." *Soviet Studies* 29: 62–85.

Kay, J. A. (1979) "The anatomy of tax avoidance." *British Tax Review*: 354–365.

Kay, J. A. (1980) "The anatomy of tax avoidance." In Collard, D., Lecomber, R., and Slater, M. (eds.) *Income Distribution: The Limits to Redistribution*. Scientechnica, Bristol.

Keenan, A., and Dean, P. N. (1980) "Moral evaluation of tax evasion." *Social Policy and Administration* 14: 209–220.

Kemp, M. C., and Ng, Y.-K. (1979) "On the importance of being honest." *Economic Record* 55: 41–46.

Kenadjian, B. (1982) "The direct approach to measuring the underground economy in the United States: IRS estimates of unreported income." In Tanzi 1982b.

Kesselman, J. R. (1989) "Income tax evasion: An intersectoral analysis." *Journal of Public Economics* 38: 137–182.

Kirchgässner, G. (1983) "Size and development of the West German shadow economy. 1955–1980." *Zeitschrift für die gesamte Staatswissenschaft* 139: 197–214.

Klein, R. (1975) *Social Policy and Public Expenditure, 1975: Inflation and Priorities*. Centre for Studies in Social Policy, London.

Klovland, J. T. (1980) In Search of the Hidden Economy: Tax Evasion and the Demand for Currency, Norway and Sweden. Norwegian School of Economics and Business Administration, Discussion Paper 18/80.

Klovland, J. T. (1983) Tax Evasion and the Demand for Currency in Norway and Sweden; Is There a Hidden Relationship? Norwegian School of Economics and Business Administration, Discussion Paper 07/83.

Kofler, E., and Menges, G. (1976) *Entscheidungen bei unvollständiger Information*. Springer-Verlag, Berlin.

Kolm, S.-Ch. (1973) "A note on optimum tax evasion." *Journal of Public Economics* 2: 265–270.

Koskela, E. (1983a) "A note on progression, penalty schemes and tax evasion." *Journal of Public Economics* 22: 127–133.

Koskela, E. (1983b) "On the shape of the tax schedule, the probability of detection, and the penalty schemes as deterrents to tax evasion." *Public Finance* 38: 70–80.

Kreps, D. M., Milgrom, P., Roberts, J., and Wilson, R. (1982) "Rational cooperation in the finitely repeated Prisoners' Dilemma." *Journal of Economic Theory* 27: 245–252.

Kurz, M. (1977) "Distortion of preferences, income distribution, and the case for a linear income tax." *Journal of Economic Theory* 14: 291–298.

Lafuente, A. (1980) "Una medición de la economía oculta en España." *Boletín de Estudios Económicos* 111.

Lai, C.-C., and Chang, W.-Y. (1988) "Tax evasion and tax collections, an aggregate demand-aggregate supply analysis." *Public Finance* 43: 138–146.

Lampert, N. (1985) *Whistleblowing in the Soviet Union*. Macmillan, London.

Landsberger, M., and Meilijson, I. (1982) "Incentive generating state dependent penalty system." *Journal of Public Economics* 19: 333–352.

Laurent, R. D. (1979) Currency and the Subterranean Economy. Federal Reserve Bank of Chicago, Economic Perspectives.

Laurin, U. (1983) Tax Evasion and Prisoner's Dilemma: Some Interview Data and a Tentative Model for Explanation. Mimeo, Department of Government, University of Uppsala.

Lea, S. E. G., Tarpy, R. M., and Webley, P. (1987) *The Individual in the Economy*. Cambridge University Press.

Lewis, A. (1978) "Perception of tax rates." *British Tax Review* 6: 358–366.

Lewis, A. (1979) "An empirical assessment of tax mentality." *Public Finance* 34: 245–257.

Lewis, A. (1982) *The Psychology of Taxation*. Martin Robertson, Oxford.

Lewis, J. (1984) *Women in England 1870–1950*. Wheatsheaf Books, Brighton.

Lipman, B. L. (1986) "Cooperation among egoists in Prisoners' Dilemma and Chicken games." *Public Choice* 51: 315–331.

Loftus, E. F. (1985) "To file, perchance to cheat." *Psychology Today* (April): 35–39.

Long, S. B. (1980) The Internal Revenue Service: Measuring Tax Offenses and Enforcement Response. U.S. Department of Justice, Washington.

Macafee, K. (1980) "A glimpse of the hidden economy in the national accounts." *Economic Trends* 316: 81–87; reprinted in Tanzi 1982b.

Mackscheidt, K. (1984) "Konsolidierung durch Erhöhung von Steuern und Abgaben?" In von Arnim, H. H., and Littmann, K. (eds.), *Finanzpolitik im Umbruch: zur Konsolidierung Öffentlicher Haushalte.* Berlin.

Maggs, P. B. (1979) "Characteristics of Soviet tax and budgetary law." In Barry et al. 1979.

Maital, S. (1982) *Minds, Markets and Money.* Basic Books, New York.

Marchon, M. (1979) "Tax avoidance, progressivity and work effort." *Public Finance* 34: 452–460.

Marrelli, M. (1984a) "On indirect tax evasion." *Journal of Public Economics* 25: 181–196.

Marrelli, M. (1984b) "L'evasione fiscale delle imposte indirette: imposte specifiche e imposte ad valorem." *Problemi di Finanza Pubblica* 6: 181–199.

Marrelli, M. (1987) "The economic analysis of tax evasion: Empirical aspects." In Hey, J. D., and Lambert, P. J. (eds.), *Surveys in the Economics of Uncertainty.* Basil Blackwell, Oxford.

Mason, R., and Calvin, L. D. (1978) "A study of admitted income tax evasion." *Law and Society Review* 13: 73–89.

Mason, R., and Calvin, L. D. (1984) "Public confidence and admitted tax evasion." *National Tax Journal* 37: 489–496.

Matthews, K. G. P. (1982) "Demand for currency and the black economy in the UK." *Journal of Economic Studies* 9: 3–22.

Matthews, K. G. P. (1983) "National income and the black economy." *Economic Affairs* 3: 261–267.

Mayshar, J. (1986) Taxation with Costly Administration. University of Wisconsin–Madison, SSRI Workshop Discussion Paper 8616.

McCaleb, T. S. (1976) "Tax evasion and the differential taxation of labour and capital income." *Public Finance* 31: 287–292.

McGee, R. T., and Feige, E. L. (1982) "The unobserved economy and the UK Laffer curve." *Journal of Economic Affairs* 2: 36–43.

McKenzie, R. B., and Tullock, G. (1978) *The New World of Economics*. Irwin, Homewood, Illinois.

Millett, P. (1986) "Artificial tax avoidance: The English and American approach." *King's Counsel* 36: 5–10.

Mirus, R., and Smith, R. S. (1981) "Canada's irregular economy." *Canadian Public Policy* 7: 444–453. Reprinted in Tanzi 1982b.

Molefsky, B. (1982) "American underground economy." In Tanzi, V. (ed.), *The Underground Economy in the U.S. and Abroad*. D. C. Heath, Lexington, Massachusetts.

Moltó, M. A. (1980) "La economía irregular. Una primera aproximación al caso español." *Revista Española de Economía* (July): 33–52.

Mork, K. A. (1975) "Income tax evasion: Some empirical evidence." *Public Finance* 30: 70–76.

Mossin, J. (1968) "Taxation and risk-taking: An expected utility approach." *Economica* 35: 74–82.

Murphy, J. H. (1959) "Selecting income tax returns for audit." *National Tax Journal* 12: 232–238.

Nayak, P. B. (1978) "Optimal income-tax evasion and regressive taxes." *Public Finance* 33: 358–366.

von Nell-Breuning, O. (1930) "Steuerverfassung und Steuergewissen." *Stimmen der Zeit* 118: 254–268.

Neck, R., Schneider, F., and Hofreither (1989) "The consequences of progressive income taxation for the shadow economy: Some theoretical considerations." In Bös, D., and Felderer, B. (eds.), *The Political Economy of Progressive Taxation*. Springer-Verlag, Heidelberg.

Newcity, M. (1986) "Recent changes in Soviet personal taxation." *Review of Socialist Law* 12: 175–196.

Niskanen, W. A. (1971) *Bureaucracy and Representative Government*. Aldine-Atherton, Chicago.

Nitzan, S., and Tzur, J. (1987) Taxpayers, Auditors and the Government: An Extended Tax Evasion Game. Discussion Paper A-105, Rheinische-Friedrichs-Wilhelms-Universität, Bonn.

Noldin, H. (1907) "Besprechung einer Dissertation von K. Wagner." *Zeitschrift für katholische Theologie* 31: 530–534.

Noldin, H. (1909) "Zur Erklärung des Pönalgesetzes." *Zeitschrift für katholische Theologie* 33: 136–141.

Ofer, G., and Vinakur, G. (1980) *Private Sources of Income of the Soviet Union Household.* Rand Publications.

O'Hearn, D. (1980) "The consumer second economy: Size and effects." *Soviet Studies* 32: 218–234.

O'Higgins, M. (1980) Measuring the Hidden Economy: A Review of Evidence and Methodology. Outer Circle Policy Unit, London.

O'Higgins, M. (1981a) "Aggregate measures of tax-evasion: An assessment—I." *British Tax Review*: 286–302. Revised and updated from O'Higgins 1980.

O'Higgins, M. (1981b) "Tax evasion and the self-employed—An examination of the evidence—II." *British Tax Review*: 367–378.

O'Higgins, M. (1985) "The relationship between the formal and hidden economies: An exploratory analysis for four countries." In Gaertner and Wenig 1985.

O'Higgins, M. (1989) "Assessing the unobserved economy in the United Kingdom." In Feige 1989.

Oldman, O. (1965) "Controlling income tax evasion." In Joint Tax Program, Organization of American States, Inter-American Development Bank, Economic Commission for Latin America: Problems of Tax Administration in Latin America. Johns Hopkins University Press.

Orland, L. (1987) "Perspectives on Soviet economic crime." In Ioffe, O. S., and Janis, M. W. (eds.), *Soviet Law and Economy.* Sijthoff and Noordhoff, Germantown, Maryland.

Pandit, V. (1977) "Aggregate demand under conditions of tax evasion." *Public Finance* 32: 333–342.

Park, T. S. (1981) "Relationship between personal income and adjusted gross income, 1947–78." *Survey of Current Business* (November): 24–28.

Park, T. S. (1983) "Personal income and adjusted gross income, 1977–81." *Survey of Current Business* (April): 28–33.

Patrizi, V. (1986) "Measures of concealed employment: Pitfalls and insights." *Economia & Lavoro* 20: 91–111.

Peacock, A. T., and Shaw, G. K. (1982) "Tax evasion and tax revenue loss." *Public Finance* 37: 269–278.

Pencavel, J. H. (1979) "A note on income tax evasion, labor supply and nonlinear tax schedules." *Journal of Public Economics* 12: 115–124.

Persson, M., and Wissen, P. (1984) "Redistributional effects of tax evasion." *Scandinavian Journal of Economics* 86: 131–149.

Pestieau, P. (1985) "Belgium's irregular economy." In Gaertner and Wenig 1985.

Petersen, H.-G. (1982) "Size of the public sector, economic growth and the informal economy." *Review of Income and Wealth* 18: 191–215.

Polinsky, M., and Shavell, S. (1979) "The optimal trade-off between the probability and magnitude of fines." *American Economic Review* 69: 880–891.

Polinsky, M., and Shavell, S. (1984) "Optimal use of fines and imprisonment." *Journal of Public Economics* 24: 89–99.

Pommerehne, W. W. (1983) "Steuerhinterziehung und Schwarzarbeit als Grenzen der Staatstätigkeit." *Schweizerische Zeitschrift für Volkswirtschaft und Statistik* 119: 261–284.

Pommerehne, W. W. (1985) "Was wissen wir eigentlich über Steuerhinterziehung?" *International Review of Economics and Business* 32: 1155–1186.

Pomorski, S. (1979) "Crimes against the central planner: 'ochkovtiratel' stvo.'" In Barry et al. 1979.

Pomorski, S., and Ginsburgs, G. (1980) Enforcement of Law and the Second Economy. Kennan Institute for Advanced Russian Studies, The Wilson Center, Occasional Paper 118.

Porcano, T. M. (1988) "Correlates of tax evasion." *Journal of Economic Psychology* 9: 47–67.

Poterba, J. M. (1987) "Tax evasion and capital gains taxation." *American Economic Review, Papers and Proceedings* 77: 234–239.

Pratt, J. W. (1964) "Risk-aversion in the small and in the large." *Econometrica* 32: 122–136.

Pyle, D. J. (1983) *The Economics of Crime and Law Enforcement.* Macmillan, London.

Pyle, D. J. (1987) The Political Economy of Tax Evasion. The David Hume Institute, Hume Paper No. 6.

Rawls, J. (1971) *A Theory of Justice.* Harvard University Press.

Rees, R. (1985) "The theory of principal and agent." *Bulletin of Economic Research* 37: 3–25, 75–95.

Reinganum, J. F., and Wilde, L. L. (1984) Sequential Equilibrium Detection and Reporting Policies in a Model of Tax Evasion. California Institute of Technology, Social Science Working Paper 525.

Reinganum, J. F., and Wilde, L. L. (1985) "Income tax compliance in a principal-agent framework." *Journal of Public Economics* 26: 1–18.

Reinganum, J. F., and Wilde, L. L. (1986) "Equilibrium verification and reporting policies in a model of tax compliance." *International Economic Review* 27: 739–760.

Rey, M. (1965) "Estimating tax evasions: the example of the Italian General Sales Tax." *Public Finance* 20: 366–386.

Rice, R. (1956) *The Business of Crime.* Gollancz, London.

Rickard, J. A., Russell, A. M., and Howroyd, T. D. (1982) "A tax evasion model with allowance for retroactive penalties." *Economic Record* 58: 379–385.

Ricketts, M. (1984) "On the simple macroeconomics of tax evasion: An elaboration of the Peacock-Shaw approach." *Public Finance* 39: 420–424.

Robinson, J. V. (1964) *Economic Philosophy.* Pelican Books, London.

Ross, I. (1978) "Why the underground economy is booming." *Fortune* (October 9, 1978): 92–98.

Rothschild, M., and Stiglitz, J. E. (1970) "Increasing risk I: A definition." *Journal of Economic Theory* 2: 225–243.

Rothschild, M., and Stiglitz, J. E. (1971) "Increasing risk II: Its economic consequences." *Journal of Economic Theory* 3: 66–84.

Ruesga Benito, S. M. (1987) "La economía sumergida en España." In *La Economiá Sumergida,* Instituto de Estudios Económicos, Madrid.

Sandford, C. T. (1980) "Tax compliance costs, evasion and avoidance." In Collard, D., Lecomber, R., and Slater, M. (eds.), *Income Distribution: The Limits to Redistribution*. Scientechnica, Bristol.

Sandmo, A. (1981) "Income tax evasion, labour supply and the equity-efficiency tradeoff." *Journal of Public Economics* 16: 265–288.

Sandmo, A. (1984) "Some results from the 'new' theory of public finance." *Empirica* 2: 111–124.

Sandmo, A. (1986) Tax Distortions and Household Production. Rheinische Friedrich-Wilhelms-Universität Bonn, Discussion Paper A-69.

Sawicki, P. (ed.) (1983) *Income Tax Compliance*. American Bar Association, Chicago.

Schleicher, H. (1971) "A recursive game for detecting tax law violations." *Economies et sociétés* 5: 1421–1440.

Schlicht, E. (1985) "The shadow economy and morals: A note." In Gaertner and Wenig 1985.

Schmähl, W. (1985) "Soziale Sicherung und Schattenwirtschaft." In Winterstein, H. (ed.), *Sozialpolitik in der Beschäftigungskrise*, volume I. Berlin.

Schmölders, G. (1959) "Fiscal psychology—A new branch of public finance." *National Tax Journal* 12: 340–345.

Schmölders, G. (1970) "Der Beitrag der Schattenwirtschaft." In *Wandlungen in Wirtschaft und Gesellschaft*. J. C. B. Mohr, Tübingen.

Schneider, F., and Pommerehne, W. W. (1981) "Free riding and collective action: An experiment in public microeconomics." *Quarterly Journal of Economics* 96: 689–704.

Schwartz, R. D., and Orleans, S. (1967) "On legal sanctions." *Chicago Law Review* 34: 274–300.

Schweizer, U. (1984) "Welfare analysis of excise tax evasion." *Zeitschrift für die gesamte Staatswissenschaft* 140.

Scotchmer, S. (1986) Equity in Tax Enforcement. Harvard Institute of Economic Research, Discussion Paper 1233.

Scotchmer, S. (1987) "Audit classes and tax enforcement policy." *American Economic Review, Papers and Proceedings* 77: 229–233.

Scotchmer, S. (1988) "The effect of tax advisers on tax compliance." In *Taxpayer Compliance*, National Academy of Sciences.

Scotchmer, S. (1989) "Who profits from taxpayer confusion?" *Economics Letters* 29: 49–55.

Scotchmer, S., and Slemrod, J. (1987) Optimal Obfuscation in Tax Enforcement. University of California–Berkeley, Graduate School of Public Policy, Working Paper 126.

Scotchmer, S., and Slemrod, J. (1989) "Uncertainty in tax enforcement." *Journal of Public Economics* 38: 17–32.

Scott, W. J., and Grasmick, H. G. (1981) "Deterrence and income tax cheating: testing interaction hypotheses in utilitarian theories." *Journal of Applied Behavioral Science* 17: 395–408.

Seidl, C. (1974) *Normative Theorie der Steuerdisziplin der Selbständigen: Eine Analyse des Zensitenverhaltens*. Verlag der österreichischen Akadamie der Wissenschaften, Vienna.

Seldon, A. (ed.) (1979) *Tax Avoision*. Institute of Economic Affairs, London.

Shavell, S. (1987) "The optimal use of nonmonetary sanctions as a deterrent." *American Economic Review* 77: 584–592.

Simon, C. P., and Witte, A. D. (1982) *Beating the System: The Underground Economy*. Auburn House, Boston.

Simons, H. A. (1938) *Personal Income Taxation*. University of Chicago Press.

Singh, B. (1973) "Making honesty the best policy." *Journal of Public Economics* 2: 257–263.

Skinner, J., and Slemrod, J. (1985) "An economic perspective on tax evasion." *National Tax Journal* 38: 345–353.

Skolka, J. (ed.) (1984) *Die andere Wirtschaft: Schwarzarbeit und Do-it-Yourself in Österreich*. Signum Verlag, Vienna.

Skolka, J. (1985) "The parallel economy in Austria." In Gaertner and Wenig 1985.

Slemrod, J., and Sorum, N. (1984) "The compliance cost of the U.S. individual income tax system." *National Tax Journal* 37: 461–474.

Slemrod, J., and Yitzhaki, S. (1987) "On the optimum size of a tax collection agency." *Scandinavian Journal of Economics* 89: 183–192.

Smith, A. (1981a) The Informal Economy in the European Community: A review of the Concepts and Evidence. *Economic Papers 3*, Commission of the European Community.

Smith, A. (1981b) "The informal economy." *Lloyds Bank Review* 141: 45–61.

Smith, G. B. (1979) "Procuratorial supervision of economic violations in the USSR." In Barry et al. 1979.

Smith, S. (1986) *Britain's Shadow Economy*. Oxford University Press, for the Institute of Fiscal Studies, London.

Smithies, E. (1984) *The Black Economy in England since 1914*. Gill and Macmillan, Dublin.

Song, Y., and Yarbrough, T. E. (1978) "Tax ethics and taxpayer attitude: A survey." *Public Administration Review* 38: 442–452.

Spicer, M. W. (1975) "New approaches to the problem of tax evasion." *British Tax Review*, pp. 152–154.

Spicer, M. W., and Becker, L. A. (1980) "Fiscal inequity and tax evasion—an experimental approach." *National Tax Journal* 33: 171–175.

Spicer, M. W., and Hero, R. E. (1985) "Tax evasion and heuristics." *Journal of Public Economics* 26: 263–267.

Spicer, M. W., and Lundstedt, S. B. (1976) "Understanding tax evasion." *Public Finance* 31: 295–305.

Spicer, M. W., and Thomas, J. E. (1982) "Audit probabilities and the tax evasion decision: An experimental approach." *Journal of Economic Psychology* 2: 241–245.

Sproule, R. A. (1985) "Tax evasion and labor supply under imperfect information about individual parameters of the tax system." *Public Finance* 40: 441–486.

Sproule, R. A., Komus, D., and Tsang, E. (1980) "Optimal tax evasion, risk-neutral behaviour under a negative income tax." *Public Finance* 35: 309–317.

Srinivasan, T. N. (1973) "Tax evasion: A model." *Journal of Public Economics* 2: 339–346.

Stern, N. H. (1978) "On the economic theory of policy towards crime." In Heineke 1978.

Steuerle, E. C. (1986) *Who Should Pay for Collecting Taxes? Financing The IRS*. American Enterprise Institute, Washington.

Stigler, G. J. (1970) "The optimum enforcement of laws." *Journal of Political Economy* 78: 526–536.

Stiglitz, J. E. (1969) "The effect of income, wealth and capital gains taxation on risk-taking." *Quarterly Journal of Economics* 83: 263–283.

Stiglitz, J. E. (1982) "Utilitarianism and horizontal equity." *Journal of Public Economics* 18: 1–33.

Stiglitz, J. E. (1985) "A general theory of tax avoidance." *National Tax Journal* 38: 325–337.

Sugden, R. (1986) *The Economics of Rights, Co-operation and Welfare*. Basil Blackwell, Oxford.

Tanzi, V. (1982a) "The underground economy in the United States: Annual estimates, 1930–80." *IMF Staff Papers*, 283–305.

Tanzi, V. (1982b) *The Underground Economy in the United States and Abroad*. D. C. Heath, Lexington, Massachusetts.

Tanzi, V. (1983) "The underground economy." *Finance and Development* (December): 10–13.

Tauchen, H., and Witte, A. D. (1985) "Economic models of how audit policies affect voluntary tax compliance." *Proceedings of the NTA-TIA* 78: 39–45.

Taxation (1984) "News Digest." 113: 325.

Taylor, M. (1987) *The Possibility of Cooperation*. Cambridge University Press.

Thibaut, J., Friedland, N., and Walker, L. (1974) "Compliance with rules: Some social determinants." *Journal of Personality and Social Psychology* 30: 792–801.

Thomas, J. J. (1985) Incorporating the Informal Sector into a Macroeconomic Model. Mimeo, London School of Economics.

Thuman, Q. (1988) "Tax payer noncompliance and attribution theory: An experimental vignette approach." *Public Finance* 43: 147–156.

Thuman, Q., St. John, C., and Riggs, L. (1984) "Neutralization and tax evasion: How effective would a moral appeal be in improving compliance to tax laws?" *Law and Policy* 6: 309–327.

Tittle, C., and Rowe, A. R. (1973) "Moral appeal, sanction threat and deviance: An experimental approach." *Social Problems* 20: 488–498.

Townsend, R. M. (1979) "Optimal contracts and competitive markets with costly state verification." *Journal of Economic Theory* 21: 265–293.

Tressler, J. H., and Menezes, C. F. (1980) "Labor supply and wage-rate uncertainty." *Journal of Economic Theory* 23: 425–437.

Tucker, M. (1980) The Underground Economy in Australia. Commercial Bank of Australia Ltd. Economic Review.

Tutt, N. (1985) *The Tax Raiders: The Rossminster Affair*. Financial Training Publications, London.

U.S. Department of the Treasury, Internal Revenue Service (1979) Estimates of Income Unreported on Individual Income Tax Returns. Washington.

Usher, D. (1982) The Private Cost of Public Funds: Variations in Themes by Browning, Atkinson and Stern. Queen's University, Institute for Economic Research, Discussion Paper 481.

Usher, D. (1986) "Tax evasion and the marginal cost of public funds." *Economic Inquiry* 24: 563–586.

Usher, D. (1987) "Theft as a paradigm for departures from efficiency." *Oxford Economic Papers* 39: 235–252.

Virmani, A. (1987) Tax Evasion, Corruption and Administration: Monitoring the People's Agents under Symmetric Dishonesty. Provisional Paper in Public Economics 87–10, World Bank.

Vogel, J. (1974) "Taxation and public opinion in Sweden: An interpretation of recent survey data." *National Tax Journal* 27: 499–513.

Walker, M. (1986) *The Waking Giant: Gorbachev's Russia*. Abacus Press, London.

Wallschutzky, I. G. (1984) "Possible causes of tax evasion." *Journal of Economic Psychology* 5: 371–384.

Wärneryd, K. E., and Walerud, B. (1982) "Taxes and economic behaviour—Some interview data on tax evasion in Sweden." *Journal of Economic Psychology* 2: 187–211.

Watson, H. (1985) "Tax evasion and labor markets." *Journal of Public Economics* 27: 235–246.

Webley, P. (1987) "Audit probabilities and tax evasion in a business simulation." *Economics Letters* 25: 267–270.

Webley, P., Morris, I., and Amstutz, F. (1985) "Tax evasion during a small business simulation." In *Economic Psychology*, Proceedings of the Tenth IAREP Annual Colloquium, Linz.

Webley, P., and Halstead, S. (1986) "Tax evasion on the micro: Significant simulations or expedient experiments." *Journal of Interdisciplinary Economics* 1: 87–100.

Webley, P., Robben, H. S. J., and Morris, I. (1986) Social Comparison, Attitudes and Tax Evasion in a Shop Simulation. Mimeo, University of Exeter.

Weck, H., Pommerehne, W. W., and Frey, B. S. (1984) *Schattenwirtschaft*. Vahlen, Munich.

Weck-Hannemann, H., and Frey, B. S. (1985) "Measuring the shadow economy: The case of Switzerland." In Gaertner and Wenig 1985.

Weck-Hanneman, H., and Pommerehne, W. W. (1988) Steuerbelastung, Finanzkontrolle und Steuerhinterziehung: Eine empirische Analyse. Mimeo.

Weigel, R. H., Hessing, D. J., and Elffers, W. (1987) "Tax evasion research: A critical appraisal and theoretical model." *Journal of Economic Psychology* 8: 215–235.

Weiss, L. (1976) "The desirability of cheating incentives and randomness in the optimal income tax." *Journal of Political Economy* 84: 1343–1352.

Wertz, K. (1979) "Allocation by and output of a tax administering agency." *National Tax Journal* 32: 143–157.

Wiles, P. J. de la F. (1987) "The second economy, its definitional problems." In Allesandrini and Dallago 1987.

Witte, A. D., and Tauchen, H. V. (1987) Tax compliance research: Models, data and methods. Mimeo, Wellesley College.

Witte, A. D., and Woodbury, D. F. (1983) "What we know about the factors affecting compliance with the tax laws." In Sawicki 1983.

Witte, A. D., and Woodbury, D. F. (1985) "The effect of tax laws and tax administration on tax compliance: The case of the U.S. individual income tax." *National Tax Journal* 38: 1–13.

Wolff, E. N. (1985) "The disappearance of domestic servants and the underground economy." In Gaertner and Wenig 1985.

Yaniv, G. (1986) "Fraudulent collection of unemployment benefits." *Journal of Public Economics* 30: 369–383.

Yaniv, G. (1988) "Withholding and non-withheld tax evasion." *Journal of Public Economics* 35: 183–204.

Yankelovich, Skelly and White, Inc. (1984) Survey of Taxpayer Attitudes. IRS, Washington.

Yitzhaki, S. (1974) "Income tax evasion: A note." *Journal of Public Economics* 3: 201–202.

Yitzhaki, S. (1987) "On the excess burden of tax evasion." *Public Finance Quarterly* 15: 123–137.

Zweifel, P., and Pommerehne, W. W. (1985). On Preaching Water and Drinking Wine: An Analysis of Voting on Tax Amnesty and (Under) Reporting of Income. Mimeo, University of Zürich.

Index

27.50

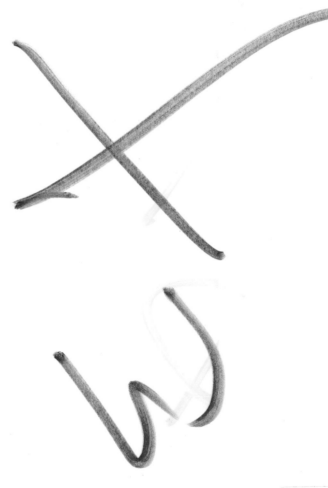